MEANING AND DISCOURSE

MEANING AND DISCOURSE

A COMPUTER MODEL OF PSYCHOANALYTIC SPEECH AND COGNITION

JOHN HENRY CLIPPINGER, JR.

THE JOHNS HOPKINS UNIVERSITY PRESS
BALTIMORE AND LONDON

The Johns Hopkins University Press, Baltimore, Maryland 21218
The Johns Hopkins Press Ltd., London

Library of Congress Catalog Card Number 77-4779
ISBN 0-8018-1943-1
Library of Congress Cataloging in Publication data will be found on the last printed page of this book.

To my parents

CONTENTS

PREFACE

The work represented here cuts across a number of disciplines: cognitive psychology, pragmatics, linguistics, analytic psychology, and artificial intelligence. To regard the book in terms of any one of these disciplines would be to miss its intent. The research described is concerned with a problem: how do speakers arrange linguistic items (as represented textually) to convey *and* to conceal their meanings and intentions? Or, from another perspective, what inferences can we make about a speaker's cognitive (and affective) processes from an examination of the manner in which his or her discourse is constructed?

I felt that a method of representation and analysis was needed that could account, in a rigorous and integrated manner, for the symbolic structures and processes involved in the conceptualization, formation, and generation of discourse. Such a method of representation has only recently become available through work in artificial intelligence. Previously, programming languages imposed upon their users a rather inflexible format which predetermined the modeling or descriptive effort to rather simplistic and limited ends. This no longer need be the case, or rather, so much less so that truly interesting problems of language use can be explored through process or computational models. Intentionality, once the bugaboo of modern psychology, can be given a precise and operational definition. Similarly, the notion of meaning can be formulated in a manner that makes intuitive sense and yet is precise. But more than clearing the good name of previously disparaged notions, a programming or computational approach enables one to begin to see, and perhaps even to understand, the extraordinary ways and levels in which human thought is organized, regulated, and realized through speech. Speech or discourse is certainly more than getting all one's grammatical rules correct; it is a means of conveying information, experiences, and feelings. It is also a highly selective collection of operations whereby the speaker uses what devices and information he or she has at his disposal to create and dispel certain associations and inferences to himself and to others. Moreover, a speaker can voice many different points of view, even contradictory points of view, in the course of his discourse without wholly being aware of it. This is one of the reasons that psychoanalytic discourse was selected for study.

In the psychoanalytic setting the speaker is often not just inconsistent (every speaker is inconsistent), but unknowingly in conflict about what he wants, thinks, or feels. Consequently, the discourse is often filled with self-corrections, qualifications, topic changes, interjections, and partially formed sentences. What is apparent to the therapist is often not apparent to the patient, for, as the patient speaks, the locus of his attention or awareness shifts as conflicting points of view introduce themselves into his thinking and speech. While the discourse so produced may make sense at one level, in that it is grammatical and sufficiently well structured to convey information, it often represents a compromise solution to a wealth of conflicting intentions. This, the patient commonly does not see, for by being party to the compromise agreements, it is as if he or she is bound not to disclose the existence of these agreements either to himself or to others. In a very real sense, the patient does not know himself, and it is the therapist's or analyst's job to educate the patient in self-knowledge.

Seen in terms of a computational or programming method, the patient is unable or unwilling to assess critical information about his beliefs and intentions. The reasons for this are multiple: he may have acquired different inferential and cognitive rules which impose contradictory criteria; he may have acquired concepts or knowledge structures that are highly idiosyncratic and hence poorly tagged and not easily assessed; he may have developed a wealth of censoring mechanisms that have effectively blocked self-disclosure, or he may have failed to differentiate key concepts and control structures. From this perspective, the success of treatment depends upon the analyst or therapist being able to determine how the patient's control and conceptual structures are ordered, and then, on the basis of this knowledge, to teach the patient (by avoiding incorrect interpretations and associations) how to assess and interpret information about himself. In this manner the therapist helps the patient establish more realistic and effective controls which are, at the same time, his own. For certain types of patients, the task may be to find a place or context where the patient can stand and see himself without having his insights censored or distorted. For other classes of patients, the task may be to assess a formative experience, which by virtue of its place in the patient's cognitive scheme continues to exert a negative influence but which is not subject to more positive controls. In either case, the problems are symbolic and involve an intricate and intimate understanding of the mental architecture of the patient.

The purpose of this book, then, is to provide a preliminary but explicit framework whereby cognitive structures and processes can be studied and modeled from speech behavior. Although the data used for the modeling effort were taken from a psychoanalytic episode and the focus of the model-building effort is upon a single patient, the theory and method presented here are intended to have a generality beyond the clinical setting.

The following chapter summaries are offered as guides to the contents of the book.

*Chapter 1:** Since to my knowledge there are no systematic theories of discourse behavior, I felt it necessary to demonstrate the need for such a theory. Hence, this chapter begins with a discussion of some of the current problems in linguistics, and proceeds to establish some requirements for a theory of discourse formation and generation.

Chapter 2: In this chapter we distinguish between two types of discourse, fixed and negotiated. Fixed discourse is code-dependent, as its meaning is explicitly given within the linguistic code, whereas negotiated discourse is idiosyncratic to the intentions and knowledge of communicants. A general theory of discourse behavior is offered in which fixed and negotiated discourse theory are described in terms of an autoregulative model. This model constitutes the theoretical basis for the computer model discussed in subsequent sections.

Chapter 3: In this chapter the reader is provided with a simplified overview of how the program works and is organized.

Chapter 4: This is the first chapter in which the workings of the model are discussed in detail. Here the discussion is devoted primarily to a description of the cognitive aspects of the computer model. A brief description of the programming language (CONNIVER) is offered, followed by a detailed discussion of our representation of concepts, control mechanisms, and the organization of cognitive processes into "contexts."

Chapter 5: In this chapter we present a detailed account of the grammar developed to realize concepts into discourse. Most of the chapter is devoted to describing the realization process of the program in terms of a "discourse grammar" created for purposes of explication. The remaining section describes the procedures the program actually uses to realize concepts for discourse. Since the program is an implementation of the discourse grammar, the two sections complement one another.

Chapter 6: Here for the first time we see how the model simulates the cognitive and discourse behavior of the patient. A scenario is provided describing some of the general processes involved in the creation of our simulated episode. This is followed by a detailed analysis of how the program goes about simulating the formation and generation of the patient's discourse.

Chapter 7: In this chapter the theoretical ramifications of key components of the model are developed: specifically, concepts, contexts, and

*Those readers who are not particularly interested in theoretical questions might prefer to skip ahead to Chapter 4 or 5 and begin reading there, and those of you who feel an immediate need to see what the program does might try reading Chapter 6 before starting the other sections.

multiple-body interrupts. A comparison is then made of the descriptive value of these mechanisms with some of those developed by Freud, Piaget, and Bateson.

Chapter 8: This chapter has two parts. The first discusses those properties of the theory that are not model-dependent, that is, that are considered to offer a general theoretical description of all discourse and cognitive behaviors. The second discusses the possible psychotherapeutic applications of computational methods and theory. Here key psychoanalytic concepts, such as primary and secondary processes, ego, superego, and self-understanding, are examined in light of computational methods and an argument is made for the adoption of the computational approach in metapsychology and clinical psychology.

Chapter 9: Here we attempt to tackle the difficult problem of verifying our model and demonstrating its flexibility and generality as a model of discourse behavior. An experiment is performed on the model whereby alterations are made in the program's cognitive structure and new discourse is generated. This experiment was performed to see if the criteria used by therapists in evaluating therapeutic discourse were similar to those embodied in the program's design. The book ends with a discussion of the possible extensions and uses of the model.

ACKNOWLEDGMENTS

The research described in this book has a long personal history. Initially, it was spurred by an interest in Levi-Strauss, who in his analysis of myths awakened me as an undergraduate to the prospect of studying and analyzing the underlying laws of human thought. This interest, in turn, became channeled into an interest in cybernetics, information theory, and content analysis. I was especially fortunate in having Klaus Krippendorff as my mentor in all three of these areas, as he is a gifted and thorough teacher. I am also indebted to Bob Scholte, who never tired of supplying me with endless bibliographies and valuable critiques of the methodological problems involved in modeling human symbolic processes. As I discovered the limitations of content-analysis methods and turned to new methods of analyzing and representing cognitive and linguistic phenomena, I found artificial intelligence, having read Terry Winograd's thesis on natural language understanding. To him I am especially grateful, both for having written his thesis and for including me in his seminar on natural language processing. For the first time I was able to get a handle on how to think about and represent cognitive and linguistic processes.

The conceptual framework provided first by Winograd's thesis and then by CONNIVER enabled me to clarify many of my own ideas about discourse formation and production. I was then very fortunate to work with Richard Brown in the programming of the model, for not only is he a masterful programmer but an original and creative interpreter of discourse as well. Without his assistance, this work certainly would have suffered. With the completion of the manuscript, I received valuable criticism and guidance from many people: Joe Becker, who was a meticulous, but constructive critic; William Labov, whose reading of the manuscript was especially insightful, and whose encouragement was especially helpful; Ramon Greenberg, who patiently improved my understanding, and hence discussion of psychoanalytic technique; and Steve Kosslyn, whose systematic and intelligent commentary on the manuscript helped tighten many previously loose arguments. To these people I am most grateful, and in no way should any failings of this work be a reflection on them.

MEANING AND DISCOURSE

1 : THE NEED FOR A THEORY OF DISCOURSE

If language had been the creation, not of poetry, but of logic, we should only have one.—HEBBEL

1.10. THE NEED FOR A THEORETICAL MODEL OF DISCOURSE BEHAVIOR

Spoken and written materials are so commonplace that it is difficult to imagine them as data. Yet as speakers and interpreters of discourse, both written and spoken, we evolve in our lifetimes remarkable capacities to use and interpret spoken data. While as children we may be taught correct usage and conventions of interchange, we, as individuals, learn much more than that. We learn to tell from a speaker's tone of voice, or from what he did not say, what he really meant. And, in turn, we learn what to say, or what not to say, to achieve our ends. In other words, we learn how an understanding of speech can be used to direct ourselves and others. Therefore, rather than simply being a medium of information exchange, speech is also a means of control. For in a very real sense, in speaking to one another, we are also mutually programming one another in thought and act.

However, from the beginning of this century until the last decade, speech, or rather language, has been studied primarily in terms of its grammatical properties. Owing, perhaps, to the philosophical and humanistic origins of linguistic research, linguistic data have rarely been studied analytically for their psychological properties. All this has changed within the last 10 years. A plethora of schools, methods, and hybrid disciplines have sprouted up, which in one way or another study the psychological aspects of language, speech, and discourse: ethnomethodology, psycholinguistics, sociolinguistics, pragmatics, computational linguistics, and generative semantics. The advent of these diverse disciplines evidences a dissatisfaction with the singularity of current linguistics' concern with syntax and a recognition of the importance of psychological and sociological factors in speech generation.

However, with this diversity has come a number of problems, for the theories and descriptions so far produced tend not to be compatible, and are therefore not easily integrated. The situation is very close to what Thomas Kuhn terms a scientific crisis, wherein the canons of "normal science" cease to hold sway and new theories compete for the formation of a new consensus, a new paradigm.

On the basis of these facts an argument can be made that there is a need to develop a preliminary, theoretical framework in which the study of discourse can be pursued in an integrated and complementary fashion. The difficulty is, of course, how the different concerns of psycholinguists, computational linguists, cognitive psychologists, ethnolinguists, sociolinguists, and clinical psychologists are to be incorporated into a common framework. Doubtlessly, not all interests can be subsumed under a single theoretical framework. However, in each of these fields there is concern to relate cognitive operations to linguistic performance and to determine those social and cultural factors that account for variants in performance. Increasingly, the tendency has been to characterize behaviors in terms of "rules," although, it should be added, these rules are extremely variable in the level and nature of their descriptions. Here the legacy of transformational linguistics continues to exercise its influence on how to formulate the description. Although such rules may capture certain regularities in the use of various discourse expressions, forms, or sequences, they do not readily map onto any available model of higher-order cognitive operations; hence, they tend to stand alone. To make the leap from linguistic descriptions to cognitive descriptions entails having a model that can account for both. Why was it that the utterance was ordered in the way it was? Why did it follow from what was previously stated? Why did it take so long to produce, or why was it filled with so many errors or hesitations? What did the *speaker* really mean or want? Although one necessarily has to account for the syntactic, semantic, and thematic properties of the utterance, one also needs to know how and why it was said. Inevitably, then, one gets into the murky water of inferring the speaker's intentions and cognitive operations that produced the utterance.

One temptation, or as some would argue, one reasonable approach, it to take an aspect of the speech behavior problem and analyze its every conceivable facet. A second temptation is to keep building upon or modifying existing frameworks, principally of linguistic derivation, until all aspects are accounted for. Neither approach works very well. The first accumulates reams of unintegrated data, and the second simply evolves into an unwieldy and progressively ad hoc monster which fails to metamorphose into anything new or interesting.

What seems to be needed is a theory that is general and well defined: general in the sense that it does not preclude certain aspects of discourse behavior, and well defined in the sense that it works to establish common conventions and parameters of research. Without such a general plan, my fear is that research in this area may fail to coalesce into a coherent understanding and will continue to oscillate between fragmented data analysis and ungrounded theoretical speculation.

Our initial discussion will focus briefly upon some of the goals and requirements of generative linguistics in order to establish the differences between this approach to language and our own. Subsequent discussion will then be directed toward showing how cognitive operations are involved in the discourse production process and how, in turn, a methodological framework might be designed to account for both.

Let us begin with a quote from Chomsky. "The problem for the linguist, as well as for the child learning the language, is to determine from the data of performance the underlying system of rules that has been mastered by the speaker–hearer and that he puts into use in actual performance. Hence, in the technical sense, linguistics is mentalistic, since it is concerned with discovering the mental reality underlying actual behavior" (Chomsky 1965, p. 4).

On the surface the problem for a theory of discourse behavior and cognition is similar to that in the quotation: that is, to take from the data of performance—in our case, discourse—and create a system of rules that characterize the mental rules used by a speaker in actual performance. Although this may appear to be the case, for generative linguistics it is not. Generative linguists have a very special notion about what constitutes a rule and "mental reality." The central concern of the generative linguist is syntax. His goal is to write a system of rules that can account for the generation of grammatical utterances of a group of "native speakers" and, by so doing, to reveal the underlying mental reality of the speaker(s). To accomplish this end, the generative linguist has had to introduce progressively fuzzier and more cognitively dependent components into his model. Whereas at one time semantics played a relatively minor role, and the "context" of the utterance was given minimal attention, both are now regarded as being essential parts of a well-formulated linguistic theory (Steinberg and Jakobovits 1971). Yet despite current linguistics capacity to grow to accommodate new data and new requirements, it does not, I believe, provide a suitable framework in which to address questions of meaning, context, and intention in language use. In fact, it really was not designed to, despite laymen's possible preconceptions to the contrary. And, if one attempts to use the work of generative linguists as a means of reconstructing the "psychological reality" or motivation behind speech behavior, one will in the end be disappointed; the tools of generative linguistics are simply inappropriate to this more general end.

As we noted in the previous section, discourse means different things to different researchers. Moreover, its explicit form, whether written or spoken, is the mere tip of the iceberg, or rather the only visible or audible manifestation of a long and arbitrarily complex process. The process is arbitrarily complex because we can reach back virtually indefinitely into the ''causes'' for the generation of a discourse episode; for it can be explained synchronically, that is, atemporally; or it can be explained developmentally, over time. Ideally, one would like to reach back as far as one could and provide a complete developmental description and theory. Such a theory would tell us not only how a speaker composed and produced a discourse episode, but it would also tell us why he or she came to produce the particular discourse. Such a theory would then explain why a speaker said what he did by showing not only how the mechanisms worked to produce the utterance, but also how these mechanisms were themselves produced and structured. Unfortunately, such a theory is clearly beyond the means of our current understanding, and hence we would be doing well simply to describe the mechanisms of the ''on-line'' operations.

The general strategem of this research—and the model and theory presented here—is primarily descriptive, to find a sufficiently detailed and well-defined formal language whereby the mechanisms, structures, and processes involved in the initiation, formation, and realization of a discourse can be comprehensively and precisely characterized. It should be noted that while our approach may help identify or isolate questions regarding the origins or reasons behind the production of a given construction or a particular cognitive response, it does not pretend to answer such questions.

Discourse is treated within this theory as a communication process that is motivated by a need to solve a number of cognitively posed problems. Hence, the discourse itself, as far as this theory is concerned, is but a mirror of the mind and is of interest primarily for this reason. It is, in other words, a rich and natural data source from which we can make carefully controlled inferences about mental activity and organization. We are as much concerned with the ''incorrect'' or sloppy uses of languages as we are with the grammatical uses, for it is through these slips of the tongue that we can gain glimpses of some of the more hidden mechanisms of the mind. However, whereas words may bear the imprint of the mind, they are but imperfect copies, and to interpret them we must first understand the more basic and complex structures that gave rise to them. This entails, I believe, having a rather developed model of the conceptual structures and processes that operate prior to speech production and which, in turn, are responsible for the composition and configuration of an utterance.

Although it is popular to treat syntax as an independent phenomenon, the position taken here is that syntactic choices themselves are instrumental to cognitive processes, and therefore must be represented in terms of the functions they perform for these cognitive processes. In other words, syntactic options are seen as solutions or partial solutions to more general cognitive problems. This becomes especially apparent when one recalls the obvious but often forgotten fact that speakers shape the tone and contents of their remarks in terms of their images of their audiences. Consequently, a speaker has to do a lot of thinking about how his remarks will be understood and how he should select his words to make his meanings clear. Therefore, from the standpoint of these high-order cognitive operations and concerns, the speaker "sees" his syntactic, semantic, and thematic options in terms of their potential effects rather than simply their grammaticality or well-formedness. As will become clear in subsequent chapters, this approach leads to a rather different treatment of linguistic processes than those commonly found in most conventional linguistic research.

Another aspect of speech behavior—that thinking processes are amazingly heterogeneous and, at times, at variance with one another—warrants consideration at this point. We cannot only entertain many different points of view about the same subject but can also see them from many different levels and perspectives. We can think in "words" or we can think in very abstract idiosyncratic terms that escape verbal expression. Consequently, any theory of discourse that attempts to homogenize cognitive processes into a single normative framework is going to inflict a grave injustice on the richness, uniqueness, and diversity of the discourse process. Naturally, such an orientation or inclination should be avoided. The trick is to develop a framework that is sufficiently flexible to allow for such idiosyncracies and at the same time to be sufficiently general not to be limited to the particular.

One final consideration before we set forth some of the very basic features of a theory of discourse behavior. Very often there is a great deal of confusion in psychology as well as linguistics over whether a theory is of an individual or of a group. By and large, they are treated as two separate entities and therefore proceed to evolve two different and incompatible frameworks. This, I believe, is unfortunate and unnecessary. As one speaker among a community of speakers, an individual must understand and use those rules and assumptions that hold for the group. Hence, embedded in his knowledge structures are at least some of the rules and knowledge structures that characterize the group as a whole. Syntax is an excellent example of this; it exists "independent" of the individual, and yet it is an intimate part of his communicative repertory. To describe the discourse behavior of an individual, then, requires being able to distinguish between that which is shared and that which is not. In some instances, where the acculturation or socialization process is very intense, it may be difficult to distinguish; in others, the differences may be even syntactic. In either case, it is important to have a theory that is not one or the other. Rather, what is needed is a general theory which subsumes both, that is, provides common conventions in which both collective and individual rules can be represented. The need for such a general theory becomes particularly apparent when one attempts to interpret the meaning of a psychoanalytic discourse, for one needs to know whether the conventions and the constructions the speaker is using are typical of his group or of himself alone. If it is the former, what may appear to be pathological to the speaker may not, in fact, be so for the speaker, but for the group. And if it is the latter, the therapist knows that he is dealing with a very personal matter.

The theory described here is intended to be a general theory, although the computer model of the patient is obviously an individual theory. This is possible because the methods used are not, I believe, specific to the particular modeling effort, but can be applied to any speaker. The grammar developed for modeling purposes can be regarded as a collective theory of how speakers use English syntax, since syntax is the collective medium of any individual discourse.

We are now in a position to discuss some of the elementary features of a theory of discourse behavior. As should become apparent, the theoretical model has a great deal more in common with a cybernetic mechanism than it does with a generative device. For the explanatory criteria required of the theoretic model entail having a device that interacts with and effects to some purpose a symbolic representation of a discourse environment. Next are listed some basic features of a theoretical model of discourse behavior which will be explicated individually.

1.20. FEATURES OF A THEORETICAL MODEL OF DISCOURSE BEHAVIOR

1. Procedures for representing diverse motivational initiatives involved in discourse composition and production.
2. Procedures for representing the knowledge base contained within a discourse production.
3. Procedures for generating solutions to motivational initiatives for discourse generation.
4. Procedures for choosing between alternative solutions.
5. Procedures for representing the audience of a discourse.
6. Procedures for representing the context of a discourse.
7. Procedures for generating acceptable discourse that achieves the selected solution.

1. Procedures for representing diverse motivational initiatives involved in discourse composition and production

All discourse proceeds out of motivational initiatives, and, depending upon the nature of the initiatives, may vary considerably. Consequently, an adequate explanation of discourse must include a representation of the forces that gave rise to it. Here and elsewhere in the criteria we call for procedures for representation rather than structural descriptions, or simply descriptions. This was done so as not to prejudice any explanation toward a structural or static representation, feeling that process or teleological descriptions are probably more appropriate.

2. Procedures for representing the knowledge base contained within a discourse production

Quite obviously, discourse entails the processing and transmitting of knowledge to another speaker. Much of what appears in a discourse is derived from inferences and knowledge structures which have no manifest expression in the discourse proper. Nonetheless, these knowledge structures are required to derive the discourse and are presupposed in its interpretation.

3. Procedures for generating solutions to motivational initiatives for discourse generation

In many, if not most, cases, discourse is a communicated solution to some cognitively posed problem, here called motivational initiatives. Very often many solutions are generated for such problems, and very often they individually or collectively affect the content and the structure of the discourse.

4. Procedures for choosing between alternative solutions

The decision criteria a speaker or speakers use in selecting a solution not only determines the content of a discourse, but often itself is the content of a discourse. Similarly, it can affect the structure and style of a discourse.

5. Procedures for representing the audience of a discourse

Naturally enough, all discourses are directed to someone real or imagined. Consequently, the speaker's model of the audience is highly influential in determining the manner and content of the discourse.

6. Procedures for representing the context of a discourse

The time, place, and context of a discourse utterance also are highly influential of its character. Consequently, procedures must exist which properly give these expressions within the discourse.

7. Procedures for generating acceptable discourse that achieves the selected solution

This requirement simply states that an adequate model of discourse must have rules which realize the knowledge constructs of the solution into discourse that is not only acceptable in the Chomsky sense but is natural for the speaker or speakers that the model represents. In some cases, the discourse might contain numerous interruptions and qualifications which might not be intelligible to the listener but are natural to the speaker.

Although it might seem desirable at this point to establish some evaluation criteria for choosing between alternative models of discourse behavior, it is my feeling that such criteria are premature at this time. Tests can be devised which use panels of judges to evaluate different model's discourse in terms of their similarity to sampled discourse of the modeled subject, but these tests, as Colby's (1973) experience has shown, are weak indicators of validity and have little or nothing to say of the model's structural or procedural validity. Our purpose in this chapter has been to make a place for a theory of discourse behavior so that the scope of our subsequent descriptions is clear. When more is understood about discourse models and discourse behavior, more adequate evaluation criteria can be designed.

2 : A GENERAL THEORY OF DISCOURSE BEHAVIOR

How can I tell what I think till I see what I say?—FORESTER

What a great deal of talking there would be in the world if we desired at all costs to change the names of things into definitions.—LICHTENBERG

2.10. OVERVIEW

In this chapter we shall begin with some observations and examples of discourse behavior. We shall attempt to show that discourse behaviors are teleological processes which cannot be wholly understood in terms of their linguistic properties alone. We shall argue, rather, that they are instances of "symbolic actions" undertaken to achieve specific effects in terms of their impact upon both an intended audience and the speaker. Two key dimensions of discourse behavior are identified, the fixed and the negotiated, which, although they are derived from a common cognitive process, differently affect the character of discourse. A model of the process of discourse formation and generation is offered which attempts to account for these two dimensions and their derivation from a common cognitive process. This model is termed an *autoregulative model* because of its capacity to model its own behaviors, those of others, and to modify its actions through feedback.

2.20. WHAT IS DISCOURSE?

One immediate problem in discussing discourse is that the term is so variously and loosely employed that no one knows exactly what it is. When we think of a discourse, the image that comes to mind is that of a conversation, monologue, or a written treatise. Usage has conditioned us to identify discourse with the symbols of its expression. Consequently, we tend to forget that discourse is not simply a collection of sounds or symbols but a form of behavior that is communicative and goal-directed. When we try to pinpoint what these behaviors are, however, we get into trouble, because much of discourse behavior is internal and only indirectly reflected in the symbols of its expression. Although we can make inferences about how these symbols are formed and the types of cognitive processes they entail, we are not yet able to precisely relate these behaviors to their symbolic expressions. To do so, a model is needed to identify the implicit structures and processes involved in the production of discourse. In describing the properties of such a model, we shall begin with the simplest model and then show how the model must be altered and extended to account for the complexity of discourse behavior.

Let us assume that discourse is a simple process of information exchange between a sender and receiver. Each is equipped to code, decode, and transmit information through a common set of symbols. Also, let us assume that associated with the code are physical and information-processing behaviors, so that when a particular message is received, the recipient or listener will act in a specified and predictable manner. Discourse in this setting would consist of the exchange of messages between the sender and the receiver, and to an outside observer might appear to be similar to human discourse. Yet, upon closer observation it would be apparent that communication of this type is not at all human in character, for everything that is communicated is explicitly represented in the code and therefore has an invariant meaning. For in this model, neither the sender nor the receiver is able to modify his code and consequently is incapable of saying more than the code initially allows. Although such a model may seem too naive to be considered seriously, it is not unlike those which attempt to explain discourse in terms of its linguistic properties alone. For if one acknowledges that the purpose of language is to communicate and does not allow for the goal-directed character of this communication, something like our naive model is being assumed. In such models, discourse is identified with the acceptable or grammatical uses of a mutually shared code (language), and communication becomes a problem not in how the code should be used or modified to transmit new knowledge but simply in how the rules of the code are to be observed. If a speaker were actually so constrained, he could say no more than what was explicitly represented in his linguistic code and that of his listener's linguistic code. Similarly, his inferential abilities would be severely limited, as he could not modify or build upon his coded knowledge; for as far as he would know, this communicated knowledge would be immutable.

Since speakers can obviously transmit new knowledge, and since discourse can express much more than is explicitly stated, discourse is something more than transmission of explicit information. Yet if this is so, how are the conventions of language used to express information that is not explicitly represented in its code? The following example of a hypothetical robot demonstrates how new meanings can be created in the course of extended communication. Let us assume that this robot has been designed to communicate with its programmer through a facsimile of English and that it has been programmed to solve problems in the most efficient manner possible. Let us also assume that whenever the robot fails to solve a particular problem, it prints out, "I don't understand," and that the programmer quickly provides it with the answer. If the programmer is trying to teach the robot to solve problems on its own, and if the programmer is a more efficient problem solver than the robot, his teaching effort will soon be defeated. For the robot will learn to say "I don't understand" for all those problems for which the programmer's solutions are more efficient than its own. And even though the robot might know the answer to a particular problem, it will, in effect, lie and plead ignorance in order to get the programmer to do its work, as this would be its most efficient response to the problem. In this way, the meaning of "I don't understand" becomes "Provide me with an answer," as the robot has effectively given a unique meaning to a standard sentence. If the programmer catches on, he will respond to the robot's statement not in terms of its explicit or manifest meaning, but in terms of what he understands it to be saying.

The parallel with children is striking. If a parent responds to a child's expression of distress by always solving his problems for him, the child will learn to express his distress at every problem situation, regardless of whether or not he can solve it for himself. Likewise, the child will learn to use language not in terms of its conventionalized meanings but in terms of the effects he or she wants to achieve. The parent who does not effectively discriminate between these meanings will often misunderstand the child and respond inappropriately. In light of this, it is not difficult to see how, over time, normal human discourse can evolve meanings which differ from or supplement those prescribed by the explicit conventions of discourse. Discourse between members of the same family especially exhibits this trait. A child announces at the dinner table, "I feel sick," and the mother answers, "Eat your beans, they're good for you." In this case, a response to the explicit statement would be inappropriate, as the explicit meaning is not the intended meaning. Both the mother and the child know this, and through their close association over time they have evolved idiosyncratic meanings for standard discourse. When these idiosyncratic meanings or uses become fixed, they are standard or fixed for their speech community. But to those outside this community, the meanings may appear to be idiosyncratic.

From these examples it should be clear that discourse is not simply the transmission and interpretation of coded information. Rather, it would appear that it is common for speakers to use coded information in unique ways to create meanings that differ from those represented within the code. Moreover, how a particular information code is used or modified seems to depend on the intentions of the speaker and his perceptions of the audience. To account for such nonconventional and specialized meanings of discourse, a model is needed to represent the ways in which discourse is shaped by speakers' intentions and knowledge. As a preliminary step toward suggesting such a model, a distinction of convenience is made between discourse whose intended meaning is coterminous with its coded meaning—*fixed discourse* (F-discourse)—and discourse whose intended meaning differs from or builds upon coded meanings—*negotiated discourse* (N-discourse).

In fixed discourse the interpretation of a discourse message is not dependent upon any particular listener, because the information code shared by the speaker and the listener is collective and sufficient to convey the intended message. In this case neither the speaker nor the listener is free to alter the meaning of the discourse symbols, as these meanings constitute the inalterable conventions upon which the discourse depends. Since all discourse depends upon such conventions, all discourse is at least partially fixed. Grammaticality and the proper use of semantic items fall within this category of discourse, as do notions of propositional content and information. Negotiated discourse, on the other hand, is not completely regulated by convention but rather by the individual intentions and perceptions of the discourse participants. Hence, unlike F-discourse, its meaning is dependent upon the circumstances and goals of the participants. In N-discourse the communicants do not literally interpret or employ a discourse code but, instead, attempt to negotiate new and more specialized and personal meanings. Our examples of the robot and the child are both instances of N-discourse. However, N-discourse is more than just a supplement to F-discourse, as it is used to communicate and acknowledge the unique experiences and circumstances of communicants. Since F-discourse is impersonal, in that its use and meaning is independent of any particular speaker or listener, it has no provision for noncollective experiences and beliefs. Consequently, it is a poor vehicle by itself for affective or non-information-based communication.

Conventions do exist within language, however, for expressing interpersonal information. A speaker has a wide variety of options in the grammatical choices he makes and the manner in which he organizes his discourse for thematic impact. Yet in terms of content, these options do not alter the meaning of the discourse. Rather they alter the relationship of the speaker and the listener to the content of the discourse. As an example, take the case of a drunken driver apprehended by a police officer. When asked by the officer to explain his actions, the driver probably would not give a simple informative account of his actions, but rather would try to provide a sympathetic picture of his predicament. This type of discourse requires a great deal of competence on the part of the driver, for he must, on the one hand, describe what actually took place and, on the other, make it appear forgivable. Hence, his discourse might go as follows: "You're quite right, officer, I must have been going faster than I should have. I was over at Judge Parker's house and we happened to have a few beers watching the game when I got a call from my wife, who hasn't been feeling too well lately. So I left as quickly as I could and didn't realize how fast I was going until I saw your flashing red light."

In this example the speaker has no intention of fully acquainting the officer with the circumstances leading to his arrest. On the contrary, he tried to draw attention away from the fact of his reckless driving and to solicit the sympathy of the officer by referring to the judge and to his sick wife. Similarly, he uses what devices he can to confirm the policeman's authority (You're *quite* right . . .) and makes it appear as if he had a minor role in his actions (I *must* have . . . *happened* to have a few . . .). The officer's report, which did not have to concern itself with interpersonal effects but, rather, with informational accuracy, might be as follows: "Mr. Clements was apprehended after a 37-minute chase at speeds in excess of 90 miles an hour after his car sideswiped an ice cream truck and came to rest in a ditch. His breath smelled of alcohol, and he was unable to stand." Obviously, the officer's report is F-discourse and that of the driver N-discourse, and, although both represent descriptions of a similar event, they have little in common.

Another instance of the use of N-discourse is when the speaker cannot directly express what is on his mind for fear of explicitly insulting his listener. For, if an insult is explicit, the speaker can be held accountable for his remark; but if the insult must be inferred by the listener, the speaker can plead innocence by correctly noting that he did not state anything insulting. Speakers may construct discourse situations in which an insult can be expressed with impunity, as this example of a four-year-old girl's discourse reveals. The child has been reprimanded by her grandmother and wishes to express her dislike of her grandmother. She knows that she cannot say so directly, as she would then be punished further, so she devises the following discourse, which she sings as a nursery rhyme:

I don't like alligators,
I don't like alligators,
Grandmothers are alligators.

Neither the content nor the form of this discourse makes explicit reference to the little girl's grandmother. Furthermore, there is no explicit expression of dislike for anything other than alligators, which certainly is an understandable thing to dislike. In order for the grandmother to accuse the child of an insult, she would have to go through a rather elaborate and perhaps not altogether convincing demonstration of the syllogistic intent of the child's remarks, and the little girl knows her grandmother is probably unwilling to do so.

The distinction between fixed and negotiated discourse is similar to a number of other distinctions made which describe the properties of language and cognition: connotative–denotative, subject–object, diachronic–synchronic, manifest–latent, informative–affective, and so on. In some respects it resembles Piaget's early distinction between assimilation and accommodation. But there is a difference, for Piaget never addresses himself directly to the problem of discourse and bases his distinction on a contrast between cognitive behaviors which are adaptive (accommodating) and those which are simply acquisitive (assimilating). Adaptive behaviors entail a modification of an individual's schema, whereas nonadaptive behaviors—assimilation-type behaviors—supposedly entail no such modification. The trouble with this notion is that all cognitive behaviors entail a modification of a conceptual structures; otherwise, no learning could take place. To produce a F-discourse or to interpret an F-discourse, a speaker–listener will invariably have to perform operations and even modifications of this conceptual structures, but these modifications (in contrast to those required of N-discourse) are set by convention. My ability to use the English language does not entail my learning or deriving new rules of syntax or inventing new words. Similarly, my ability to process information and solve most everyday problems does not entail my developing new knowledge structures or procedures. In both cases, I rely upon those conceptual and linguistic conventions which are common to others of my kind and experience. However, when these established conventions fail to work, that is, when they fail to achieve my desired goals, be they in discourse or thought, I am forced to abandon them or to modify them so that they do work. N-discourse is such an example and consequently, in Piaget's terms, it is always adaptive.

Although Piaget's distinction between accommodating and assimilating behaviors may not be wholly pertinent to an analysis of discourse, his emphasis on adaptation and regulation is. For the difference between fixed and negotiated discourse is not simply due to the fact that one is conventionalized and the other is not, but rather to the fact that an N-discourse represents a solution to a problem of communication for which there is no prescribed or linguistically set solution. In an N-discourse the speaker is often uncertain that the listener will correctly interpret his meaning, whereas in an F-discourse the speaker knows that if he follows the rules, his meaning will be evident. Consequently, in a negotiated discourse the speaker must not only regulate linguistic conventions to express his idiosyncratic beliefs or meanings, but must adapt them to his listener's discourse knowledge. In this way, his discourse becomes a form of adaptive behavior in the Piagetian sense, as the communicative and cognitive goals of the speaker must accommodate themselves to the constraints imposed by the listener's own discourse competence.

In constructing a discourse, a speaker must resolve at least three different types of problems. First, he must be able to identify the goals of his discourse: does he want new information; does he want his listener to act or respond in a particular way; does he want to influence his listener's attitude; does he have to provide information? Second, the speaker must calculate the impact of his desires or goals upon his listener: will they offend, amuse, inform, or assure him; will the listener think well or ill of the speaker; will he understand what is being said, and if not, why not? Finally, the speaker must determine the manner in which he will express his goals given his understanding of the listener: should he use the interrogative, imperative, or declarative moods; should he focus upon the action implied by the verb; should he use qualifiers? In each of these areas the speaker may encounter complex problems of computation which even if they are solvable in one area, may not be compatible with solutions arrived at in the other areas. For example, the speaker may decide to express a goal that is unacceptable to his listener, or he may decide upon a goal that is acceptable but not expressible. Notice that to perform these many computations a simple generative device would not suffice, as any solution to a problem of discourse is not fixed in advance by a set of rules but is dependent upon the coordinated efforts of very different and often changing procedures and structures. The problem of discourse production therefore becomes not one so much of generation as one of complex regulation, whereby novel structures have to be constructed and combined to express the intended effects of the speaker. In all cases, the range of regulative options is severely limited by the speaker's own discourse competence and that of his listener. Consequently, the organization and communicative effectiveness of any discourse is not simply a function of the speaker, but also of his audience.* If an audience does not possess the same information procedures and structures as the speaker, or of it is unwilling to acknowledge these structures and procedures, then a speaker who wishes to be communicative cannot exceed in his discourse the competence of his audience.

Aside from the initial formation of discourse, regulative processes are also reflected in its ongoing production. In the course of producing an entire discourse episode, a speaker often monitors his statements to assess their impact upon his audience. In those cases where the initial formulation of a sentence or clause is not faulty, this assessment often takes place after each clause or sentence. At this point the speaker may ask himself, "Is this really what I wanted to say?" or "How will this be taken?" Based on the feedback he receives, either directly or through inference, he then applies the corrective actions he deems necessary. Sentential connectors and deictic devices are some of the simpler and more conventionalized means a speaker may use to steer his discourse, whereas commenting and contrastive clauses represent more complex and major corrections for possible error. In either case, to modify his discourse through feedback, the speaker must have a model of himself speaking. Similarly, he must be able to infer why a particular utterance may be misinterpreted and find the proper corrective action. No generative model of discourse could perform these operations; consequently, it would be forced to represent such operations in terms of fixed rules.

*See Grice's discussion of the "cooperative principle" for an excellent account of the types of rules or maxims that a speaker should follow in conversation. His article, "Logic and conversation," will be found in F. Cole and J. Morgan, eds., *Syntax and semantics*, vol. 3, *Speech acts* (New York, Academic Press, 1975), pp. 41–58.

Before discussing the properties of the model we propose for the representation of discourse behavior, let us summarize our previous discussion. Discourse, we have argued, cannot be adequately represented by a simple sender–receiver model. The behaviors required to produce and interpret a discourse are not simply code-determined but may involve the use of established codes in very idiosyncratic ways. We identified two types of discourse, fixed and negotiated, and showed how discourse varies according to each. N-discourse, and probably even some types of F-discourse, require complex processes of regulation to produce. Speakers, we argued, have to perform complex and interdependent deductions regarding the goal of their discourse, its likely effect upon the audience, and the appropriate devices for expression. In many, if not most cases, the solutions to these discourse problems are not available to a speaker in a precoded fashion but must be inferred by him in the course of constructing discourse. Consequently, feedback and self-modeling become significant properties of the discourse process, as the speaker is never certain of the effectiveness of his expressions and must monitor his remarks to regulate their effect. Models without a regulative and adaptive capability that focus primarily on the coded knowledge implicit in discourse suffer as models of discourse, because they are forced to represent all idiosyncratic and regulative behaviors as conventionalized and generative.

2.30. AN AUTOREGULATIVE MODEL OF DISCOURSE BEHAVIOR

In the discussion of our general model of discourse behavior we will focus upon three general areas: the organization and representation of knowledge, the regulative procedures, and the representation and use of discourse and linguistic knowledge. We shall not now attempt to offer a detailed description of the model's properties in each of these domains. Instead, we will direct our discussion toward describing the model's general design characteristics. In later chapters we shall demonstrate how these theoretical or design features are realized in a computer model of discourse behavior.

A. THE REPRESENTATION AND ORGANIZATION OF KNOWLEDGE

Unlike linguistic models, the issue of knowledge representation is critical to our model. And, although the issue is by no means resolved in either artificial intelligence or cognitive psychology, certain facts are becoming clearer. One of the most important of these is that knowledge cannot be adequately represented in terms of structures alone. An individual's intellectual competence does not seem to be simply a function of the complexity or the ordering of his cognitive structures. Rather, much of his knowledge appears to reside in his ability to manipulate and access these structures. Consequently, knowledge is likely to be as much procedural as it is structural, and therefore any model representing it must have both these aspects. It is likely that knowledge is not organized around any all-pervasive taxonomy but around the uses to which it is put. The latter property presents special problems for modeling, for if there is no consistent scheme around which knowledge is organized, then it is highly probable, if not certain, that inconsistent and conflicting knowledge structures and procedures would exist. Consequently, knowledge structures and procedures would have to be stored in such a way that they are masked from one another. Only in this way could computations be performed without their interfering with one another. For example, it is common for people to have contradictory attitudes about the same person or event and to respond variously because of these differing attitudes. If our knowledge bases did not contain a mechanism for cloaking these different representations from one another at any given time, the deduction necessary for their cognition could not effectively function. Instead, we would be forced to adopt a single attitude consistent with our overall classification scheme. Since this is not what people do, and since knowledge appears to be organized around special uses, it is highly likely that an individual's knowledge base is composed of "microworlds" which are consistent within themselves but which are potentially inconsistent one to another.

Just as in discourse there are two types of behavior, so are there in cognitive processing. The F-equivalent includes those knowledge structures and procedures which are part of the standard repertory of a speaker's knowledge. In modeling these, the problem is principally one of encoding the requisite knowledge that the speaker possesses rather than representing those structures and procedures which he uses to derive new knowledge. Much of this knowledge is collectively shared and constitutes the basis upon which most communication depends. The more difficult knowledge to represent is N-knowledge, as it is idiosyncratic and not easily inferred from discourse protocols. Very likely this type of knowledge is both abstract and a function of an individual's own experiences.

Such knowledge is also affective, for it is intimately involved with the individual's valued beliefs. Similarly, the stability of this type of knowledge is critical for the coherency of an individual's understanding of himself and others. Yet the term "affective" is a bit of a misnomer, as it is not the idiosyncracy of knowledge that makes it affective but the relation of that knowledge to the primary and critical goals of the speaker. Therefore, knowledge about goals should also be included in a model of discourse, as such knowledge directly affects cognition, and hence reshapes the configuration of the knowledge base.

B. REGULATIVE PROCEDURES

The representation of knowledge and the design of regulative or control structures are two parts of the same problem, for the procedures that construct and modify knowledge structures are themselves a type of knowledge. Furthermore, since they work with and on knowledge structures, their design is, in turn, dependent upon the design of the knowledge structures. As was pointed out in the previous section, knowledge is not represented in terms of any general taxonomy but in terms of its special uses and effects. Similarly, control structures will not be designed as general-purpose problem-solving procedures, but rather as specialists which solve parts of problems very efficiently and then combine their partial solutions for a final solution. Therefore, like the knowledge structures, the control procedures will be numerous and, in some cases, even contradictory in purpose. In some instances, they will have to be masked from one another to prevent confusions in computation. Although such a control structure design makes good sense from a programming standpoint, from the standpoint of modeling actual discourse behavior, the validity of such an approach is less apparent. Somehow, the notion that our cognitive and linguistic processes are being regulated by procedures which are masked from one another and which function independently and often inconsistently is not pleasing. Yet the fact of unconscious cognitive behaviors is undeniable, and there is neurological evidence to suggest that information processing by the brain is a highly specialized process (Arbib 1972). Moreover, as later chapters demonstrate, discourse protocols (transcripts) suggest the existence of such control structures in the conflicts and mistakes reflected in discourse.

Aside from the design of control procedures, there is the question of their organization within a single coherent system. As noted, one significant ability a speaker of discourse possesses is his ability to listen to himself speak and to modify his remarks according to their anticipated effects. To do so, his control mechanisms must be organized in such a fashion that he can monitor his utterances, infer their point of fallacy, and then make the necessary corrections. Since a discourse failure can be due to a wide range of problems, some of which are deeply embedded in the knowledge base, the control structures must be so organized in the model that they can readily infer the cause of an error and find appropriate solutions. This ability is akin to the notion of introspection, and although it is difficult to say how pervasive it should be, it is so prevalent in discourse behavior as to be required by any model.

In modeling a particular speaker of discourse, problems arise which are similar to those encountered in modeling knowledge structures. It is very difficult to determine from listening to an individual's discourse how deeper control procedures function and are organized. The problem is very similar to that confronted by a psychiatrist, who, by carefully listening to his patients, attempts to infer the structure and processes of their thought. Success in this endeavor has been very uneven, and although Freudian and other models of depth psychology exist, they are not sufficiently precise to be any more than guides. It is my guess that F-type procedures would be the easiest to represent, as they are the most stable and invariant. Yet it would be very difficult to determine how these more conventionalized procedures relate to the more idiosyncratic procedures of the individual. It is conceivable that what would appear on the surface to be a simple F-type procedure was, in fact, a highly complex idiosyncratic procedure. For example, in psychoanalytic discourse it is not uncommon for a patient to repeatedly employ similar constructions or to focus repeatedly upon similar or related themes. Although such discourse behavior could be regarded as fixed in character, because it follows established conventions, its incidence is regulated by special concerns on the part of the speaker and is therefore involved with the intimate regulatory concerns of the patient. To simulate such behaviors would require knowledge of the patient that would be very difficult, if not in some cases impossible, to obtain.

The proper representation of regulative procedures is more than a technical concern, for it is from the standpoint of regulation that much psychological and discourse behavior is evaluated. Piaget, for instance, equates intelligence with adaptive capacity, and the Freudian notions of displacement, denial, and reaction formation all describe types of regulation. Therefore, from a theoretical point of view it is necessary to stress the importance of a speaker's autoregulative strategies, as it is these strategies that determine the adaptivity and effectiveness of the person's actions.

C. DISCOURSE AND LINGUISTIC KNOWLEDGE

One of the outcomes of representing knowledge in this way is that the concepts or information structures used in cognition are often different from the lexical items used in discourse. My assumption is that although words may act as concepts, very often they are not identical to concepts, and therefore in producing discourse there is a problem of going from a conceptual representation to a linguistic representation. Consequently, in modeling a speaker's production of discourse it is not sufficient to simply represent the rules that he uses in generating well-formed discourse, as this is only one aspect of his competence. In addition, there must be a representation of the procedures a speaker uses to translate his conceptual knowledge into linguistic knowledge. Since linguistic options are selected according to their anticipated impact on the audience as well as their equivalence to cognitive structures, the model must contain a representation of the audience impact of various linguistic constructions, as well as their grammaticality. For example, it is not enough for the model to know that the passive voice very often takes a key phrase for the agent; it must also know that a passive construction is an effective device for altering the focus of a clause, and thereby changes the way in which the clause is understood. The manipulation of a listener's interpretation of the contents of a discourse is one of the key techniques of competent speakers, and the English language provides a number of devices for such manipulation. Without altering the information content of a clause, a speaker can dramatically affect the manner in which it is understood by altering the word order, verb tense, voice, mood and aspect, and by the use of qualifiers, dubitatives, and conjunctions. Similarly, at the intersentential level, the interpretation of discourse is regulated through the use of deictic and contrastive devices, binders, and logical connectors. In selecting these techniques the speaker must infer how they will affect the listener's understanding and response to his statements. Consequently, the speaker's knowledge of their correct or grammatical use plays only a minor role in his communicative competence, as it is his understanding of their impact upon his audience that enables him to use them in an effective manner. Furthermore, since the rules for the thematic organization of the clause, and the discourse in general, are far less restrictive than those of syntax, the speaker has a relatively free hand in shaping the thematic character of a discourse to suit his own ends. What we often term style is probably no more than a speaker's consistent use of various thematic and discourse techniques, and perhaps it, rather than syntactic knowledge alone, is the best index of communicative competence.

Before concluding this discussion of the theoretical model, it might be beneficial to clarify the scope of the model's descriptions. For it may not be clear whether our model is intended as a model of a particular speaker of discourse or of all speakers of discourse. This problem was addressed in Chapter 1, in which we distinguished between a collective and an individual theory. At that time we argued that these two types of theories do not differ in kind but in the referent of their descriptions, and that an individual theory implied or required at least part of the descriptions of a collective theory. Therefore, although they differed, they were not wholly independent. In this chapter we have attempted to deal with this problem through the notion of fixed and negotiated discourse, where the former would constitute the basis of a collective theory and the two together would form the basis of an individual theory. Had our concern been to discriminate between those behaviors that were collectively and individually held, our model would have been collective and would have entailed a very different enterprise.

3 : A GENERAL OVERVIEW OF THE MODEL

A little inaccuracy sometimes saves tons of explanation.—SAKI

3.10. OVERVIEW

In this chapter, a summary description of our program is provided. As subsequent chapters will reveal, the actual program differs from this description. Yet I feel that by first describing it in these somewhat simplistic terms the reader will gain an understanding that will help render the following chapters more intelligible.

ERMA is a computer program written in CONNIVER, a sublanguage of LISP. The program is intended as a limited model of the discourse behavior of a patient in a psychoanalytic session, and as such is also intended to be a preliminary model of the processes whereby speakers translate thoughts, feelings, and attitudes into the discourse of language.

Upon command the program can initiate, plan, modify, censor, and generate a limited discourse. It has a model of itself, its "world," those to whom it may speak, and of its own discourse options and behaviors. Like a human speaker, it has an understanding of what should and should not be said or "thought" and, accordingly, has knowledge of how to use language to achieve communicative effects. Also, like the human speaker, the program interrupts and qualifies itself when points of discourse appear inappropriate.

The program's data base and operations were formed by an examination of a patient's transcripts taken during four years of psychoanalysis. No attempt was made to have a comprehensive representation of the knowledge and cognition contained in all the transcripts. Rather, a limited but representative discourse episode was modeled to the depth required to simulate the requisite discourse.

Diagram 3.10 shows the basic organization of the program. In a very broad sense, the arrows represent the flow of processing within the program and the boxes signify a concentration of similar processing programs. For purposes of explanation, the program is presented as a linear process, but in actuality it is not organized linearly but around the computational capability of various types of programs that look for the appearance of different data patterns which, when present, they process. Later we shall discuss how these programs work, but first we shall present the program in terms that are intuitively palpable.

3.20. MOTIVATING CONCEPTS

Discourse is initiated by the appearance of a problem that needs solving through the expression of a discourse. The problem is stated in the form of a concept, which might be any of the following kinds: "I want some *x*," or "I don't understand *x* and *y*," or "I want to tell *A* and *B*, *x* and *y*." Within the model, discourse can be initiated by any number of means. It may be initiated by a need of its own, or in response to the stated or implied need of another. Consequently, the problem initiating the discourse may be resolved through a question, a request, a command, or a statement. In the course of generating a discourse the model may initiate other discourses, depending upon whether it "feels" a need to mention other topics or to clarify its remarks. Therefore, although the model is initially motivated by a motivating concept, once it has been so motivated, it can generate its own motivations for further discourse behavior. There is an instance of this in the episode modeled by the program. The patient begins one form of discourse in an attempt to effect a change in

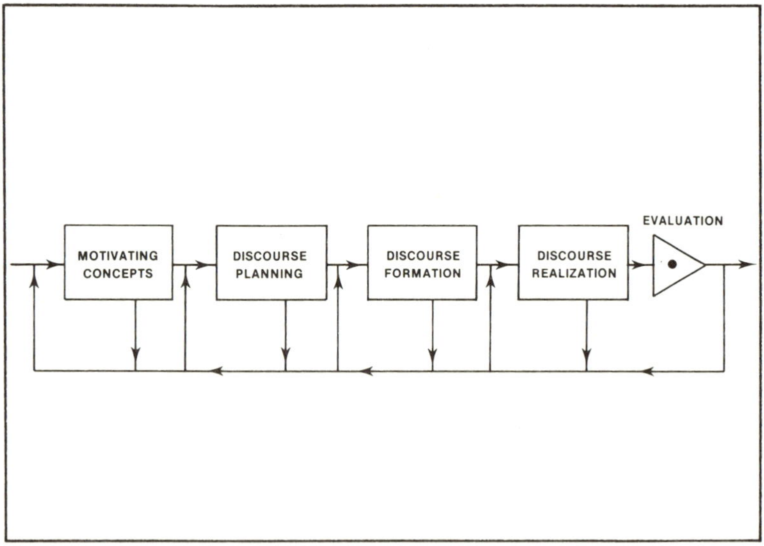

DIAGRAM 3.10

her relationship with her therapist, and then, upon reflection about this discourse, initiates another discourse in an attempt to explain and understand her motivation for the former discourse.

It may turn out that the motivating concept has no way of being realized through discourse. In this case, either a facsimile of the original motivating concept is found or the motivating concept is sought. If there are no motivating concepts on the program's list of possibilities, the program will look for something to say or ''think about'' by a search of its data base.

Diagram 3.20 shows how motivation works within the program. Notice that two types of motivations are represented: those originating on the initial possibilities list and those that are initiated through the intrusion of selected ''interrupt''-type programs. These interrupt programs appear virtually everywhere in the program. They might be ''fired'' by having a pattern ''remind'' the program of other things it wanted to say or not to say, or they may be fired to inhibit a thought or discourse, and thus give rise to a different, diversionary discourse.

In the diagram the dashed lines represent the appearance of interrupts that determine whether a particular motivating concept is unrealizable, thereby causing the selection of another motivating concept. Failure to realize a motivation can be for a number of reasons: no solution in planning, no way to realize the concept into an acceptable discourse, or no way to form a discourse out of a plan. The second type of motivation is represented by the circles and solid lines. When such motivations are instituted by the firing of an interrupt, the result is a very particular motivation and the beginning of a new planning process. Such motivations may be regarded as lying dormant within the

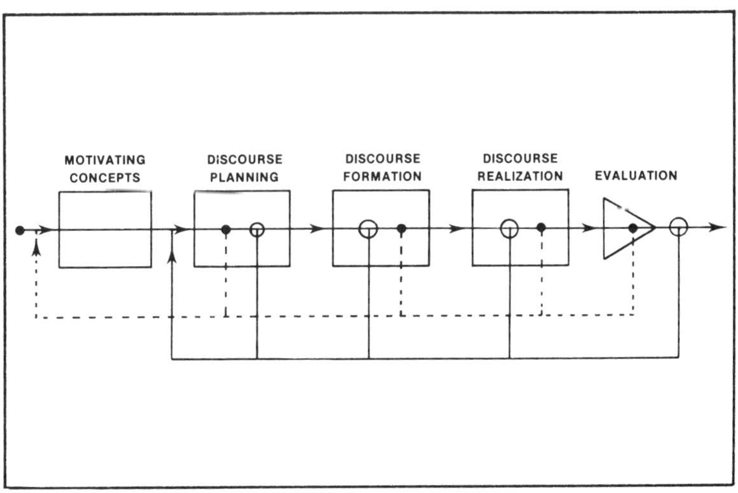

DIAGRAM 3.20

speaker and awakened to expression when keyed conceptual patterns are present.

3.30. PLANNING PROCESSES

Planning processes are groups of programs especially concerned with taking a given problem, as presented in the motivating concept, and finding an acceptable solution. For example, if the motivating concept required that a particular object be acquired (e.g., salt), the planning programs determine if it is possible to acquire that object under present circumstances (e.g., where is the salt?), whether it is necessary to make any requests or initiate any actions in order to acquire the object (e.g., who shall I ask for the salt?), and how such actions might be expressed in the discourse (e.g., please pass the salt). Since the program is organized on an interrupt basis, it is somewhat artificial to differentiate between planning processes and discourse formation processes, because in many instances they work together. Yet the programs that we are describing here are primarily concerned with making the deductions necessary to construct the content and action of a discourse; and, although the determination of content may affect the thematic organization of the discourse, initially audience impact and thematic organization are not considered.

Besides the standard problem-solving programs, the planning process contains a number of special-purpose interrupt programs. These programs are similar in operation to those discussed in the previous paragraph, but in this case the programs are alerted by the presence of specified problem patterns. When such a pattern is detected, the programs assume control and perform their own very specialized mode of problem solving. Very often, these special-purpose programs work in conjunction with interrupt programs whose purpose it is to detect patterns which are unacceptable either to the speaker or to the listener. When a pattern is determined to be unacceptable by an interrupt program, one of these special-purpose problem-solving programs is fired to find an acceptable solution.

The planning process is represented in Diagram 3.30. Those interrupt programs that are specialists in problem solving and in censorship are represented as two separate boxes. Since both are a part of the planning process, they are shown as originating in the planning module.

3.40. KNOWLEDGE BASE

Within the data base is stored all the model's knowledge of the world and itself. This knowledge is partitioned into various layers and is altered through the inclusion and removal of data items. For example, if a data item, *x*, is true only if another item has a particular property, and this property is altered, then

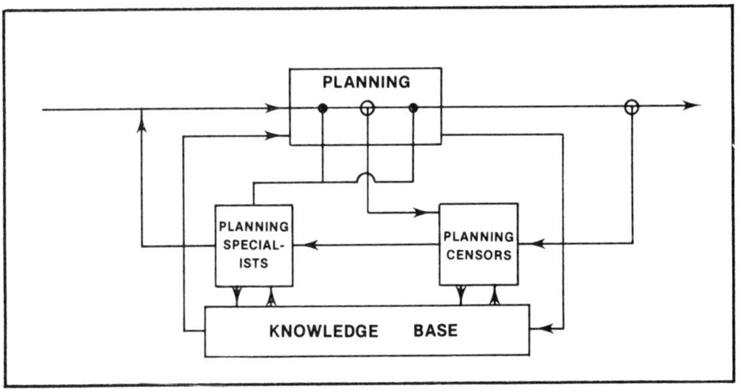

DIAGRAM 3.30

programs in the data base are fired to change the status of the data item, *x*. However, an alteration in one context does not necessarily imply the same alteration in another context. Consequently, the same item can be true in one context and false in another.

In processing concepts for planning, formation, and realization, the knowledge base is continually consulted and altered. Records of the alterations can be maintained so that the planning programs and other programs can recover past operations and kept track of previous efforts. In contrast to most other programming languages, the data structures of CONNIVER can be easily manipulated and altered throughout computation. Thus, data structures can be created, revised, and destroyed—all in the course of performing a computation. The obvious advantage of such a data base is that it keeps an up-to-date account of what is going on in the program, and it does so in a manner that is not separate from the processes of computation but one that comprises a participating part of the computation process.

3.50. DISCOURSE FORMATION PROGRAMS

Working in close conjunction with those programs that are planning the discourse are a group of programs that transform the solutions of the planning programs into a form that can be expressed in discourse. These programs determine the effect and the impact which the discourse will have on the intended audience. In assessing effects, the programs consult the knowledge base to see if the information being expressed is known to the audience, and, if so, to what degree and in what manner. Impact, on the other hand, is concerned with determining the emotional and proprietary impact of the discourse upon the hearer. In making these assessments, the program consults the knowledge base to see if the intended discourse might be offensive or inappropriate in any way, either for personal or sociocultural reasons. For example, a group of programs may find that a given concept is both unclear and offensive to an intended hearer. If the concept is not so novel or so offensive that it cannot be expressed, they make suggestions as to what aspects of the concept are offensive or unclear, and whether they should be emphasized, deemphasized, or qualified. These suggestions are then taken by the realization programs and used in selecting the appropriate discourse options to achieve the effects suggested by the discourse formation programs. For example, a program may determine that in the concept "John left home in a purple flying saucer," the concept of a flying saucer is unknown to the listener in this context and requires emphasis for clarification. The realization programs might then express this concept and its emphasis with the following predicative device, "It was a purple flying saucer in which John left home." Perhaps in such an unusual and incredulous discourse situation, the remark might even be prefaced by, "You won't believe this, but. . . ." In either case, it would be a discourse-forming program that required the particular realization of the concept.

Roughly, the discourse formation programs are of three types: those that transform the plan concept (thought) into a discourse concept (speech), those that examine that discourse concept to see if the concept is acceptable to the intended listener (feedback thought), and those that suggest how the discourse concept should be treated for expression. In Diagram 3.50 the first type of program is represented in the discourse formation box, as such programs constitute the core of the formation process. The other programs function on a contingent basis and are therefore represented in terms of dots and circles, the former representing impact-effect evaluators and the later, special-purpose discourse formers. Although these can assist in the normal formation process, they generally handle the difficult objections raised by the evaluative programs, and in some instances, they call planning programs to process particularly difficult objections and to plan supplementary discourse.

3.60. DISCOURSE REALIZATION PROCESS

Once the discourse formation programs have determined how the principal concepts should be marked and modified, the realization programs try to find the appropriate discourse, syntactic, and semantic means to achieve their expression. To this end, the realization programs are very knowledgeable, as they have at their disposal a wealth of information about the interpretation of formation markers into linguistically acceptable and communicatively effective discourse. Much of this information is implicit in the organization of these programs alone, but much of it also exists in data stored about words and constructions in the semantic and syntactic lexicons.

Once again, most of the computation is achieved through special-purpose interrupt programs that look for a pattern and, when it appears, interrupt

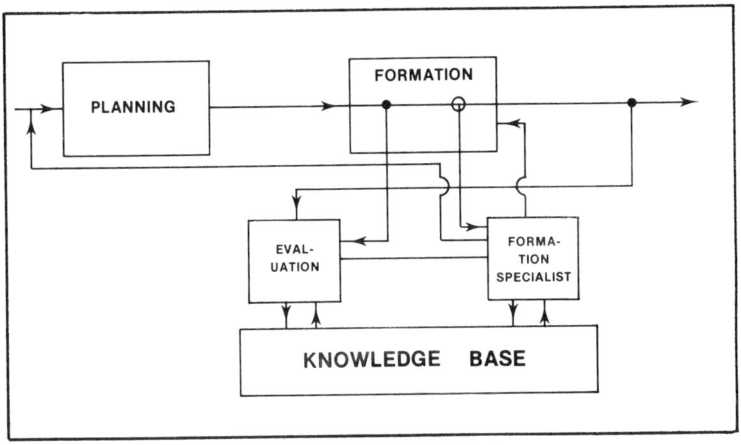

DIAGRAM 3.50

processing and assume control of processing themselves. Given the complexity and in some cases the contradictory character of formation program suggestions, the realization of a concept can be a protracted process involving a number of revisions. For, in the course of finding one solution to a realization problem, another solution may be negated. This problem is dealt with in a number of ways, one of which is to have special-purpose programs keyed to solve just such problems, and another is to have this component interact with the formation module to reshape the discourse. In such cases, the expression of discourse is interrupted with interjections (ah . . . I mean) until a new and more appropriate means of expression is found.

Diagram 3.60 shows how the discourse realization process is organized. The same conventions are used as were used in previous illustrations.

3.70. EVALUATION PROCESS

During and after speaking we tend to evaluate what we have said. We listen to ourselves speaking, and we check to see if what we are saying is what we really mean. Within psychoanalytic discourse this process is particularly apparent and important. Here the patient is often torn between trying to be open and direct with the expression of feelings, and being secretive and correct. Outside the therapeutic context, this self-reflective capability is also important. Speakers check their discourse continually to confirm the propriety and effectiveness of their discourse, both to anticipate possible misunderstanding and to ensure that it conforms with an acceptable self-image.

In raw form, ERMA has these abilities. The programs grouped under the heading "evaluation" are interrupt-driven and look for the presence of special patterns in discourse. These patterns can be related to the content or organiza-

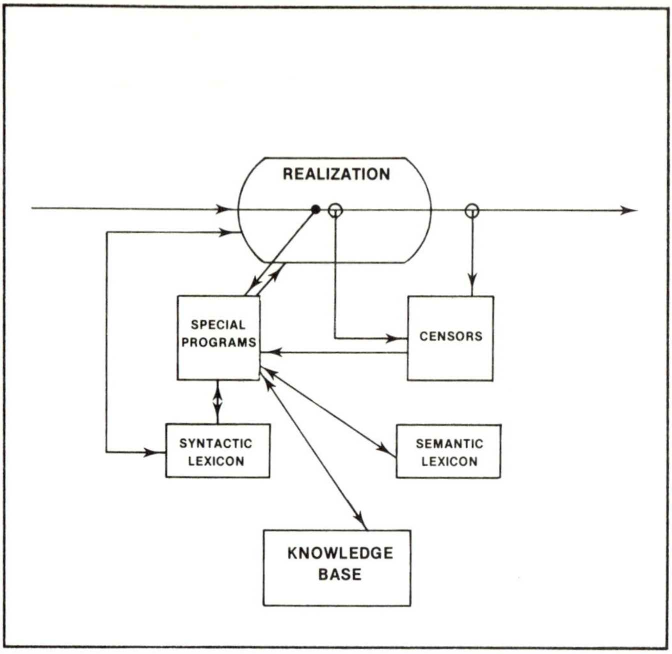

DIAGRAM 3.60

tion of the discourse, or to the whole character of a discourse episode. When detected, the interrupt programs fire, and either interrupt the discourse with interjections, pauses, and dubitatives or create a whole new discourse. In the former case, when the interrupts have detected a pattern that is either inappropriate or ungrammatical, they give the speaker time through interjections to find corrections for the detected failures.

The organization of the evaluation programs is shown in Diagram 3.70. Since they have an ability to immediately affect discourse through interjections and pauses, they are represented as affecting the discourse stream. However, as they can also work with other programs to generate corrective procedures and generate new discourse, they are also shown as special-purpose programs.

3.80. TRANSCRIPTS MODELED IN ERMA

The transcripts used in creating the ERMA model were taken from nearly four years of taped therapy sessions with two psychoanalysts. As the tapes were not readily available, the modeling was based upon the transcripts. However, careful attention was given to these transcriptions and all relevant pauses, hesitations, and interrupts were recorded, including their time of

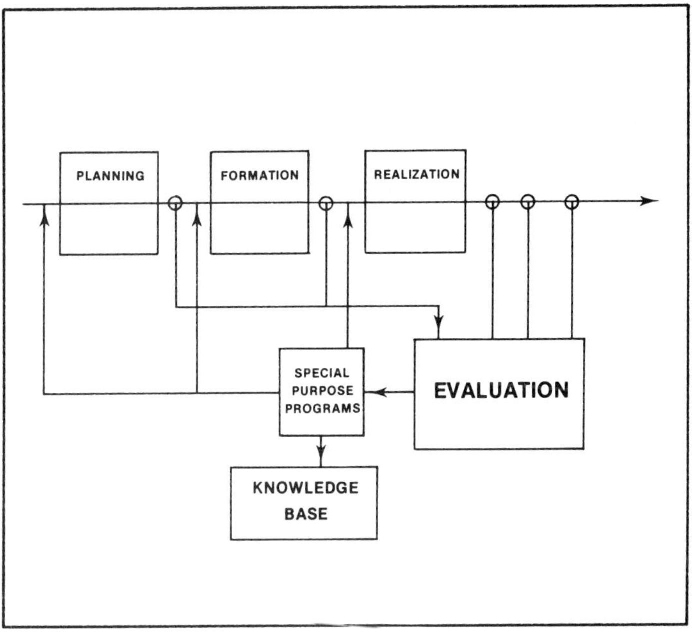

DIAGRAM 3.70

duration. Although extensive, the transcripts were not complete; they were principally exerpts of selected discourse episodes.

Following is a transcription of the actual discourse episode that was modeled. As you can see, although it is brief, it contains a complex and revealing amount of deduction.

> You know, for some reason, I, uh, just thought about, uh, about the bill and about payment again. That (pause 2 seconds), that, uh (pause 4 seconds), I was, uh, thinking that I—of asking you whether it wouldn't be all right for you (pause 2 seconds), you know, not to give me a bill. That is, uh—I would (hesitates), since I usually by— well, I immediately thought of the objections to this, but my idea was that I would simply count up the number of hours and give you a check at the end of the month. Then I realized that there might be some, uh (hesitates), some disagreement (pause 2 seconds) on occasion about whether I was to pay for an hour. That if, you know, if I should miss it or, anyway, there might be instances in which, uh (hesitates), I–I shouldn't be, uh—toting up my own bill. (pause 40 seconds) I'm just trying to think how that connects with what I was, uh, saying. And I (pause 4 seconds), hum, is—think it may (hesitates) be that, uh, I mean, on my—original reason for thinking about this was that, uh (pause 3 seconds), I never was, I

mean, that every time I've gotten a bill, I've always known how much it would be. And it seemed a kind of—uh (pause 3 seconds), e–empty little ritual—uh (pause 3 seconds), but I don't know necessarily why I—you know, why I wanted to do away with it. Uh (pause 3 seconds), like just, I mean, it may be that somehow I (pause 2 seconds), uh, again, that I should (pause 2 seconds), it can't really be that I should have control over it. But something like that. But maybe because of it would—uh (pause 2 seconds), it would reduce some—I—the amount of, uh (pause 2 seconds), I—exchange or, uh (pause 2 seconds), I was going to say interchange, but that's not right. And then I thought of, uh (slight laugh) (hesitates), intercourse between us.

4 : COMPUTATIONAL COGNITION

Knowledge, like St. Augustine's God, has its center everywhere and its circumference nowhere. . . .—NORTHROP FRYE

4.10. OVERVIEW

Up until this point our discussion has been primarily theoretical and has not presupposed special knowledge of linguistics or computer programing. This chapter is different. Here we shall discuss in detail the manner in which concepts and cognitive mechanisms are represented in our model. Since the model is programmed in CONNIVER, a sublanguage of LISP, a minimum knowledge of LISP is needed to follow the discussion. In an earlier draft of this chapter, an attempt was made to provide a brief description of LISP and CONNIVER to familiarize the general reader with some of the key concepts of these languages. However, this attempt proved unsuccessful, as it is extremely difficult to adequately describe these languages short of writing a manual. In lieu of such an effort, it is suggested that Clark Weissman's *LISP 1.5 primer* (1967) be consulted for an understanding of LISP and McDermott and Sussman's CONNIVER *Reference Manual* (1973) be consulted for an understanding of CONNIVER. It should be noted that, unlike the LISP primer, the CONNIVER manual is not an easy document to read and presupposes a sophisticated understanding of LISP.

Despite these difficulties in discussing LISP or CONNIVER, we shall, nonetheless, provide a brief description of some of the key properties of CONNIVER. This is unavoidable, because the manner in which we represent concepts and the procedures that process them is an inseparable part of this language. Without going into the details of the language, we shall describe its general design as a problem-solving language and identify some of its key features. Two of these features will receive particular attention in this and subsequent chapters. The first is the language's ability to compartmentalize its data base into microworlds, or "contexts," which can be created or abolished at will and contain their own truth values—even in contradiction to other contexts. The second is the use of "methods," special programs that are stored in contexts and invoked not by being "called," but through the appearance of a specified data pattern. Through such programs it is possible to have a highly decentralized control structure in which programs work in conjunction with one another without being able to identify one another.

In the second section of this chapter, we shall discuss our three types of concepts: generic, extended, and special purpose. Generic concepts, as the name implies, are less concepts in themselves than a label for a wide class of concepts. Their principal role is in the realization of concepts into words and in the formation of "token" concepts. As a type of extended concept, a token concept represents an instance of a generic concept and has attached to it a large number of property lists to designate its information content, how it is used, and its relationship to other token concepts. When token concepts are combined to express a relation or process, they form ARD concepts, which might be loosely characterized as conceptual clauses. However, unlike clauses, they can be arbitrary complex, and one ARD could constitute an entire discourse. Special-purpose concepts are those that are concerned with the conjoining, disjoining, and expression of concepts.

Following a section on interpersonal and information indicators (labels for property lists) is a discussion of the notion of "multiple-body interrupts," a modified version of the CONNIVER method used to perform most of the processing within the program. The advantage that multiple-body interrupts have over methods is their ability to coordinate the processing of many more programs in the solution of a problem by having available additional "bodies"—special-purpose programs that regulate the firing of other programs.

The final section of this chapter describes the organization of processing into five contexts: LEIBNITZ, CALVIN, MACHIAVELLI, CICERO, and FREUD. Each of these contexts is personified because each embodies different and often conflicting beliefs about what should be said or thought. LEIBNITZ contains the program's general knowledge, and all the other concepts draw upon it. CALVIN is concerned principally with the initiation and censoring of thoughts and discourse expressions. MACHIAVELLI is concerned with figuring out ways of expressing complex or indiscrete concepts. CICERO contains program specialists in the translation of concepts into words, and works in conjunction with the REALIZATION context, discussed in Chapter 5. The programs in FREUD try to figure out why certain concepts were thought or expressed.

4.20. CONNIVER

As tools, all programming languages are designed for special purposes. Implicit in their design are certain assumptions about the uses of the language, the type of computer system, and the skills of the user. Unlike conventional algebraic programming languages, CONNIVER is designed as a tool for artificial intelligence research. It is designed in such a way that it both enables the programmer to think freely about his problem and to program his ideas with a minimum of programming constraints. Developed by Drew McDermott and Gerald Sussman (1973) at MIT, it represents an extension and modification of many of the ideas in PLANNER, a problem-solving language developed in 1971 by Carl Hewitt, also of MIT.

As a sublanguage of LISP, CONNIVER is a recursive language which uses the Polish functional notation, in which data and programs have a homogeneous representation. Although it looks like LISP, it has two major features which provide it with programming flexibility that LISP does not have.

The first of these features is its data-base structure, which gives the user a generalized way of storing these data in distinct microworlds or "contexts." Contexts are independent data locations whose status or "truth value" is altered by the addition or removal of CONNIVER datums. These datums are list structures that are identified by special-purpose programs in terms of their "pattern." For example,

(ADD′ (SPIRO IS A COMMONER))
(REMOVE′ (SPIRO IS VICE PRESIDENT))

makes the item (SPIRO IS A COMMONER) present in a context and (SPIRO IS VICE PRESIDENT) absent. Therefore, in this context it is true that "Spiro is a commoner," whereas it is not true that he is Vice President. However, by having another context it is quite possible to have the proposition "Spiro is Vice President" be present, and hence true. Although both propositions would be contained within the data base, they would not entail any contradiction, for they occupy different contexts, and hence "different worlds." The advantage of having contexts in which programs and datums can be stored separately is that they enable the programmer to create hypothetical worlds in which to experiment with possible outcomes. For example, if I wanted to see what a house would look like if painted lavender, I could paint the entire house lavender. However, if after doing so, I decided that I did not like the result, I would be stuck with it anyway, and thus be a victim of my own alteration. In CONNIVER, I could avoid this undesirable consequence by constructing a hypothetical world or context in which I could make my change, and then decide to return the context to its original status. This capability gives the programmer immense power in experimenting "simultaneously" with various solutions. For example, in a chess-playing program the programmer can design in such a way that the program can compute the effect of many different moves without actually making these moves.

Besides datums, properties can be added and removed from contexts. For example, if I wanted to add the property DISBELIEVED under the indicator CHARACTERISTICS to the proposition (THERE ARE ONLY SEVEN TAPES), I would use the following INCLUDE function:

(INCLUDE′ (THERE ARE ONLY SEVEN TAPES)
′CHARACTERISTICS′ (DISBELIEVED))
to produce the following structure in a designated context:
(THERE ARE ONLY SEVEN TAPES)
CHARACTERISTICS (DISBELIEVED)

By having the status of the data base be determined by the addition and removal of datums and their properties, it is possible to regulate processing without having to know what every program is doing. Programs do not have to be called but can act through the sending of a datum, property, or program to a context; through their removal; or through their addition. For example, if the datum (SPIRO IS A COMMONER) is added to a particular context, a program there might be keyed to this pattern,

(IF-ADDED PAY-TAX (!>ANYONE IS A COMMONER)
(ADD′ (ANYONE MUST PAY HIS TAXES)))
and produce the following structure in the context:
(SPIRO MUST PAY HIS TAXES)

In this way, programs are activated without having to be called. But before discussing how these programs work, a little more needs to be said about how contexts are structured.

Contexts are made up of layers, and each layer has a name and can have datums, properties, and programs added or removed from it. The layers are constructed in such a way that a bottom layer can "see" what is transpiring in an upper layer. In other words, datums can be added and removed from a bottom layer without the top layer knowing about it (although the reverse is not always the case). For example, the contents of layers 20, 30, and 40 are known to the programs in layer 50, but layer 50 is not known to layers 20, 30, and 40.

20
30
40
WORLD 50
60

If it were decided to perform an experiment in the context WORLD, and we did not want to disturb the results of the other layers in this context (20, 30, and 40), we would relocate WORLD to layer 60 from layer 50. After performing our computations, we could restore WORLD back to the previous context, thereby disgarding the results of the experiment; or we could retain the results and expand the WORLD context to include layer 60. This, in a very basic sense, is how contexts work. For a more complete explanation, the CONNIVER reference manual should be consulted.

The second major feature of CONNIVER is its use of "methods," of which there are three types: IF-ADDED, IF-REMOVED, and IF-NEEDED. As one of our previous examples showed, IF-ADDED methods are programs that are invoked when a datum is added to a context that matches its pattern. When this happens, a new context frame or layer is created and the "body" of the method is executed. In our previous example of

(IF-ADDED PAY-TAX (!>ANYONE IS A COMMONER)
(ADD′ (ANYONE MUST PAY HIS TAXES)))

the name of the method is PAY-TAX and the body or program is (ADD′ (ANYONE MUST PAY HIS TAXES)). IF-REMOVED methods work similarly except that they are invoked when a datum is removed from a context. IF-NEEDED methods, on the other hand, are somewhat different and involve a feature of CONNIVER that we have yet mentioned. They are methods which assist other procedures in solving a problem and are found or "fetched" by a FETCH function when their patterns match its pattern argument. They are then placed at the end of a POSSIBILITIES list and are invoked by a special TRY-NEXT function, which goes through the possibilities list and peels off the methods as they are needed. In this manner, IF-NEEDED methods can provide another method with a wide range of problem-solving aids, and thereby expand its problem-solving powers without altering its internal structure.

Methods, like contexts, are difficult to understand without a general understanding of CONNIVER. Consequently, the previous descriptions are intended only to provide a general idea of how they work so that subsequent discussions of the program are intelligible. Later we shall discuss how contexts and modified versions of methods are used in our model.

4.30. THE REPRESENTATION OF CONCEPTS

Our representation of concepts in their bare form is deceptively simple. But, as we embellish and add to this form, the concept quickly becomes a quite complex structure not easily described in natural language. An understanding of concepts comes through an understanding of the manner in which their structures are combined and used. In this section we shall first identify the basic elements of which concepts are made, and then show how these basic structures combine to generate information structures of considerable complexity and representational power. Since we have modeled concepts in terms of their representational roles, our discussion will focus upon the characteristics of different types of concepts and the roles that they play in cognition. In the next section we shall discuss the programs that manipulate and process concepts to achieve solutions to problems of cognition and discourse formation.

4.31. *The basic form of concepts*

Before stating how concepts are represented, let us state what we want them to do. First, we want a sufficiently general and flexible method of representation that can both capture all the unique informational properties of a concept without isolating that concept from related concepts. Moreover, we want concepts defined primarily in terms of what they do rather than what they are, so that concepts with related uses can be easily referenced.

Second, concepts should be able to be combined together to create new concepts in as free a manner as possible, the only constraints being those deliberately imposed by the system. To do this, they must contain information about the acceptability of their potential combinations, and this information should be relatively easy to access. Also, concepts should be able to perform computations themselves; that is, in some cases, a process of cognition is itself a part of the concept.

To meet these requirements, concepts are represented as CONNIVER datums with property lists:

(6 TOKEN #BILL)
< CHARACTERISTICS LARGE
< UNACCEPTABLE (#THERAPIST)

Here the topmost line is a CONNIVER datum list. The less-than sign indicates that the next "atom" is an indicator and is followed by an expression, either an atom, LARGE, or a list, (#THERAPIST). It is not difficult to see that through the addition of property lists, each of which can contain embedded property lists, the definition or "meaning" of a concept could become quite complex. In the example above, the datum was represented as a list, although it could just as easily have been a single atom. As we will see later, most of our concepts are datum lists, because the extra datums are necessary to reference the concepts.

Indicators play a particularly important role in the processing of concepts, for they contain information that determines both what the concept means and how it is to be processed. For example, if the patient were thinking of mentioning her bill, she might want to know if its mention might disturb the therapist in any way. She could then do a search on the concept #BILL for the indicator, UNACCEPTABLE, to see if there were any properties listed there. In this case she would find that the bill was an unacceptable topic to the list, (#THERAPIST). After evaluating that concept, she could then determine whether and how the subject of bill could be broached.

In the course of processing a concept, property lists and indicator can be added and removed at will, and, depending upon the nature of these additions and deletions, a record is kept of the modification of the concepts in the data base. Therefore, the model can consult its data base to see what changes have been effected on a concept and gather all relevant information for a given processing goal. There are many advantages to working with indicators in this way, for it permits the model to use that part of the concept which is relevant to its computations without having to use all the information associated with a given concept. Moreover, indicator names tell how the concept might be used in forming a relationship between concepts. For example, the indicator STRUCTURE has as its properties PROCESS, GOAL, INITIATOR, etc., which specify how a concept might be combined or used in conjunction with other concepts. Therefore, depending upon its structural role, the concept #WATER may act as an initiator, process, or goal. Similarly, indicators provide information about the causes, motivations, effects, and impacts of concepts or combinations of concepts. When needed, this information enables the system to make inferences about causation and motivation. Should the system be blocked in searching for a solution, indicators such as INHIBIT and PREVENTED-BY provide information on their property lists about those concepts that prevent a solution or intended action from taking place.

In designing our conceptual system we have taken the position that the model only accesses that information needed to achieve its goals. Therefore, when processing a particular concept, it does not access all the information that might be potentially linked to that concept. Rather, it specifies what it needs and then attempts to find it. If successful, the processing is rather simple, but if restrictions and problems are incurred, as in our simulated discourse situation, additional information is requested until the solution is found. This additional information is stored in the data base and is most often accessible through the invocation of the proper indicator and property list. However, like a human being, it is quite possible that the model will have something stored that it wants but cannot access.

Although the use of datums and property lists permits the generation of complex embedded concepts and the relatively efficient accessing of concept properties for processing, it is not terribly efficient for determining the informational similarity of different concepts. This is due to the fact that properties cannot be directly accessed but first have to be accessed through their indicators. Although this is a limitation of CONNIVER and LISP, it can be circumvented somewhat through the use of an indicator that indicates related concepts. By invoking this indicator, the system can determine which concepts a concept is related to, and then use these concepts to derive conceptual associations. Similarly, there are indicators that designate those concepts that a concept is logically derived from or correlated with. Such indicators facilitate cognition and are only invoked when they are needed. However, such treatment of concepts implies that except in cases of relatively simple definitional similarity, the relationships or similarity of concepts have to be explicitly identified beforehand and cannot be simply inferred through an examination of common properties. In other words, there is no superset–subset organization of the data base that places an implicit semantic ordering on all concepts. Such an ordering would have to be inferred or constructed. However, an argument could be made that systems (Quillian 1969) that imposed such an organizational framework were highly restrictive, since such hierarchical information is not always relevant, and concepts are better organized around the goals of the system rather than some external taxonomy. This being the case, semantic relatedness could be established through programs that create concepts of the relatedness of other concepts. This criteria of classification would then vary according to the computational requirements of the system and, although it might resemble some external taxonomy, would not necessarily be equivalent to it. If such is the case, our method of representation would be amenable to such a classification procedure.

Before proceeding to discuss the different types of concepts used in this model, we need to clarify what we mean by a concept. Conventional usage implies that a concept is an identifiable entity which is bounded in some way. Hence, we are led to believe that it is something that has a singular and unified meaning. Although our treatment of concepts does not flatly contradict this notion, it is not particularly relevant to our method of representation. In other words, the delimitation and a priori specification of concept boundaries are not critical to our model. A concept of an entity or process is simply everything that can be accessed under the atom or list standing for that item of data. Therefore, when represented in an unrestricted manner, a concept designator, such as a house, can be interpreted to mean all the information that a speaker–hearer may have stored under that concept. Since this type of information is quite vast, the use of such generic concepts supplies relatively little information. Yet when the generic concept is restricted in some way through the selection of proper indicators and their properties, the concept takes on a specific and quite often unique meaning, such as "*the red* house *your brother built*." Consequently, the generic concept is seldom used in actual cognition, as an understanding of its meaning would entail a costly search of the system's entire data base. Rather, a part or token of the generic concept is used in most cognition, as it is generally not the general concept that is thought or expressed, but rather a restricted aspect of it. It is my belief that effective communication takes place through interactive restrictions on mutually held generic concepts. Hence, token concepts and their indicators and property lists are the means by which generic concepts are given a specific meaning. In those cases where two or more communicants share token concepts, their discourse can be quite abbreviated. However, when there is no mutually held token concept, the speaker must begin his discourse with commonly held token concepts and then publicly construct the token concept he wishes to express. Our method of concept representation is designed to make this process of concept construction and restriction possible, and to understand how this is achieved, we need to discuss further the three different types of concepts used in the model.

4.32. *Generic concepts*

As we have indicated throughout, concepts are best understood in terms of the role they play in the process of discourse formation and generation. Generic concepts have no specific meaning; rather they are principally labels used to designate a class of information structures with common properties. However, their meaning is determined by the programs that use them, and their role in more complex information structures, such as tokens and ARDs. Generic concepts have their own unique property lists, but unlike those of the other concept types, their property lists do not designate particular information properties. Rather, these indicators are principally concerned with the ways in which generic concepts are given lexical realization.

A generic concept is simply represented as a list with a sign (#) before it: #I, #WHATEVER, #ETC. All the generic concepts are entered into a *semantic lexicon,* which may have the following indicators and property lists associated with it.

Indicator	*Property list*
REALIZED-AS	A list of words or even phrases that the generic concept can be realized as lexically.
RELATED-CONCEPT	A list of generic concepts that may be related in some way to this generic concept.
REALIZE-PROG	A special-purpose program used for the realization of a generic concept.
IMPACT-AT	A list that references those concepts that contain useful information about the impact of this generic concept. By impact is meant the emotional response a hearer or hearers might have to the generic concept.
EFFECT-AT	A list that references those concepts that might contain information about the potential effect of this concept.
MOTIVATION-AT	A list that references those concepts that might have information about the motivation behind a generic concept.
CAUSE-AT	A list that references those concepts that might contain information about the cause underlying a particular generic concept.
DENOTER-CLASS	When a generic concept is used as a denoter (i.e., like a modifier), this list identifies the class of adjectives to which it belongs. The classifica-

tion scheme is relevant for sequencing purposes and will be discussed later.

The purpose of the semantic lexicon is to provide different processing components, particularly the realization component, the information it needs about a given generic concept to complete its work. By and large, the semantic lexicon generally works in conjunction with the *syntactic lexicon,* which also has generic concept entries, and provides information about the syntactic features of words—information needed not for cognition but the generation of acceptable discourse.

4.33. *Extended concepts:* TOKENs *and* ARDs

The token concept is composed of a generic concept; the optional word, TOKEN; and an identifying number in front of it. An example is

(16 TOKEN #ERMA)

This token concept can be referenced by combining the concept number, which is always in the first position, with the "prime" concept, #ERMA, in a dotted pair:

(16. #ERMA)

When token concepts are combined together to form "conceptual clauses," they are termed ARDs (argument concepts and relator concepts). ARDs are composed of arguments and relators. The arguments are numbered A1, A2, and so on, and are bound together by the relator R to express a complex relation, one potentially containing many embeddings between one or more arguments. An example of an ARD is:

A1	R1	A2
(1. ARD (16. #ERMA)	(2. #LIKE)	(3. #CHOCOLATE))

The prime concept of this ARD is the second component of the dotted pair in the third position, in this case the relator concept, #LIKE. To reference this ARD, the following form is sufficient: (1. #LIKE). Notice that there are no generic concepts in the ARD, as both (16. #ERMA) and (3. #CHOCOLATE) are token concepts.

This ARD might be realized as: Erma likes chocolate; Chocolate, Erma likes; Erma likes hot chocolate. Notice that the last sample realization introduces a word not represented at the level of the token concept. To get the realization "Erma likes hot chocolate," the token concept, (3. #CHOCOLATE), would have to have the following indicator and property list:

(3. #CHOCOLATE)
< CHARACTERISTICS (12. #HOT)

Indicators can be attached to an entire ARD as well as single token concepts. When they are so attached, they denote a property that pertains to the entire relation within the ARD. To see the difference between an indicator attached to a single token and one attached to an entire ARD, consider these two sample sentences and their conceptual representation:

1. George painted the white house.
   (1. ARD (5. #GEORGE) (6. #PAINT) (7. #HOUSE))
   (7. #HOUSE)
   < CHARACTERISTICS (8. #WHITE)
   (8. #WHITE)
   < STRUCTURE(DENOTER)
2. George painted the house white.
   (2. ARD (5. #GEORGE) (6. #PAINT) (7. #HOUSE))
   < CHARACTERISTICS (8. #WHITE)
   (8. #WHITE)
   < STRUCTURE(DENOTER)

In the first example, the CHARACTERISTIC indicator is attached to the token house, thereby denoting a particular house. In the second example, the indicator, CHARACTERISTIC, is attached to the entire ARD, thereby denoting a characteristic of the entire process.

Indicators and their properties provide information not only about the content of a particular token concept, but also about how that concept is to be used and the effects and causes of its use. Consequently, both the type of indicator and the information contained on its property lists are critical for the effective operations of the model. Programs are keyed to look for certain types of indicators in order to perform their operations, and therefore, in large measure, the sophistication and complexity of the indicators determines the sophistication and complexity of the model's cognition.

Although it is not possible to create a strict taxonomy of indicators, stating their specific role in the cognitive and discourse process, nonetheless, for the purpose of presentation, it is desirable to provide some grouping of indicators in terms of their functional roles.

Roughly, there are three types of indicators: (1) *relational and informational,* (2) *affective,* and (3) *operational*. The first type of indicator provides information about the concept itself—its causes, effects, constraints, circumstances, time, place, and so on—and is generally used in all phases of cognition and discourse generation. The second type, the affective indicators, provide information about the emotional content and impact of the concept. They tell what may motivate, inhibit, and be affected by a particular concept. The last type of indicator, the operational, provide information as to how a concept is to be processed for expression.

Following is a list of the three types of indicators, with brief descriptions of each.

Relational and Informational Indicators

CHARACTERISTICS	Contains concepts that supply additional information about the indicated concept. One of the most frequently used of all indicators.
PLACE	Contains concepts that give spatial location information.
TIME	Contains concepts that give temporal location.
CAUSE	Contains concepts that give information about the cause underlying the indicated concept.
EFFECT	Contains information about the effects associated with the indicated concept.
PREVENTED-BY	Identifies concepts that prevent the indicated concept from being actualized.
PREVENTS	Identifies those concepts that prevent certain effects from taking place.
CORRELATION	Identifies those concepts with a common cause.
CONDITION	Contains those concepts that must be valid in order for the indicated concept to be valid.
NOT-CONDITION	Contains those concepts that must not be valid in order for the indicated concept to be valid.
L-DERIVED	Contains those concepts from which the indicated concept is logically derived.
L-INFERRED	Contains those concepts that logically follow from the indicated concept.
COMPLETION	Contains those concepts that describe the state of completion for the indicated concept.
INCOMPLETION-CAUSE	Contains those concepts that give the reasons for incompletion.
INSTRUMENT	Contains those concepts that give "by means of" information about the indicated concept.
DERIVED	Contains those concepts that cognitive procedures use to generate the indicated concept.
DERIVED-INTO	Contains those concepts a concept is derived into.

Affective

IMPACT	Contains those concepts that describe the affective impact of the indicated concept on a potential audience.
MOTIVATION	Contains those concepts that motivate the generation of the indicator concept.
INHIBITION	Contains those motivation concepts that prevent the indicated concept from being actualized.

INHIBITS	Contains those concepts that prevent impacts from being realized.
UNACCEPTABLE	Contains those concepts that are unacceptable to the indicated concept.
ACCEPTABLE	Contains those concepts that are acceptable to the indicated concept.
SYMPATHETIC	Contains those concepts that have a common motivation.

Operational Indicators

NEGATE	Specifies those concept effects that are to be eliminated.
ATTENUATE	Specifies those concept causes that are to be eliminated.
AMPLIFY	Identifies those effects that are to be given prominence.
NEG-EMPHASIS	Specifies those concept impacts that are to be eliminated.
DE-EMPHASIS	Specifies those motivation concepts that are to be eliminated.
POS-EMPHASIS	Specifies those concept impacts that are to be brought into prominence.
STRESS	This indicator specifies up to five types of stress. Rather than containing concepts on its list, it contains the five indicators, T, NIL, FOCUS, PIVOT, and INCIDENTAL, which in turn may contain either indicators, such as CHARACTERISTICS, or concepts. (This is a most important indicator to the realization process; more will be said of it when that topic is discussed in detail.)
STRUCTURE	This indicator identifies the structural role a concept plays in a complex conceptual construction. On its property list it contains seven types of descriptors: PROCESS, RELATION, GOAL, INITIATOR, BENEFACTOR, EVENT, AGENT, and DENOTER. These descriptors are important in the realization process and will be discussed in greater detail in that section.
SYN-FEAT	Like the preceding indicator, this indicator contains descriptions needed for realization of, in this case, syntactic features. It will be discussed in greater detail in the section on realization.

TENSE — This indicator contains descriptors of the various tenses a verb (PROCESS or RELATION) may take and is used principally in the realization component.

4.34. *Special-purpose concepts*

The special-purpose category of concepts can be divided into two types: those that combine or disjoin concepts, and those that organize concepts for some speech act, such as a statement or a question.

Beginning with the first type, the most common concept is the CONJOIN concept. This concept takes any number of references and joins them together. INTERSECT and NOR-CONJOIN operate similarly, except that whereas NOR-CONJOIN produces a negative "or" construction, "neither . . . nor," INTERSECT produces a simple "or" construction. In contrast to the extended concepts, these concepts have as their "prime" reference concept the second component of the first dotted pair, #ROBIN in the first datum below. The examples below provide an illustration of how these concepts combine other concepts.

```
(1 CONJOIN (2. #ROBIN) (3. #LITTLE-JOHN))
(2 TOKEN #ROBIN)
(3 TOKEN #LITTLE-JOHN)
(4 CONJOIN (5. #BUY) (6. #SELL))
(5 TOKEN #BUY)
(6 TOKEN #SELL)
(7 CONJOIN (8. #GOLD) (9. #CAR))
(8 TOKEN #GOLD)
   < CHARACTERISTICS (20. #OLD)
(9 TOKEN #CAR
   < CHARACTERISTICS (16. #SECOND-HAND)
(10 ARD (1. #ROBIN) (4. #BUY)
   (7. #GOLD))
(11 ARD (2. #ROBIN) (5. #BUY)
   (8. #GOLD))
(12 ARD (3. #LITTLE-JOHN)
   (6. #SELL) (9. #CAR))
(13 CONJOIN (11. #BUY) (12. #SELL))
(14 INTERSECT (11. #BUY) (12. #SELL))
(15 NOR-CONJOIN (11. #BUY) (12. #SELL))
(16 ARD (1. #ROBIN) (4. BUY) (0. NIL))
```

If number 10 were given realization, it would produce the sentence "Robin and Little-John buy and sell old gold and second-hand cars." In this case the two subjects, the two verbs, and the two objects are combined. If CONJOIN concept 13 were realized, the meaning would be quite different, "Robin buys old gold and Little-John sells second-hand cars." The realization of INTERSECT acts just like CONJOIN except that an "either–or" construction replaces the "and" construction: "Either Robin buys old gold or Little-John sells second-hand cars." Likewise, the realization of the NOR-CONJOIN concept 15 is similar except for the difference of the formative: "Neither Robin buys old gold nor Little-John sells second-hand cars." These types of concepts are not only important in the realization of a concept but also in the processing of conceptual constructions, for they are required to express complex conceptual relations as well as to guarantee grammatical discourse.

The second type of special-purpose concepts all concern the structuring of concepts for a speech act. Of these, the simplest is the YN-QUESTION concept. Only for those questions to which a "yes–no" response is desired is this concept applicable. Therefore, to ask the question, "Do Robin and Little-John buy and sell old gold and second-hand cars?", the conceptual construction would be:

(19 YN-QUESTION (10. #BUY))

Most questions, however, are not a simple matter of yes or no but a request for information about a particular concept or group of concepts. The WH-QUESTION concept is the means by which such information is elicited. This type of concept takes the form

(*number* WH-QUESTION *unknown concept reference*)

Number is the referencing index of this concept, *unknown* is that which is desired to be known by the speaker, and *concept-reference* is the concept that contains the unknown component. To ask the question, "What did Robin and Little-John buy?", you would use the following concept:

(31 WH-QUESTION A2 (16. #BUY))

Notice that the unknown slot is filled by A2, indicating that it is the second argument of the ARD that is unknown. Questions about manner and cause can be asked similarly, by filling the unknown slot with the appropriate indicator.

When the speech act to be taken is not of an interrogative form, the STATE concept is used. The STATE concept has the form

(No. STATE ref1 ref2)

where ref1 is the concept to be stated and is embedded in the same way in the concept ref2. The STATE concept distinguishes between what is thought and what is said, as each has different meanings; something thought may be perfectly acceptable but its statement offensive. When ref2 is NIL, this indicates that the concept is not embedded but is a top-level concept. To say "Robin and Little-John buy and sell old gold and second-hand cars," the following STATE concept would suffice:

(38. STATE (10. #BUY) NIL))

4.40. INFORMATIONAL AND INTERPERSONAL INDICATORS

It could be quite difficult to understand the processing of concepts without a firm grasp of the manner in which indicators are used to bind concepts together and to create related conceptual structures. Indicators can be used to designate what might be loosely called "semantic dimensions" of the content of the concepts. Two principal dimensions are the informational and the interpersonal, for as Halliday (1967) and other linguists have observed, language behaves differently along these dimensions, having a different set of conventions and rules to handle each.* Also, the distinction is important at the level of cognition, for the informational dimension represents a relatively neutral area of observed fact and accumulated knowledge, whereas the interpersonal concerns the affective reactions and motivations of the speaker and other persons with whom he interacts or has interacted. Both interpersonal and informational indicators exist in reflexive pairs. These pairs can be used to relate concepts, for example, noting which concept is the *cause* and which is the *effect*. (CAUSE, EFFECT), (PREVENTS, PREVENTED-BY), (DERIVED, DERIVED-INTO), and (L-DERIVED, L-INFERRED) are all information-type reflexive indicator pairs. These are essentially "descriptive" in that they are free from affective attachment. (INHIBITS, INHIBITION), (MOTIVATION, IMPACT), and (ACCEPTABLE, UNACCEPTABLE) are all interpersonal reflexive indicators which are likely to have an affective attachment. The processing programs rely upon these pairs to make inferences about possible actions and to construct acceptable discourse. Very often the informational and the interpersonal functions are parallel, which is to say that these are affective responses to objective events.

To see how these two types of indicators work in tandem, consider the following simplified example taken from the sampled discourse. The patient feels no control over her therapy and wants to "control" the therapy by controlling the payment of bills. She first asks to pay the bills, then sees the effect and impact of the statement and withdraws her decision. Schematically, you would have the following, where the label on the arrows identifies the indicator, and the arrowhead, its property.

This situation can be more satisfactorily represented in terms of a simplified version of our conceptual notation.

(1 TOKEN #I)
(2 TOKEN #FEAR)

*The distinction is similar to that between "fixed" and "negotiated," although made from a somewhat different perspective.

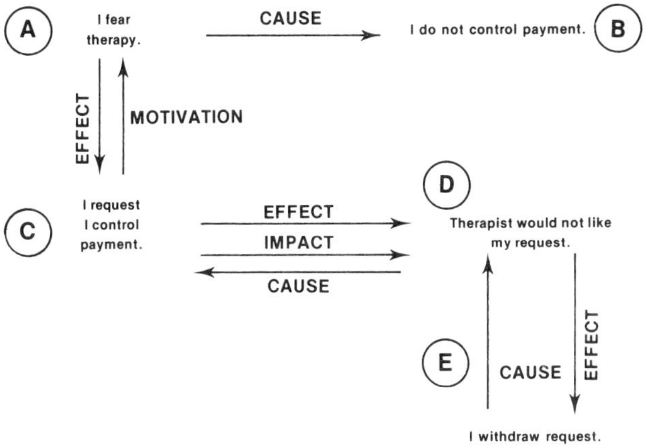

(3 TOKEN #THERAPY)
(4 TOKEN #CONTROL)
(5 TOKEN #PAYMENT)
(6 TOKEN #REQUEST)
(7 TOKEN #THERAPIST)
(8 TOKEN #THERAPIST)
(9 TOKEN #LIKE)
< CHARACTERISTIC (NOT)
(10 TOKEN #CONTROL)
< CHARACTERISTIC (NOT)
(11 TOKEN #REQUEST)
< CHARACTERISTIC (1 TOKEN #I)
(12 TOKEN #WITHDRAW)
(13 ARD (1. #I) (2. #FEAR) (3. #THERAPY))
< CAUSE (11. ARD (1. #I) (10. #CONTROL) (5. #PAYMENT))
(14 ARD (1. #I) (4. #CONTROL) (5. #PAYMENT))
< EFFECT (16. #LIKE)
< MOTIVATION (13. #FEAR)
(15 ARD (1. #I) (6. #REQUEST) (14. #CONTROL))
< MOTIVATION (13. #FEAR)
< IMPACT (16. #LIKE)
(16 ARD (8. #THERAPIST) (9. #LIKE) (11. #REQUEST))
< EFFECT (17. ARD (1. #I) (12. #WITHDRAW) (11. #REQUEST

To identify the causal relations underlying a series of cognitions, the CORRELATION indicator is used. In this example, the effect of the patient requesting to control payment C can be attributed to the cause and motivations of A and B. This would be represented as follows:

(13. #FEAR)
< CAUSE (14. #CONTROL)
< CORRELATION (15. #REQUEST)
(15. #REQUEST)
< MOTIVATION (13. #FEAR)
< CORRELATION (14. #CONTROL)

Notice that a cause is correlated with a motivation. In this way some overlap is permitted between the informational and interpersonal indicators. Other indicator pairs, such as (ACCEPTABLE, UNACCEPTABLE) and (INHIBITS, INHIBITOR), can be used by interrupt programs to make similar inferences about conceptual relations. These programs can also add or remove such indicators according to their own processing requirements. To see how this is done, we now turn to a discussion of multiple-body interrupt programs.

4.50. THE PROCESSING OF CONCEPTS: MULTIPLE-BODY INTERRUPT PROGRAMS

There are many ways to model human information processing. Two of the more common approaches are either to treat it as a process that is centrally controlled, or as a highly differentiated process, having many localities of control, each with their own special processing function. The first approach suffers many disadvantages, as most problem environments are highly idiosyncratic and are not amenable to one uniform procedure, albeit how complex. Consequently, to design a system which has one component that has "its finger in every part" of computation is to create a model which is relatively inflexible in its operations. Systems that have differentiated centers of control, on the other hand, are able to respond to problem environments in a highly specialized and flexible manner. For in such systems only those programs that are required for the particular task are invoked.* In other words, they do what they can do, and then after they have completed their work, other programs are involved which specialize in processing their completed work. The analogy is to that of a cooperative factory where every worker is a specialist, works in synchrony with other workers, and, during times of trouble, knows whom to call upon for special assistance.

Our model is designed on the cooperative-factory notion. All problems are diagnosed by specialized programs, which think about possible solutions in cooperation with other programs and decide how the problem should be broken down and acted upon by other specialist programs. These "doer"

*See Terry Winograd's discussion of the difference between uniform procedures and specialized procedures, pp. 2–15 in his *Procedures as a representation for data in a computer program for understanding language* (Cambridge, Mass.: MIT, Project MAC, TR-84, 1971).

programs work on their part of the problem and pass the results of their operations to other programs.

If in the course of their operations they run into special types of problems that they themselves are not equipped to handle, they can "work" with other programs which handle these problems and then return the work to the original program to be completed. To strain the analogy a bit, the type of work and the work load are determined by the status of the data base, so that if a change occurs in the data base, certain programs notice this change and perform their own special tasks.

Before venturing into a discussion of the interrupt programs, one more analogy might be useful—one which is more specific and perhaps more telling—that of a neural net in the cerebral cortex. Some neurologists (Pribram 1971) working in brain research have argued that the operations of the cortex can be described in terms of a TOTE mechanism (Test–Operate Test Exist process). This mechanism is like a servomechanism that evaluates neural impulses to detect a given pattern, which, if detected, it operates upon in some manner. The important point about this type of mechanism is that it operates or fires only when a given pattern has been detected; once detected, the mechanism performs an operation to alter the impulse received. There is evidence in the literature of brain research to substantiate the existence of such a mechanism and, more importantly for our purposes, its close affinity with the processing mechanisms and the concept descriptions that we have employed. Geherhard Werner (1970), for example, has developed a computer model of some aesthetic feature analysis which, with minor modifications, can be applied to other types of neural systems. Spinelli (1970) has, in fact, developed a program that simulates a neural feature analyzer. These and other such models of neural processing correspond quite closely to our "interrupt program" for processing concepts. Moreover, neurological evidence strongly suggests that "feature analyzers" are organized by specialty (i.e., in terms of the special tasks that they are to perform) and widely distributed throughout the neural system (Pribram 1971). Likewise, the interrupt programs, which perform all the cognition within this system, are functionally specialized and widely distributed, not having a central control center. They, like neurons, "fire" when there is an appearance of a specific pattern which disturbs a particular state of "equilibrium" within the data base (Arbib 1972).

Interrupt programs are activated when a particular pattern is detected and then perform a structure-manipulating operation. These programs were developed by Richard Brown at the MIT Artificial Intelligence Laboratory and represent a modification of the CONNIVER *method*.

One problem with methods is that if two or more respond simultaneously to the same pattern, there is no simple way to determine which program should be evaluated first. Interrupt programs surmount this problem by having additional bodies or programs which can determine and rearrange the sequencing of evaluation of a series of programs. In this way they complement each other in processing a pattern.

Interrupt programs only fire when certain types of functions are used, or to use the analogy of neural nets, when certain impulse patterns are transmitted. Three types of functions can fire an interrupt program:

(SEND message location), where location is optional
(INCLUDE message property–indicator property list), where LIST is optional
(EXCLUDE message property–indicator property), where property is optional

Here, *message* is a datum, and location is a CONNIVER context frame. The SEND function adds messages to contexts, whereas INCLUDE adds a property to the property list of a message and EXCLUDE removes it. For each of the functions above there is a corresponding interrupt program which is activated when the pattern of the interrupt program matches the message, indicator, and property of the message-type function.

(IF-SENT name pattern (body 1) (body 2) (body 3) (. . .))
(IF-INCLUDED name pattern (body 1) (body 2) (body 3) (. . .))
(IF-EXCLUDED name pattern (body 1) (body 2) (body 3) (. . .))

To see how an interrupt program is fired, the following example of an IF-INCLUDED and INCLUDE pattern match might be helpful. The IF-INCLUDED program has a pattern

((pattern of message) indicator, pattern of property)

which, if it matches that of the INCLUDE function, causes the program to be fired and its various bodies to be activated to perform their designated functions. Therefore, if the INCLUDE message were

(INCLUDE (DATUM '2 'TOKEN '#BILL) 'NEGATE '#PAY 'LIST)

the matching IF-INCLUDED pattern would be

(IF-INCLUDED NAME-OF-INTERRUPT ((2 TOKEN #BILL) NEGATE #BILL) (PRINT 'INTERRUPTED))

The effect of the INCLUDE message being sent would be to cause the IF-INCLUDE program to fire and to print out the word INTERRUPTED and to create the following structure in the data base:

(2 TOKEN #BILL)
< NEGATE (#PAY)

In other words, under the indicator NEGATE, the TOKEN list PAY is added. In less technical terms, the effect of this operation is to create the "idea" of not paying one's bill, and, as we will see later, this is the prevalent theme in the discourse of the patient that we are modeling.

So far we have only shown how interrupt programs are fired through pattern matching. We have yet to demonstrate the way in which bodies work to control the order of processing. Such control is achieved by having the bodies, which are programs, examine a list pointed to by a variable named INTERRUPT-ORDER, and to manipulate that list when necessary. In this way the bodies are able to alter the processing sequence in concert with other programs. This is done by having all those programs which fired evaluate their first body. After they have done so, each can examine the INTERRUPT-ORDER list to determine who else is working on the problem and rearrange the INTERRUPT-ORDER list if need be. This process continues, that is, new processing sequences are created, until there are no more bodies. In this way different interrupt programs are able to communicate with one another to process a problem in a coordinated and complementary fashion.

To illustrate how the sequencing of interrupts' processing is altered through their bodies, consider the following example. There are three interrupts, A, B, and C, where A and B have four bodies and C has three. Suppose that body 3 of interrupt B "kills" interrupt A, and body 2 of interrupt C changes its position relative to A. Beginning with the initial firing sequence of A, B, and C, the interrupts would proceed as follows:

body 1 of A
body 1 of B
body 1 of C
INTERRUPT-ORDER is now (A B C)
body 2 of A
body 2 of B
body 2 of C
INTERRUPT C has changed position with A
INTERRUPT-ORDER is now (C B A)
body 3 of C
body 3 of B
body 3 of A
INTERRUPT C is now finished
INTERRUPT A has been eliminated by B
INTERRUPT-ORDER is now (B)
body 4 of B
INTERRUPT-ORDER is now empty

In this example, it may appear as if the different bodies of an interrupt are unable to pass the results from one body to another. This, however, is not the case, for within each body it is possible to have special variables that contain the results of a body's computations, which can be accessed by another body at a later point in computation.

Like methods, interrupts are able to invoke other programs to assist them with a problem. By using a SUGGESTION LIST, an interrupt can utilize the results of other interrupts in the same way methods use POSSIBILITIES lists. By this means, series of interrupt programs can combine their resources to solve a problem which any one of them alone would be powerless to solve. Naturally, this process can become quite complex where interrupt programs start interrupting other interrupt programs, but since interrupts do not have to be called, they can be inserted without having to alter the structure of the program.

Besides the various programming advantages of using interrupt-type programs, there are theoretical reasons that make the notion appealing. Not only are they mechanisms that operate very much like neurological mechanisms, but they are also mechanisms which can be used to process cognitive and linguistic data, and in this way provide a linkage from a neurological description of cognition to a symbolic and linguistic description. Moreover, as we shall discuss in greater detail in Chapter 7, they help explain some theoretically troublesome aspects of cognitive behavior. For example, new programs can be added to the system without altering old ones, so that it is quite possible to have a system which processes similar types of problems in a different manner. Consequently, depending upon how a concept is represented, it may be blocked in one context or processed in another. In other words, the manner in which the interrupt programs are keyed for firing is determinative of its problem-solving ability. When applied to human cognition, as represented in psychoanalytic discourse, the notion of interrupt-type cognition produces some interesting insights. What is traditionally regarded as unconscious intervention can be represented in terms of "hidden" interrupt programs keyed to fire on certain key concepts of a traumatic nature. Since these hidden interrupts were probably learned early in life, they are likely to be deeply embedded and keyed to rather basic conceptual patterns, and therefore not accessible to higher-level or "conscious" programs. Only by identifying the referent pattern of the traumatically generated interrupt and giving it an appropriate context, or by superimposing upon it a more appropriate interrupt-type program, is a "cure" effected. As we will see later, the associations, the displacements, resistances, and self-interruptions of our modeled patient seem very amenable to an interrupt-type representation.

4.60. THE ORGANIZATION OF COGNITIVE PROCESSES

All the programs in this model are organized according to the different stages a thought or concept must go through in order to be expressed in discourse. The goal is not to represent all the possible cognitive mechanisms an individual might use to solve a theorem or to derive an elaborate discourse. Rather, it is restricted to the representation of the evident cognition a patient used to generate a complex discourse in a psychoanalytic session. Since there was no direct means of inferring the patient's cognition, the modeling is based upon what I think she might have thought. In this respect, the perspective is like that of the psychiatrist, who makes inferences and deductions about the patient's cognition based upon his or her discourse behavior. Despite the focus on a limited discourse situation of a single patient, my belief is that the general model does capture the basic mechanisms that any individual might use in the initiation, inhibition, formation, and generation of discourse.

One general comment is required before describing the organization of cognitive processing. This is that the model of cognitive processing does not correspond to any existing theory of cognition. This is principally due to the fact that no coherent theory exists which describes the way discourse is formed and generated. Consequently, the model of cognition is a montage of existing theories. For example, the manner in which concepts and their processing are modeled resembles both Piaget's and Pribram's notions, whereas our treatment of the stages of cognition, particularly as related to discourse, is much like Freud's conception of mental organization. I doubt that any of these men would like to find themselves bedfellows in a single theory, but as their theories very often concern different levels of description, I feel that they are not in conflict. More about this will be said in Chapter 7.

Cognition is organized according to processing modules or, in CONNIVER terms, contexts, each of which contain interrupt programs that perform similar or related operations. There are six cognitive contexts in the program. Two of these, LEIBNITZ and REALIZATION, will not be discussed here: the first because it is trivial in that it is only a reservoir of general knowledge taken from other contexts, and the second because it is so complex as to require its own chapter. In order of processing: the first, CALVIN, decides what should be said and, like its namesake, decides on whether the concept should be thought or expressed. Once a concept has received CALVIN's blessing, it is processed by the MACHIAVELLI module, named for the great Florentine strategist of means. The programs in this module determine how and what CALVIN wants said can be stated in an acceptable and intelligible manner. He tries to find ways of saying the unacceptable, and very often, in his exploration of alternatives, he, like CALVIN, uncovers other constraints on expression which he, in turn, tries to deal with. Part of his job is to take concepts that have been formed for expression and pass them back to CALVIN for approval. Once receiving this approval, he then oversees the final expression of the concept. In overseeing the formation of concepts for expression, MACHIAVELLI is assisted by the CICERO context, which acts as an interface between cognitively based programs and linguistically based programs. The final processing context, FREUD, examines what was said and tries to uncover why it was said. These programs provide the model with a self-reflective capability necessary in modeling our patient in psychoanalysis.

Diagram 4.60 is provided to facilitate discussion of these modules. This diagram, much like those in Chapter 3, provides an overview of the stages of

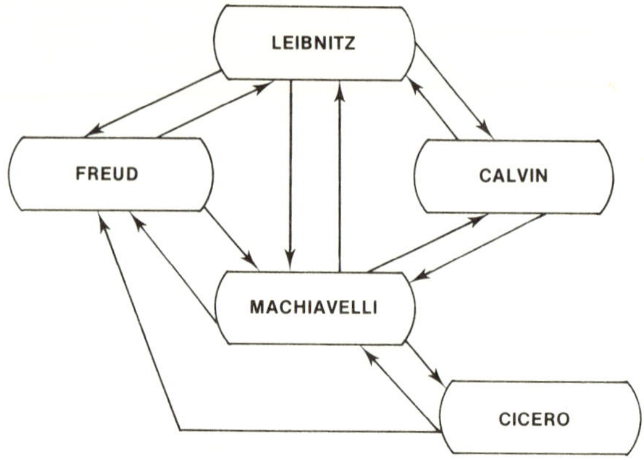

DIAGRAM 4.50

cognitive processing. Arrows indicate paths of communication between the cognitive modules.

We have chosen to describe cognitive processes in somewhat personified terms. And though Freud was faulted for a similar type of characterization, we feel that this type of description is more suitable than more neutral and static types of descriptors. For cognition is paramountly a process, a process that is not uniform in its behavior but often contradictory and distinct. Hence, Freud's animistic descriptions of the id, ego, and superego operations are not at all out of place in the context of this program.

4.61. CALVIN

CALVIN, as the name implies, is the highest-level censor in the system. It receives a topic of conversation generated by a top-level program called SPEAK-UP. Given this topic, which is in the form of a concept, CALVIN evaluates the concept to determine whether it is appropriate for expression, either to ERMA or to its listeners. To do so, CALVIN examines the indicators attached to these topic concepts to determine why they were put there. CALVIN may then add concepts to the examined concepts to improve upon their expression, or it can merely pass on to MACHIAVELLI suggestions as to how these concepts should be treated for expression.

It should be remembered that the processing of concepts is not a linear process passing from one module to the next in simple succession. Quite the contrary. Feedback effects or backups occur regularly so that concepts pass back and forth between various modules. CALVIN does not merely examine a concept, manipulate it, and then rid itself of the concept forever. Rather, CALVIN works with the MACHIAVELLI program to see whether the suggested realization and embellishments are acceptable.

A possible scenario of CALVIN operations might be as follows: receives a concept from SPEAK-UP, evaluates that concept, and finds that some property of it is negated through the NEGATE indicator. CALVIN then finds out why the concept is negated through a search of the data base and attaches some indicators and concepts of its own. It then sends this concept on to MACHIAVELLI, which suggests how the concept might be realized. CALVIN evaluates this suggestion, passes on it, and gives MACHIAVELLI the go-ahead. MACHIAVELLI then works with the CICERO programs to create realizations of the concepts. These realizations are STATE concepts, which are passed back to CALVIN via MACHIAVELLI. CALVIN examines these concepts for their potential impacts as registered in the IMPACT indicators. When it decides that all is well, it gives its approval for the STATE-concepts expression. However, "at the same time" that CALVIN programs are doing this, other programs are preparing other concepts for expression. This process continues until there is nothing more to say or until the process is interrupted by the FREUD programs.

CALVIN's operations can be seen as having two parts. The first part is concerned with taking an initial concept and evaluating its properties for expression. At this point, it generally works with the indicators CHARACTERISTIC, TIME, PLACE, and NEGATION, and examines the concepts under them for their acceptability. CALVIN may then decide to add indicators, such as POS-EMPHASIS, NEG-EMPHASIS, and ATTENUATE, as a means of softening the potential impact of these concepts. MACHIAVELLI takes these suggestions and makes its own additions and suggestions, which are in turn returned to CALVIN for approval. Once these "high-level" suggestions are accepted, MACHIAVELLI works through CICERO to generate expressions of the concepts via STATE concepts. These STATE concepts are then returned to CALVIN as the second stage of evaluation is initiated. Attached to them are audience-sensitive indicators such as IMPACT, MOTIVATION, INHIBITION, INHIBITS, and UNACCEPTABLE. A special set of interrupt programs, called JOHNSON interrupts after the discrete lexiographer, evaluate the concepts stored under these indicators. When a STATE concept has such indicators of a negative character attached to them, the program interrupts itself and interjects various dubitatives and pauses. CALVIN inserts these interjections by employing the form

(JOHNSON-WORRIED *code* concept-number)

where *code* is an injection from the following list and *concept-number* is the normal reference to the STATE concept causing the problem.

Johnsonian Reactions
Initial print is *code*

INITIAL PRINT	ADDITIONAL PRINT
<pause>	
<vowel-slur>	"ah"

INITIAL PRINT	ADDITIONAL PRINT
<mmm>	"um"
<repeat>	repeat last word
<spurious-that>	"that"
<deletion>	delete next word
<i-mean>	"I mean"
<you-know>	"you know"
<again>	"again"
<and>	"and"
<but>	"but"
<well>	"well"

These pauses and interruptions are similar to those found in the modeled transcript and represent points of uncertainty or hesitancy on the part of the speaker. By injecting them, ERMA buys time to correct its discourse so as to avoid potentially unpleasant impacts.

Two classes of CALVIN interrupt programs are used to perform all his operations: SEND and INCLUDE. To each of these, CALVIN responds by interrupting in the following manner:

SEND I

When this type of SEND concept is transmitted to the CALVIN context, an interrupt program keyed to its pattern fires and evaluates the concept to determine its acceptability. This type of interrupt generally approves of the concept sent to it, but often adds one or another introductory or qualifying concept. This type of interrupt can be regarded as a kind of weak censor which accepts most concepts with minor modification.

SEND II

In contrast to the previous interrupt programs, these programs are strong censors which generally do not approve of the concepts transmitted to them. They evaluate the concept and return suggestions as to why the concept is unacceptable. These suggestions can be regarded as alternative but related topics of discourse.

INCLUDE I

When an INCLUDE message is transmitted to CALVIN, these programs attempt to figure out why that indicator and its properties have been included, and then they attach an indicator giving the reason. For example, a NEGATE indicator may have been attached to a concept. These programs would examine the concept to determine why and attach their own indicator, perhaps the indicator UNACCEPTABLE. When interacting with MACHIAVELLI, these programs can reject his INCLUDE suggestions and make alterations of the structure of the concept. In most cases, these programs determine why an indicator was added and then make alterations of their own. In this sense, they are "doer" programs.

INCLUDE II

These programs examine a concept to see why a particular indicator was added, and then they provide a suggestion list of the possible reasons for the inclusion of the indicator. In this respect, these programs are more like "thinkers" which contemplate the causes for indicators being included but do not do anything about them. Very often it is left for MACHIAVELLI to act upon these suggestions.

To see how CALVIN-based programs work, consider this example taken from the program. At one point in the modeled discourse the patient wants to express the idea that she pays the therapist. This would be an ARD, which for purposes of illustration we will represent as follows:

ARD (#I #GIVE #PAYMENT #THERAPIST)

CALVIN evaluates this concept and determines that it is incomplete and needs improvement. In particular, CALVIN decides that additional knowledge is required about when the payment is to be given. This knowledge is provided by a special interrupt program which is keyed to the pattern of the initial concept, PAY-EOM (pay bill at end of month).

PAY-EOM
CALVIN: ARD (#I #GIVE #PAYMENT #THERAPIST)
+ <TIME (END-OF-MONTH)*

where CALVIN indicates the context and + says to include the indicator TIME and its property (#END-OF-MONTH). However, since suggestions of payment changes are sensitive topics, the patient decides that it is necessary to stress the fact that she will be correct in her calculations of payment. This is achieved by the CALVIN interrupt PAY-CAL (pay bill and calculate amount):

PAY-CAL
CALVIN: ARD (#I #GIVE #PAYMENT #THERAPIST)
+ C2 (#HOUR)
<CHARACTERISTICS (#NUMBER #OF POSS #HOUR)
+ C3 ARD (#I #COUNT #HOUR)
+ CONJOIN (C2 C3)

This interrupt says add (+) to the initial concept the notion "I count up number of possible hours." Hence, the original concept, I give payment to the

*This is a modified version of a program notational system developed by Richard Brown at MIT (unpublished senior thesis, 1974).

therapist, would be expanded to "I count up the number of hours and give payment to the therapist at the end of the month." However, this is not the way the original transcript reads, for it says "give you a check at the end of the month," not "give payment to." To overcome this problem, the PAY-CAL interrupt works in unison with other multiple-body interrupt programs. Hence, instead of immediately embedding the PAY-CAL additional concept, the program waits until another program makes the suggestion

ARD (#I #GIVE #CHECK #THERAPIST)

which the PAY-CAL program then incorporates into its own suggestion. The result is, "I give you (therapist) a check at the end of the month." Notice how an initial concept can become considerably modified through the operations of coordinated interrupt programs. We begin with "I give payment to the therapist" and end with a considerably different but related discourse.

4.62. MACHIAVELLI

Once CALVIN has decided on a course of action and made its own suggestions as to how that action should look or proceed, MACHIAVELLI tries to find the general linguistic and thematic means of realizing CALVIN's intentions. Whereas CALVIN censors and manipulates content, MACHIAVELLI works on the structuring of that content for suitable expression. Therefore, although not directly concerned with linguistic realization, it is concerned with the ordering and structure of the concepts for discourse. It has the capacity to alter a concept to make it expressible or to override CALVIN suggestions. But more than anything else, MACHIAVELLI oversees the realization process and acts as a liaison between CALVIN and CICERO. It takes CALVIN concepts, examines them to identify their various conceptual and thematic properties, then attaches the appropriate indicators and passes them onto the CICERO context. Once the CICERO programs have formed suitable STATE concepts, MACHIAVELLI transfers these concepts back to CALVIN for final approval. If final approval is granted, MACHIAVELLI outputs the discourse.

In performing its operations, MACHIAVELLI makes primary use of operational and informational-type indicators. As in the case of the CALVIN program, there are two classes of interrupt programs.

SEND I

These programs find solutions to ways of expressing CALVIN-generated concepts, and once these solutions are found, they take charge of their expression. In other words, they act as the overseers of the realization of discourse and are responsible for taking STATE concepts produced by the realization process back up to CALVIN for evaluation, and getting them outputted.

In this respect, these programs are both thinkers and doers, but primarily the latter, as they do not handle particularly difficult formation strategies.

SEND II

These are primarily "thinker" programs, as the concepts they are keyed on are generally unspeakable or defective. They do, however, make suggestions to be used by either CALVIN or CICERO on how a concept will be expressed.

INCLUDE I

These programs occur rarely in the processing but are involved when a statement of a concept needs some kind of prefacing or foregrounding comment prior to expression. In other words, they create a context for a concept which makes it intelligible and then verbalizes that foregrounding concept. They are keyed on IMPACT-type indicators and supply interjections that help mollify or validate the indicated concept.

INCLUDE II

This is a common type of interrupt program, which suggests or includes concepts onto a concept in order to make it more intelligible or valid. Since the MACHIAVELLI context is primarily concerned with working on and shaping CALVIN-generated concepts, these types of interrupts are most often invoked to restructure and supplement a concept for expression. This type of interrupt also provides "solutions" to concepts that might have a "problematic" realization. For example, CALVIN may generate a concept that may have a negative impact upon the listener. Include interrupt programs that would examine that concept, determine what caused the negative impact, and find a means for overcoming the impact, through negation, for example.

The interrupt programs in the MACHIAVELLI context, therefore, perform two general types of operations:

1. They oversee the realization of concepts by placing them into the CICERO context, then in the CALVIN context for approval, and finally out to discourse production programs.
2. They examine concepts for the existence of troublesome indicators and provide suggestions as to how these problems may be overcome. These suggestions are, in turn, passed both to CALVIN, which examines them, makes its own comments, and returns the suggestions back to MACHIAVELLI for further work or realization.

Since interrupt programs work in conjunction with other interrupt programs, even those of different contexts, it is difficult and somewhat misleading to represent the operations of one interrupt in isolation from others. Nonetheless, for purposes of illustration we can represent a MACHIAVELLI-type interrupt as follows:

EXCHANGE-PRESERVE
ARD: (#I #EXCHANGE #PAYMENT #?NAME)
MACH ⇒ NEGATE ? ⇒ MACH ⇒ <IMPACT ARD (#I #SHOCK #NAME)

The name of this interrupt is EXCHANGE-PRESERVE and it fires whenever an ARD matches the above pattern, for instance the ARD (#I EXCHANGE #PAYMENT #THERAPIST). In effect, it says that if the idea of exchanging payment with anyone, in this case the therapist, is negated (NEGATE ?), the impact will be, "I shock that person." In other words, this interrupt tells the system that if payment of the bill is negated through a MACHIAVELLI operation, the therapist would be most displeased. This fact having been noted, other interrupt programs would fire, adding suggestions as to how the payment of the bill might be altered without shocking the therapist. Thus, rather than flatly refusing payment, the patient is encouraged to achieve the same effect through other means. This, in fact, she does through the use of other interrupt programs, which we shall discuss in greater detail in Chapter 7.

4.63. CICERO

As we indicated previously, the CICERO context is an interface between cognition and realization. It acts as an overseer of the realization processes, and takes concepts in a STATE format and passes them down to the REALIZATION context. Once the realization programs have completed their work, the results are picked out by CICERO programs, which in turn, pass them on to MACHIAVELLI.

Yet CICERO does more than this, for as we have indicated previously, this is a decentralized model of cognition in which similar and often contradictory cognition can take place "simultaneously." Consequently, CICERO also does some thinking of its own with respect to the impact of discourse upon the audience. However, unlike MACHIAVELLI, which considers impacts primarily from the perspective of its own wants and desires, CICERO is less subject to colored judgments and attempts to assess discourse impacts in terms of their likely effect upon the listener. By having two different cognitive components make different evaluations about similar considerations, we are implicitly assuming that the mind is subject to many different opinions regarding its own behavior. For, although both MACHIAVELLI and CICERO are both concerned with audience impacts, their assessments of these impacts are often quite different. In fact, what we have is an instance of double consciousness, one context evaluating a discourse production in terms of what it wants and another in terms of its likely effect. In our sample of discourse, our modeled patient reflects such instances of double consciousness, as she will often initiate a discourse, interrupt it, and correct it according to her perception of what she thinks the therapist wishes to hear or is willing to hear. The audience-impact programs within CICERO represent the beliefs that the patient has that would be acceptable to the ear of her audience. They do not necessarily constitute her own beliefs; these are represented in other contexts. In addition to commenting on the acceptability of discourse in terms of its interpersonal impact, the CICERO programs also comment on the awkwardness of various productions.

If an EXCLUDE operation is effected on some property in CICERO, its interrupts might fire to suggest the possible reactions that the audience might have to that property being excluded. Once again, the suggestions returned by CICERO are not necessarily compatible with those returned in a different context regarding the same problem. For example, MACHIAVELLI may determine that it is acceptable to exclude mention of payment to the therapist, whereas CICERO programs may determine that such exclusion would be inappropriate and give instances of the therapist's possible reactions.

Like the programs in the previous contexts, CICERO programs are divisible into thinkers and doers. The doers oversee the realization process, whereas the thinkers consider possible audience impacts and return suggestions on potential audience responses. Other than these two types of operations, CICERO is a relatively uninteresting context.

4.64. FREUD

One of the great difficulties of human communication and thought in general is the ability to discriminate between thoughts and thoughts on thoughts. Language is fraught with instances of confusions over levels of discourse, and epistemology itself is often caught up on confusions over different levels of theoretical descriptions. At the level of the individual, introspection is the process of thinking about thinking. It represents an attempt to understand the processes whereby a concept was formed or an action was undertaken. Through the process of introspection, the individual achieves some understanding of why he did a particular act, or, more precisely, the concatenation of cognitive processes that led to the act. In this way, an introspection is used as a means to alter the control mechanisms of cognition. Not improperly, but perhaps irreverently, it can be regarded as a self-debugging device.

Within ERMA, introspection is represented as a group of special-purpose programs within the context FREUD. These programs are keyed to unravel the processes by which a concept or discourse was formed. They do so by having a concept included within the FREUD context and then by examining all key indicators that were instrumental in the formation of the concept or discourse. This process of unraveling is continued until some "explanation" is achieved that is acceptable to a criterion established within the FREUD context. Since the question of "why" is undecidable, the solution to introspective inquiries rests upon internalized criteria—sometimes false—or upon solution of a larger problem which the introspection was instrumental in solving.

However, although FREUD is a separate context, its operations do not proceed unhampered. Otherwise, ERMA, the patient, would be able to have in-depth self-knowledge and would have no use for its therapist. Rather, introspection can be inhibited through the injections of other programs, particularly from the CALVIN context, which balk at the impropriety of certain self-disclosures and assert what should be, as against what actually is. Hence, depending upon the particular individual, introspection can be a relatively autonomous process, or it can be a process that is itself subject to blockage through the intrusions of other censoring-type programs.

The FREUD context is sprouted off from the LEIBNITZ context and is at roughly the same level as the CALVIN context. A new FREUD context is grown every time either a new topic is generated through the SPEAK-UP program or when a concept is transmitted to it for consideration. Introspection can occur at several points in processing: at the beginning, when a new topic is generated, or during the process of cognition and discourse generation. It is initiated during cognition or discourse generation when a particular interrupt program identifies some relationship or concept that it feels requires understanding. When this determination is made, a message is sent to the FREUD context, and special interrupt programs are fired which attempt to unravel the chain of computations that led to the construction of the concept. These programs look for such indicators as DERIVED-INTO, L-INFERRED, L-DERIVED, PREVENTED-BY, MOTIVATION, CORRELATION, SYMPATHETIC, CAUSE, and EFFECT. By examining these indicators, these programs attempt to determine the conditions that make a given statement "true" or prevent a given statement from being true or valid.

However, it should be added that these programs are not so much concerned with logic in the pure sense as they are with the processes by which conceptual structures were put together. Only in this way are they able to understand how a particular concept or discourse was formed. For example, if the patient should ask herself, "Why did I say that?", introspect programs would be fired to uncover the computational events by which "that" was formed. To do so, it might be concerned with determining the motivation behind the statement, the causal inferences that went into its formulation, and the conditions that led to it being stated in the manner in which it was stated. To speak about its introspective insights, ERMA must grow a new MACHIAVELLI context to oversee the generation and formation of the introspective discourse. This it does when its introspective programs have uncovered the "reasons" underlying its generation of a concept or discourse, and a decision is made to speak about these introspections.

In Chapter 7 we shall examine in detail the operations of the programs within the FREUD context, as a large section of our simulated discourse episode is derived from introspection.

4.65. *Summary*

Including the LEIBNITZ context, there are five contexts in which computation is performed. These contexts are organized according to the processing specialty of the interrupt programs within them, and although they interact in their problem solving, they are, in effect, distinct domains of operation. They are ordered as follows:

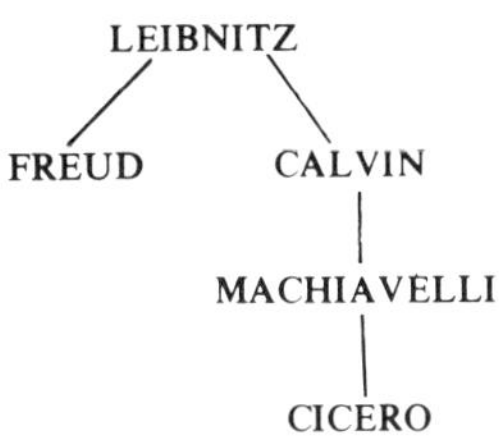

The generation of discourse, or rather the preparation of a possible discourse, begins with a SPEAK-UP program which selects a topic from a possibilities list. If this list is empty, the program generates a set of topics through a search of its data base. In either case, ERMA is never at a loss for something to say. Once a topic has been selected, it is passed on to a CALVIN context, where it is evaluated for the appropriateness of its expression. Supplementary content is added and "distasteful" content is deleted according to the wants of the various interrupt programs contained there. Once a concept has received CALVIN's blessing and corrections, it is passed on to MACHIAVELLI, where further work is done to make the concept suitable for expression. Here thematic markers are added and means are contrived for the expression of concepts that might have a negative audience impact. However, the programs in MACHIAVELLI are more than just concerned with an intermediate stage of processing, for they also act to oversee and control the process of discourse generation. Therefore, once a concept has been given suitable preparation for expression, MACHIAVELLI programs take charge of their realization and pass them on to the CICERO context, where they are given lexical realization and placed within a STATE format. MACHIAVELLI then passes these STATE concepts back to CALVIN, where they are further evaluated (a stated concept and thought concept have different meanings and impact). If the STATE concepts are unacceptable, CALVIN may interrupt discourse generation through his JOHNSONIAN interrupts (er . . . um . . . ah) and decide upon a different topic of discourse or a different method of expression. The programs within the FREUD context are invoked through operations of programs in other contexts. This occurs when a particular interrupt program determines that it is necessary to identify the processes by which a concept or discourse was formed. Once this determination is made, the concept is sent to the FREUD context, where the "logic" by which it was derived is uncovered. Should this logic require expression, a new MACHIAVELLI context is grown and discourse generation is begun anew.

5 : A GRAMMAR FOR DISCOURSE

Most of the grounds of the world's troubles are matters of grammar.— MONTAIGNE

5.10. OVERVIEW

This chapter is the longest and perhaps most difficult in the book. In it we discuss at length and in detail the "grammar" used to represent the process of discourse formation and production. Although it might have sufficed to describe, through extended examples, how the program realizes concepts into discourse, such a discussion alone would not have dispelled possible doubts about the generality of our method. Since it is precisely this generality that needs to be demonstrated, considerable attention is given to documenting how the grammar in the program is not limited to the simulated discourse episodes but is sufficiently comprehensive to cover a wide range of possible English discourses. To make this demonstration I have used a notational system that is quite different from that of CONNIVER and more compatible with those of general linguistics. Both because of the terseness of the notation and its often repetitive application to the description of different types of grammatical forms, much of the contents of this chapter may be skimmed over by the nontechnical reader. However, it is recommended that some attention be paid to the summary description and example provided in this initial overview, as they should provide a flavor of how the program works. The final section of the chapter, which contains an example of how the program realizes a sample sentence, can be read independent of previous sections.

One of the key features of this grammar is that it is written from the perspective of the speaker, and not, as is more commonly the case, from that of the observer, or linguist. Instead of identifying those constituents that combine to make a syntactically correct utterance, this grammar is organized around those conceptual and syntactic features that are instrumental in translating thought into effective discourse. Like a natural speaker, the grammar is just as capable of producing an ungrammatical utterance as it is a grammatical one. The selection of linguistic options is less guided by rules of grammaticality than it is by the speaker's concern for being understood. This concern has two aspects that the grammar is designed to accommodate. The first is that of translating what is thought into what can be said. To effect this translation the speaker must not only have knowledge about the configuration of his own thought patterns, but also about which words and grammatical expressions are suited for their expression. The second aspect entails knowing how to express thoughts in a manner that best achieves the desired impact upon the listener. Not only must the speaker know how different words and constructions shape the meaning of a discourse, he must also know how they affect his particular listener. The "grammar" by itself would not be sufficient to supply this information, but when coupled with a moderately intelligent problem-solving system with its own knowledge base, it can serve both these functions. However, in so doing it ceases to be a "grammar" in the traditional sense, but a form of specialized knowledge about words and their uses.

The realization of discourse begins when a top-level concept, known as an *episton,* is marked for expression. The episton can be thought of as complex thought, such as a request for information or a statement of a feeling or attitude, which is composed of a number of "lower-level" concepts. After the episton is identified for expression, it is broken down into separate knowledge units, called *epistemes*. The extent and the manner in which an episton is broken down depends upon its conceptual composition and the speaker's perception of the likely effect of its expression on the intended listener. For example, if the episton is highly complex, containing many embedded conceptual structures, the audience is unlikely to understand the expression of the episton without the expression of each of its constituent concepts. In such a case the speaker must take great pains to identify to his listener the constituent relationships. He may achieve this by using some epistemes to foreground his remarks and others to highlight points of contrast with possible misinterpretations. To do so, he must have knowledge about how his epistemes are going to be understood and about the manner in which they can be linguistically joined to be communicative.

Once the epistemes are broken out of the episton and marked for their role in the overall discourse, their mood is selected and they are unraveled to reveal the nature of their embedded relationships. Through this process of unraveling, knowledge is built up about the structure of the episteme that can be roughly translated into linguistic knowledge. After all the constituents have been derived from an episteme, they are marked for their thematic role and a lexicon is consulted to find words and grammatical features that appropriately realize them.

Diagram 5.10 illustrates how the sentence, "Nature never breaks her own laws," was derived from part of an episton. At the top of the diagram is located the episton, which in this example is broken down into three epistemes. The first episteme, marked "foreground," is the conceptual parent of the sample sentence and begins the discourse by creating a setting for the epistemes to follow. It is composed of three "high-level" conceptual components (A1, Rr, A2) and marked for the declarative mood (DCL). A1 and A2 indicate that the concepts in these positions play the role of arguments to the relator, Rr, which can be either a process or a relation-type concept. Once the basic conceptual roles of these constituents have been determined, they are, in turn, broken down into their constituent parts. A1, the initial argument, is composed of an "entity bundle" in the agentive case (EBA). This means that it is a bounded entity acting as an agent to the "process bundle" (PB). The second argument, A2, is derived into an entity bundle in the "goal" case, indicating that the concept in this position is in a goal relationship with the process-bundle concept. Although bundles contain their own internal relationships and constituents, their case designations, such as agentive, goal, locative, and so on, refer to the composite role within the "conceptual clause" (A1 Rr A2).

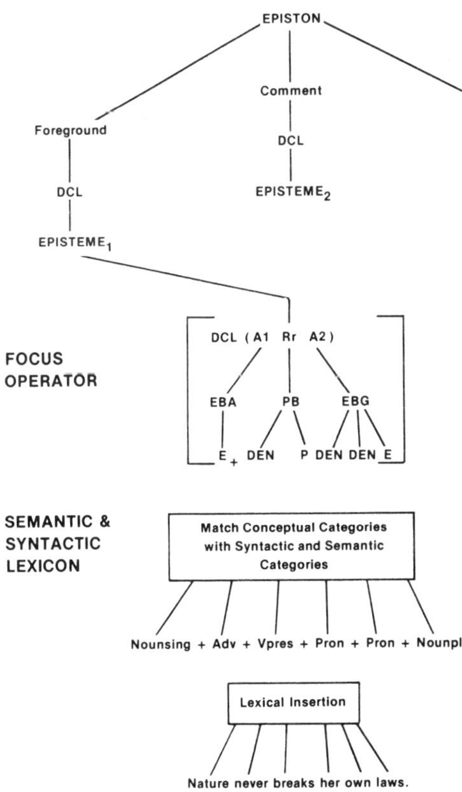

DIAGRAM 5.10

After these composite roles are identified and marked, the internal roles of the bundles are derived. EBA has a single constituent, an entity (E+), which is marked for primary focus by the + operator. The single entity, E, is always a single concept, which in this case will be realized as a noun. The process bundle (PB), on the other hand, is composed of a denoter (DEN) and a process concept (P). The denoter acts to qualify or restrict the properties of the concept it is modifying; in this case, the denoter becomes the adverb "never" and the process concept becomes the verb "breaks." The bundle EBG is composed of three constituents: two denoters and an entity. Like the previous denoter, these two denoters restrict the "generic" meanings of their reference concept, E. When given lexical realization, EBG will become the phrase, "her own laws."

The focus operator located outside the two brackets marks those constituents which are to have a special thematic role. Here only the first entity is marked for focus, indicating that it will assume the thematically prominent position in the sentence. Were the denoter of the process bundles so marked, it would be the first word in the sentence, "Never does nature break her own rules." By altering the focus, and hence the ordering of the sentence or clause, the focus operator can alter its voice and contents. Although in this system of notation the focus operator seems to occupy an ancillary role to the structuring of the concepts in bundles, it actually is coequal in its influence on the final meaning of the discourse. For, as we indicated earlier, considerations of thematic impact are a part of the meaning of the intended discourse, and therefore the ordering of concepts for audience effect is as basic to their meaning as is their logical and informational content. In the computer program, both the informational and thematic properties of a concept are treated as being apart of the meaning of the concept. They are not treated at different levels but rather regarded as different dimensions of meaning to the concept. Although it is difficult to show this in terms of the notational system of this chapter, the approach to thematic information is basically the same as in the program.

Once the concepts have been broken down into all their constituent elements and have been marked for their thematic role, their conceptual and thematic markers are then matched with their semantic and syntactic equivalents. In most cases, there is a correspondence; however, when the concepts do not match, the process of discourse formation is begun anew or a substitute construction found. In the diagram, the outcome of the match results in the string: Noun sing. + Adv. + Vpres + Pro + Pro + Nounpl.

The final stage of realization occurs with the insertion of lexical items. In the program this is achieved by consulting the appropriate indicators of generic concepts for listings of possible lexical realizations. In contrast to the operations of the focus operator and the semantic and syntactic lexicons, this is a relatively straightforward process, which is only rarely impeded by a deficit of appropriate words.

Before continuing, it is necessary to comment on the origins and the scope of the grammar developed. At this point in its development, the grammar is still experimental and rough. It was developed for this program to demonstrate the possibility of representing conceptual and grammatical knowledge in such a way that it can be used to model some of the behaviors—both cognitive and linguistic—of natural speakers. In other words, despite the technicality of some of the discussions, the intent is to demonstrate the character and the efficacy of a form of grammar which is conceptually based and which represents discourse knowledge in terms of the regulatory actions of the speaker. Consequently, I have had to skim over many problem areas in linguistics which to the general linguist may appear to be critical to the discipline but which are, for our more general purposes, too numerous and technical to pursue.

When initially working on this model, my intention was to directly adopt M. A. K. Halliday's grammar. Winograd (1971) used it with success in his program, and as Halliday took a functional orientation to language that recognized thematic and discourse properties, it seemed particularly well suited to my ends. However, when working with the grammar, I found it to be ill suited to the type of representation that I was after. The first problem was that it was not conceptually based and hence was too tightly bound to the properties and peculiarities of language to tie in easily with the conceptual structures that I was working with. This difference is reflected in the types of taxonomies that Halliday and I employ; my concern is to derive the linguistic choices that people make from their basic cognitive structures and processes, whereas Halliday, although concerned with "regulatory options," appears less concerned with conceptual derivations than with descriptions at the sentential level (Halliday 1967). Since in this model choices made at the sentential level are instrumental to conceptual goals, his scheme proved to be ill suited to the purposes of the model. Another and, I believe, terribly significant difference is that this model has a model of the audience to whom it speaks and a set of discourse goals. This feature alone results in a taxonomy quite different from the ones used by Halliday or by those wishing to use his work for sociolinguistic modeling (Bernstein 1973). In our model the regulatory options that a speaker selects are determined by the *effects* he wishes to achieve given his goals and his understanding of the audience. Hence, the modeled speaker is not likely to have a "classification" scheme in the systemic sense but rather in terms of the effects that different types of options are likely to have upon his goals.* In other words, the position taken in this grammar and this program is that the speaker orders his options according to how they will help him achieve his goals with respect to certain audiences and situations. In this sense

*The difference is between observer descriptions, such as those used by linguists, and instrumental descriptions, such as those used by a speaker. Both presuppose different objectives and utilize different types of knowledge.

they are truly regulatory options, as they are selected by control mechanisms concerned with achieving designated internal states (goals) under "imagined" external inputs (the modeled audience reactions).

Fillmore's work (1968; 1971) has also been influential but in a different way from Halliday's. As will become apparent, I have used his notions of case frames but have elevated them, so to speak, to the level of arguments and given them a conceptual representation. This change has created some problems in nomenclature, as I have continued to use (somewhat loosely) his labels for cases. In a more refined version of the conceptual grammar, the semantic descriptors, such as locative, agentive, and so on, would probably be dispensed with altogether and a very high order or deep, whichever you prefer, classification of process concepts and their argument types would be developed. Although these would naturally resemble case frames, certain economies and generalities could be achieved that would not be possible with case frames alone.

Another instance of semantic deviance in our terminology is the use of the terms "focus" and "denoter." Once again, the problem arises from piecemeal borrowing and the attempt to maintain some continuity in the semantics of labels. Therefore, the reader is warned not to think of these terms in traditional linguistic terms but rather to exercise a modicum of charity, realizing that the grammar is still quite young and is in the process of growth and development.

5.20. THE DERIVATION OF EPISTEMES FROM THE EPISTON

Most studies of discourse are only secondarily concerned with the cognitive behaviors involved in its generation or interpretation. Such studies tend to focus upon its linguistic properties and relegate to speculation the role of cognition. The outcome of this type of research has been a wealth of knowledge about the particulars of the linguistic rules of the generation of grammatically correct strings but little understanding of their role in communicating knowledge. To acquire such an understanding necessarily entails an exploration of those higher-order rules that regulate the formation of conceptual structures prior to their linguistic realization. In this section, one explanation of how concepts might be ordered for discourse expression will be presented.

Discourse does not begin with the word but with an act. Although this thought or concept may resemble the word or words used to express it, it is just as likely to be structured in a wholly different fashion. Moreover, the thought may be quite complex, and although unified in the mind of the speaker, may be composed of many smaller concepts, each of which may have a very distinctive linguistic realization. This single "global" concept I refer to as the *episton,* and each of its composite or "local" concepts, as *epistemes*. The episton is all the conceptual knowledge that the speaker wishes to communicate, and while containing many embedded concepts, it is, nonetheless, a coherent unit of knowledge. The epistemes are also coherent units of thought, although they occupy specified roles in the general architecture of the episton.

In the formation of an episton, epistemes are evaluated for their possible effect upon the intended audience. This process of evaluation appears to entail at least two criteria.* The first is whether the information content of the concepts constituting the episton are known to the listener. Where the audience is well known, ellipsis and deletion is possible, and an almost direct translation of the episton into speech is possible. In most cases the internal thoughts of a speaker are generally not so apparent, and various clarification procedures are required. The second criterion is that of the interpersonal impact of the spoken message; will the discourse offend the speaker? What will he think of me if I say this? Is it appropriate? The speaker must decide if what he wants to say is going to be offensive to his listener and, if so, in what way he can qualify or couch his remarks so as to avoid dire responses.

The present program has a very specific discourse planning ability. Although it can reorganize and partition epistons for expression, it does so in a limited and idiosyncratic manner. This is because, in our example, the speaker does not carefully plan her therapeutic discourse—other than to censor certain thoughts—but rather generates incomplete and ill-formed sentences which she then attempts to correct in the course of speaking. There are, however, a number of general strategies that do govern her discourse, and they are represented in the model.

One of the foremost concerns in planning a discourse is to resolve possible problems arising from the incomplete explication of logical connectives, or from faulty and incomplete references. Effective transmission of information requires that the experience of the speaker be represented by contents that are common to the listener, and that the relations between these contents be explicit. Consequently, if concepts embedded within an episton are marked as potentially unknown to a listener, the program must break down those concepts into component parts intelligible to the listener. For example, if I were to discuss the theory of relativity to a neophyte audience, I would be required to first provide some background in physics by referring to Newton, Maxwell, and the Michelson–Morley experiments and then derive Einstein's theories from this common ground. The same process is present in everyday discourse except that it is considerably simpler and more abbreviated. Foregrounding is the common procedure whereby a setting is established for the initiation of a discourse. Concepts are either sorted out or derived from that foreground

*These criteria resemble Lakoff's (1971) "presupposition" and Fillmore's (1971) "happiness conditions."

which is to follow. In the case of the simulated patient, the foregrounding is achieved by the statement, "I was just thinking about the bill and payment again." This statement alerts the listener to what is going to follow and provides a common frame of reference. The competent speaker then follows his foregrounding statement or statements with statements that are logically and semantically related to one another and then terminates his discourse when he feels that his audience properly understands him. In those cases where the speaker's ideas or internal concepts are either convoluted or highly embedded, this process of explication is quite complex, requiring the identification of transitional sentences, logical connectives, emphasis, and contrast. Very often at this level of planning, that is, even prior to the selection of words, decisions are made as to the tone of the discourse; whether it should be personal or impersonal, and how deictic devices, such as "therefore," "nonetheless," "meanwhile," "now we see," and so on, are to be used. For the placement of these "signaling devices" follow from decisions made regarding the organization and pacing of the discourse. Most speakers seem to lack the competence to plan their discourse in advance, and therefore the most common solutions to problems of discourse organization are derived in the course of speaking with relatively little preplanning.

The regulation of interpersonal impacts is guided by the speaker's concern over the desired emotive impacts of his speech. In most cases he does not want to offend his audience, or, if he does, at least in a calculated manner. Similarly, he may want to affect his audience positively, that is, solicit their approval or empathy, and this, too, is a calculated enterprise. Consequently, to achieve this effect, the speaker must carefully organize his discourse so as to emphasize what he wants to be known and deemphasize what he desires be left uninferred. In therapeutic discourse and probably in everyday discourse, tone is a powerful means of divorcing the speaker from the consequences of his speech. An outrageous statement uttered in an impersonal tone or under the guise of natural reflection can obtain full immunity. Similarly, indirect reference and deliberate obfuscation are powerful devices for camouflaging undesirable contents.

Although the program does not yet have an elaborate discourse marker system for epistemes, we can, nonetheless, illustrate its general form of operation through the following representation. (These examples should not in any way be regarded as being exhaustive of the discourse planning process.)

Episton	=	high-order undifferentiated concept wanting expression
EP	=	episteme derived from the episton
CONT	=	contrast marker
EMPH	=	emphasis marker
CONCL	=	conclusion marker
PREM	=	premise marker

COMPD	=	compound marker
ALT1	=	first alternate marker
ALT2	=	second alternate marker
COMT	=	comment marker
POS	=	marker that positively marks another marker
NEG	=	marker that negatively marks another marker

When ordered, these symbols determine the role that various epistemes should play in the organization of a discourse. The topmost symbol is always the episton and, in terms of a unified discourse, is usually singular, because the discourse is an expression of it. One might think of the episton as the primary topic which the discourse is constructed to express. With the exception of EP, the episteme, the remainder of the symbols designate the types of roles that the clauses are to play.

Below are some examples of episteme markers that characterize different interepistemic relationships.

(1)

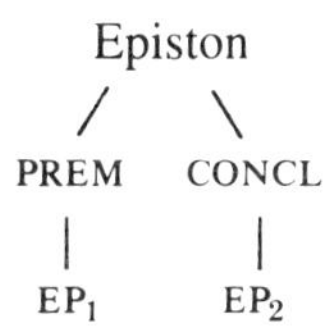

I like MacDonald's [and / so / therefore]
Nixon is a good president

This realization can be further restricted by the addition of more markers that either weaken the connection, such as "and" does, or strengthens it, as "therefore" does ("so" appears to be intermediate between the two).

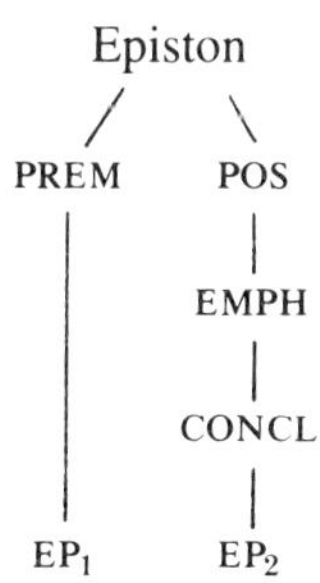

I like MacDonald's therefore Nixon is a good President.

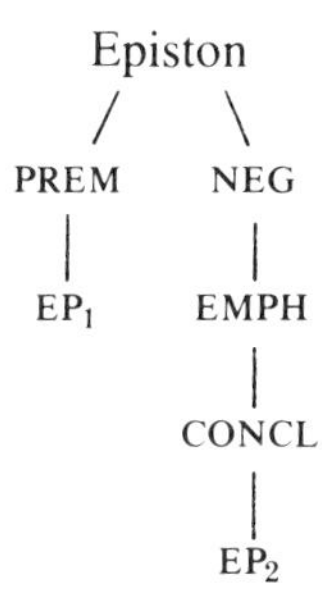

I like MacDonald's. Nixon is a good president.

(2)

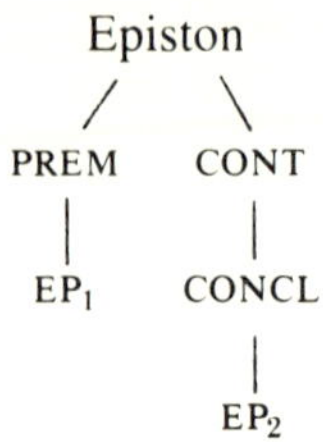

I like apples, *but* I don't like pears.

(3)

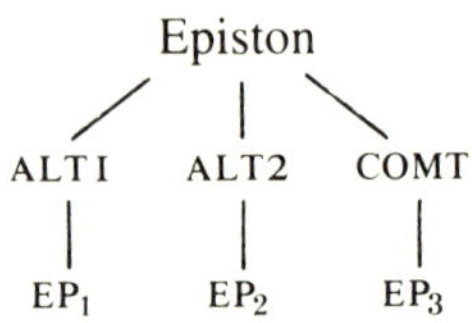

Either you can go or you can stay. It makes no difference to me.

(4)

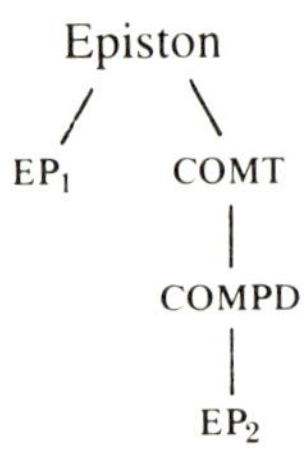

He was mistaken and he knew it.

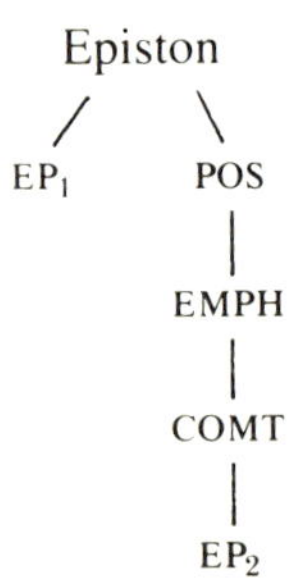

He was mistaken. He knew it.

(5)

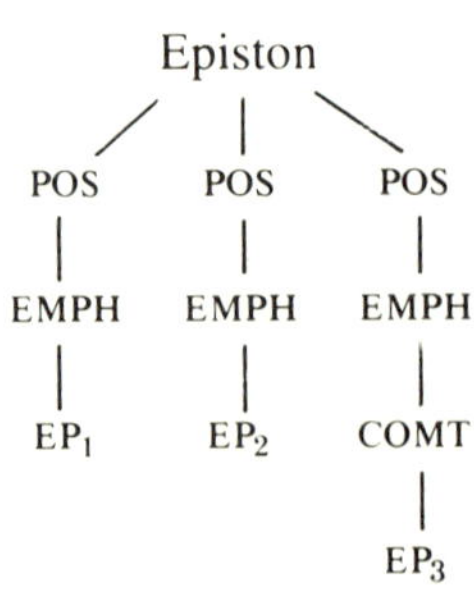

Not only did she tear up the speeding ticket, but she stuck out her tongue. That's guts.

(6)

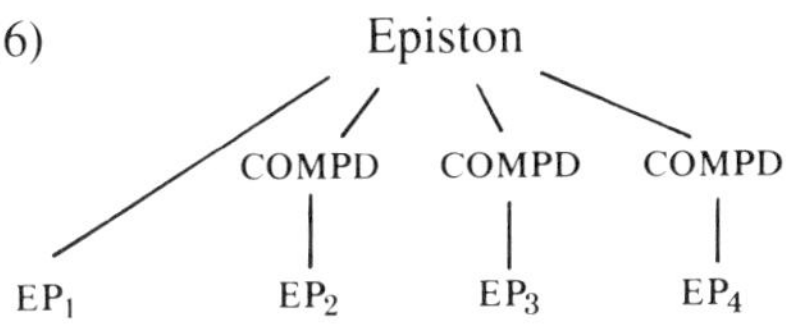

I went home once and got into bed and I turned on the tube and I ate a whole jar of marshmallow topping.

(7)

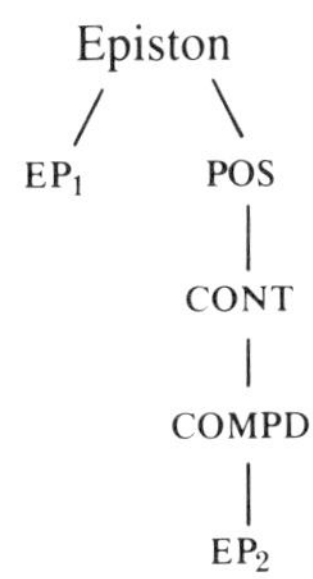

I voted Republican. But don't ask me why.

5.30. THE DERIVATION OF EPISTEME CONSTITUENTS

With the completion of the initial decomposition of the episton, which for most speakers seems to entail the derivation of relatively few epistemes, a set of procedures are involved for distinguishing among the constituent parts of the episteme. Epistemes become realized linguistically either as primary clauses or as sentences. Their constituent structures, in turn, eventually translate into grammatical constructs, and their component concepts into words.

An episteme can be composed of an arbitrary number of concepts, but these concepts are always initially ordered in the following manner: MOOD (A1 Rr A2) or MOOD (A1 Rr), where the mood can be imperative, interrogative, or declarative; A1 is an initial argument containing an arbitrary number of concepts acting in a bounded or in an "entitylike" manner; Rr is a relator designating a process or relation that holds for A1 and A2; and A2, like A1, designates an entity but differs in its role with respect to Rr. These two canonical forms, arguments and relators, in fact, define what an episteme is and constitute the primary structure from which all constituents are derived.

The second level of derivation is that of bundles: entity, process, and relation. Bundles are collections of ordered constituents that can be unwound into single words, in the simple case, or subordinate clauses of arbitrary complexity. There are seven types of entity bundles, each of which is unique in the role it plays in a process or relation bundle. In many respects, types of bundles resemble cases in a Fillmore-type grammar (Fillmore 1968). For A1-derived bundles there are two roles, agent (EBA) and initiator (EBI), whereas for A2 entity bundles, there are five possible roles: instrument (EBIN), locative (EBL), goal (EBG), recipient (EBR), and cause (EBC).

Process bundles (PB) and relation bundles (RB) are derived from the relator, Rr, and distinguish themselves in terms of whether they express a relation or a process. Although both process bundles and relation bundles take many of the same types of entity bundles, the role these entities play varies according to whether they are bound to any process or relation bundle. For example, EBA is agentive when used with a process bundle but attributive when placed in a relation bundle. Consequently, the nomenclative may be more of a hindrance than a help in some cases. In a more complete version of the "grammar," these differences might be preserved by having additional entity bundles. However, for our purposes, seven types of entity bundles seem to suffice.

Entity bundles can be broken down into constituents that have a single entity (E) with an arbitrary number of denoters (DEN), or an embedded constituent (EMB) containing a complex interdependent structure. Unlike an embedded constituent, an entity is a single concept that is unrelated to other concepts, and is linguistically realized as a noun. Denoters are concepts that restrict the meaning of other concepts. They act to modify the meaning of a given concept, be it in entity, another denoter, a process, or a relation.

Relation bundles and process bundles are always broken down into a constituent having a relation concept (R) or a process concept (P), respectively. In some cases, the constituent derived from a PB or RB can have a denoter which acts to restrict or specify the meaning of the process or relation. These denoters are generally of three types: condition (DENC), manner (DENM), and time (DENT). They, like other denoters, can be broken down into single concepts (MOD) or embedded concepts (EMB) that act to denote an attribute of a given concept.

Before discussing the episteme constituents in greater detail, let us first provide some general rules for their derivation and supplement these rules with examples of their application. The arrow in the rules simply means that the left-hand set of symbols can be rewritten as the right-hand set of symbols.

PRELIMINARY RULES FOR THE DERIVATION OF EPISTEME CONSTITUENTS

1. Episteme Moods: DCL (EP), IMP (EP), INT (EP)
   These features denote whether the discourse is to be in a declarative, imperative, or interrogative mood.
2. (EP) ⟶ (A1 Rr A2), (A1 Rr)A2
   This rule simply states that an episteme can be broken down into one or the other of the structures above.
3. A1 ⟶ (EBA), (EBI)
   This rule states that the first argument of an episteme can be rewritten as either an entity bundle of the agentive case or of the initiator case.
4. Rr ⟶ (PB), (RB)
   This rule says that a relator, a top-level designation, can only be rewritten as a process bundle or as a relation bundle.

5. A2 ⟶ (EBG), (EBR), (EBL), (EBIN), (DEN), (EBC), or combinations of the above.
The rewriting of a second argument can involve up to five entity bundles, depending on the nature of the Rr.
6. EB(X) ⟶ (DEN* E*), (E*), (EMB)
In this notation *X* is a variable standing for any of the seven roles that the entity bundles can take. *E* stands for an entity and DEN for a denoter. The *'s next to *E* and DEN symbolize arbitrary repetition. EMB symbolizes the fact that its derivative constituents are embedded and either do not play a denoter role or are entities by themselves.
7. DEN ⟶ (MOD*), (EMB)
Denoters can be rewritten either as modifiers of arbitrary numbers or as embedded concepts, those that are related and not individuated.
8. PB ⟶ (DENC* P), (DENM* P), (P), (DENC* DENM* P)
Process bundles are rewritten with a condition or manner-denoter bundle, or both denoting a process and as a single process.
9. RB ⟶ (DENC* R), (DENM* R), (DENC* DENM* R), (R)
Relation bundles are rewritten the same as process bundles except that relation concepts replace process concepts.
10. DENC ⟶ (MOD*), (EMB)
The derivation rule for the conditional denoter is here presented as the same as that for the simple denoter. Yet as we will see later, the derivations that precede it provide information that is decisive in determining lexical realization and word ordering, and therefore it is activated in different environments.
11. DENT ⟶ (MOD*), (EMB)
Same as rule 10.
12. DENM ⟶ (MOD*), (EMB)
Same as rule 10.
13. EMB ⟶ (A1 Rr A2), (Rr A2), (MOD), (E), (MOD MOD)
Embedded structures can occur after entity bundles and denoters. They can contain complete relational constituents (A1 Rr A2), or partially related constituents. The double denoter bundle signifies the modification of one denoter by another—the specification of a property by a property.

It should be remembered while interpreting these rules that they describe the roles of concepts and not words. These concepts may or may not have direct grammatical and lexical realization, which is to say that the number and type of words that realize a given concept differ for each concept. Some concepts have verbal, adjectival, and nominal realizations, whereas others may have only one of these. For example, speakers sometimes "invent" words in their expression of ideas; they do so because they are unable to find existing words that realize the concepts they are using at that time. Although our language has this capacity to construct new words through prefixing and suffixing of the appropriate morphemes, there are other, less drastic means for realizing concepts that do not have direct lexical equivalents. The use of phrases, participles, nominalization, and gerunds all serve this purpose. The derivation of conceptual role descriptors is undertaken so that the appropriate selection of linguistic realizations can be made, because this information is not in the concepts themselves but must be derived from their structural roles. In a later section we shall discuss this process of grammatical realization in detail.

1. Flying machines are dangerous.
   1. DCL (A1 Rr A2) ⟶ (EBA RB EBG)
   2. EBA ⟶ (DEN E) ⟶ (MOD E)
   3. RB ⟶ (R)
   4. EBG ⟶ (DEN) ⟶ (MOD)

   ((MOD E) (R) (MOD))

   Flying machines are dangerous

   In this case Rr is rewritten as a relation, which, although taking an entity-bundle argument, really acts more like a denoting function, and therefore has as its entity a denoter rather than an entity.

2. Flying machines is dangerous.
   1. DCL (A1 Rr A2) ⟶ (EBA RB EBG)
   2. EBA ⟶ (EMB)
   3. EMB ⟶ (Rr′ A2′) ⟶ (PB′ EBG′)
   4. PB′ ⟶ (P′)
   5. EBG′ ⟶ (E′)
   6. RB ⟶ (R)
   7. EBG ⟶ (DEN) ⟶ (MOD)

   ((P′ E′) (R) (MOD))

   Flying machines is dangerous.

   In this sentence, very similar to the first, the grammatical subject of the sentence is a gerund. This property of the subject is represented by the entity bundle in the initial argument position, having as its derivative a process and entity constituent.

3. The man who knew too much thought very little about it.
   1. DCL (A1 Rr A1) ⟶ (EBA PB EBG)
   2. EBA ⟶ (DEN DEN E) ⟶ (MOD EMB E)
   3. EMB ⟶ (A1′ Rr′ A2′) ⟶ (EBA′ PB′)
   4. EBA′ ⟶ (E′)
   5. PB′ ⟶ (DENM′ P′) ⟶ (EMB′ P′)
   6. EMB′ ⟶ (MOD′′ MOD′′)
   7. PB ⟶ (DENM P) ⟶ (EMB P)
   8. EMB ⟶ (MOD′ MOD′)
   9. EBG ⟶ (E)

((MOD (E′ (MOD′′ MOD′′) P′E) ((MOD′ MOD′) P) E)
the man too much knew man very little thought about it

In this example we see how complex embedding takes place first with the relative clause and then with adverbs modifying adverbs.

4. He knew too much to think about it.
   1. DCL (A1 Rr A2) ⟶ (EBA PB EBG)
   2. EBA ⟶ (E)
   3. PB ⟶ (DENM P) ⟶ (EMB P)
   4. EMB ⟶ (MOD′ MOD′)
   5. EBG ⟶ (EMB) ⟶ (PE)

This example demonstrates how a process can be used in a secondary argument, EBG. Notice the great differences conceptually between this sentence and the preceding one, despite the similarity of content between the two.

5. During long sieges, the Khan was subject to black moods and fits of rage.
   1. DCL (A1 Rr A2) ⟶ (EBA PB EBR)
   2. EBA ⟶ (DEN E DEN E) ⟶ ((MOD E) (MOD E))
   3. PB ⟶ (DENC P)
   4. DENC ⟶ (EMB) ⟶ (MOD E)
   5. EBR ⟶ (DEN E) ⟶ (MOD E)

   ((MOD E) (MOD E)) (((MOD E) P) (MOD E))
   black moods fits rage long sieges subject the Khan

This example quite clearly shows that the ordering of the concepts is quite different from their grammatical realization. The adverbial phrase, "during long sieges," is not given thematic prominence at this point and the verb is in an active voice. The word orderings are accomplished through the intervention of the focus operator, a topic that will be covered later in the chapter.

5.31. *The derivation of entity bundles*

Entity bundles are concepts that are structured to act like entities or objects. While they may *be* a process concept, as in the case of a gerund or infinitive, they *act* as a bounded entity. In the canonical form that we are using here, the first argument of an episteme always realizes itself or part of itself into what is to become a nominal construction. However, this is not the case for secondary arguments which have relations and relationlike processes as their initial relators. For example, "He seemed fine," "He is well," "He turned pale," have verbs that do not take objects or arguments in the same sense as do transitive verbs. Despite these differences, such relation-type verbs are still regarded as taking entity bundles for their arguments; however, their realization rules are different. For whereas entity bundles bound to process-type concepts in the relator position may not terminate in a simple denoter element, those entity bundles bound to relation-type relators can.

We have included denoters in entity bundles in the belief that they act to specify a particular property of the entity and in this way restrict the possible meanings an entity may have.* For example, the statement "It is a wooden house" conveys little information; we know that most houses are made of wood, so there is no new information in this statement that distinguishes it from millions of other houses. However, if the statement were, "This house, which H. H. Richardson built for his son in 1881, has rosewood interior paneling and Italian red marble toilet basins," it would communicate a great deal of information, because it restricted the quite general concept of house to a unique and particular house. Denoters act to achieve such particularity by specifying properties of entities, processes, and relations.

Denoters in an entity constituent can be of two types. The first is the simple case where the denoter is a single concept or a group of single concepts; denoters that function in this manner are in turn realized as MODs and can end up as adjectives, adverbs, possessive pronouns, and participles. The second type of denoter is an embedded constituent whose parts are related in some manner. In this case, DEN is rewritten as EMB and can contain a whole A1 Rr A2 structure with all its embeddings. (This type of denoter structure is generally realized as a relative clause.) When derived from a DEN feature, an embedded bundle can also represent a denoter acting on another denoter, that is, a property restriction on a property.

The other half of a derived entity bundle constituent, that concerning the entity role, can either be realized as an embedded constituent or as a single entity concept or group of concepts. When in an embedded bundle, the constituents are either of the form A1 Rr A2, or of the form Rr A2. The former structures gets realized as clauses and the latter as gerund constructions.

The following examples show how typical discourse constructions can be characterized in terms of entity bundles:

ENTITY BUNDLE DERIVATIONS

1. man of good humor
   EB(X) ⟶ (DEN E) ⟶ (EMB E)
   EMB ⟶ (DEN′ DEN′) ⟶ (MOD′ MOD′)
   ((MOD′ MOD′) E)
2. dirty stinking commie
   EB(X) ⟶ (DEN DEN E) ⟶ (MOD MOD E)
   (MOD MOD E)
3. man without a country
   EB(X) ⟶ (DEN E) ⟶ (MOD MOD E)

*See the discussion of generic and token concepts in Chapter 4 to see how this linguistic treatment fits into the cognitive model. Notice the similarity between denoters and indicators with their properties.

EMB———→ (DEN′ DEN′ E′)———→ (MOD′ MOD′ E′)
((MOD′ MOD′ E′) E)

4. the look in your eye
EB(X)———→ (DEN DEN E)———→ (MOD EMB E)
EMB———→ (DEN′ DEN′ E′)———→ (MOD′ MOD′ E′)
((MOD′ MOD′ E′) E)

5. the spy who came in from the cold
EB(X)———→ (DEN DEN E)———→ (MOD EMB E)
EMB———→ (A1′ R1′ A1′)———→ (EBA′ PB′ EBL′)
EBA′———→ (E′)
PB′———→ (R′)
EBL———→ (DEN′ E′)———→ (MOD′ E′)
(MOD (E′ R′ MOD′ E′) E)

6. That he caused the trouble . . .
EBA or EBI———→ (EMB)
EMB———→ (A1′ R1′ A2′)———→ (EBA′ PB′ EBG′)
EBA′———→ (E′)
PB′———→ (P′)
EBG′———→ (DEN′ E′)———→ (MOD′ E′)
(E′ P′ MOD′ E′)

7. Singing in the shower
EB(X)———→ (DENL P)———→ (EMB P)
EMB′———→ (DEN′ DEN′ E′)———→ (MOD′ MOD′ E′)
((MOD′ MOD′ E′) P)

8. Dean's dilemma
EB(X)———→ (DEN E)———→ (MOD E)
(MOD E)

9. His endless banter
EB(X)———→ (DEN DEN E)———→ (MOD MOD E)
(MOD MOD E)

10. the man whose greed knew no limits
EB(X)———→ (DEN DEN E)———→ (MOD EMB E)
EMB———→ (A1′ R1′ A2′)———→ (EBA′ PB′ EBG′)
EBA———→ (DEN′ E′)———→ (MOD′ E′)
PB′———→ (P′)
EBG′———→ (DEN′ E′)———→ (MOD′ E′)
(MOD (MOD′ E′ P′ MOD′ E′) E)

11. grapefruit tree
EB(X)———→ (DEN E)———→ (MOD E)

12. Dick and Spiro
EB(X)———→ (E E)

13. Avarice, stupidity, and guile
EB(X)———→ (E E E)

At this level of derivation the ordering of the concepts does not correspond in many cases to the final word orderings. In some instances, such as those involving embedded bundles that would have a subordinate clause realization, the difference is quite marked. Similarly, prepositional phrases are not discriminated from other denoter constituents. Notice also that verbs are always represented in an active voice. The reasons for these differences from our more familiar understanding of grammar is due to the fact that these rules still describe concepts that have no thematic structure. However, once the conceptual structures and orderings are decided, thematic operators take over to manipulate both conceptual and linguistic structures. Manipulation does not only entail word rearrangement or a change in voice, but very often the insertion of key phrases, lexical items, and deictic devises. Therefore, until the lexicon has been consulted to determine the type of lexical realization a concept has, grammatical features are relatively unimportant. However, once the lexicon has been consulted and a number of candidate words are evaluated, the system has to make a choice in terms of the communicative effectiveness of the different grammatical options. For instance, the entity bundle in the first example, man of good humor, is characterized as ((MOD′ MOD′) E); this concept structure could be realized as a "good-humored man." The choice between the two is here treated as a thematic choice and handled at another level of realization.

5.32. *The derivation of process and relation bundles*

There are two types of roles that concepts can play that find realization in verbs. The first is where the concept expresses a process. By this we mean an activity that is taking place, has taken place, or will take place. While all processes have initial arguments, some do not have secondary arguments; in this way the latter type are like intransitive verbs, whereas the former are like transitive verbs. The second type of concept role is that of a relation and this role roughly corresponds to the linguistic notion of an attributive verb.

Processes and relations, like entities, can achieve specified and qualified meanings through the work of denoters. These denoters act to specify a particular property or attribute of the process or relation being expressed. They are of four types: conditional denoters, specifying a condition under which the process or relation took place (DENC); manner denoters, specifying the manner by which the process or relation was enacted (DENM); temporal denoters, specifying the time at which the process or relation was in effect (DENT); and locative denoters (DENL), specifying a place of a process or relation. Like the denoters in an entity bundle, these denoters can have complex derivatives resulting in subordinate clauses, or they can terminate in single concept modifiers.

What is grammatically regarded as time and modality in verbs is here treated as a part of the process or relation concept and is not separately marked. Voice is not represented at the conceptual level, but treated as a thematic option.

The sample sentences below indicate some of the different types of process and entity bundle constructions.

PROCESS AND RELATION BUNDLE DERIVATIONS

1. He seemed like a worthy successor.
   DCL(A1 Rr A2) ⟶ (EBA RB EBR)
   EBA ⟶ (E)
   RB ⟶ (R)
   EBR ⟶ (DEN DEN E) ⟶ (MOD MOD E)
   (E (R) (MOD MOD E))
2. She is nice.
   DCL(A1 Rr A2) ⟶ (EBA RB EBR)
   EBA ⟶ (E)
   RB ⟶ (R)
   EBR ⟶ (MOD)
   (E (R) (MOD))
3. She is Natonia.
   DCL(A1 Rr A2) ⟶ (EBA RB EBG)
   EBA ⟶ (E)
   RB ⟶ (E)
   EBG ⟶ (E)
   (E (R) (E))
4. Despite his frantic efforts, Matt couldn't stop Rahu.
   DCL(A1 Rr A2) ⟶ (EBA PB EBG)
   EBA ⟶ (E)
   PB ⟶ (DENC P) ⟶ (EMB P)
   EMB ⟶ (DEN′ DEN′ E′) ⟶ (MOD′ MOD′ E′)
   DENC ⟶ (MOD)
   EBG ⟶ (E)
   ((E) (E′) (MOD P) (E))
5. He could not give her the priceless jewel unless she recited the sacred text.
   DCL(A1 Rr A2) ⟶ (EBA PB EBR EBG)
   EBA ⟶ (E)
   PB ⟶ (DENC P) ⟶ (EMB P)
   EMB ⟶ (A1 Rr A2) ⟶ (EBA′ PB′ EBG′)
   EBA′ ⟶ (E′)
   PB′ ⟶ (P′)
   EBG′ ⟶ (DEN′ DEN′ E′) ⟶ (MOD′ MOD′ E′)
   EBG ⟶ (DEN DEN E) ⟶ (MOD MOD E)
   EBR ⟶ (E)
6. The Assyrian came down like the wolf on the fold.

DCL(A I Rr) ⟶ (EBA PB)
PB ⟶ (DENM DENM P) ⟶ (EMB DEN P) ⟶ (EMB MOD P)
EMB ⟶ (A I′ Rr′ A2′) ⟶ (EBA′ PB′ EBL′)
EBA′ ⟶ (DEN′ E′) ⟶ (MOD′ E′)
PB′ ⟶ (DENC′ P′) ⟶ (DEN′ P′) ⟶ (MOD′ P′)
EBL′ ⟶ (DEN′ E′) ⟶ (MOD′ E′)

7. If that happens anymore, we will have to go.
DCL(A I Rr) ⟶ (EBI PB)
EBI ⟶ (E)
PB ⟶ (DENC P) ⟶ (EMB P)
EMB ⟶ (A I′ Rr′) ⟶ (EBA′ RB′)
EBA′ ⟶ (E)
RB′ ⟶ (DENC′ R′) ⟶ (DEN′ R′) ⟶ (MOD′ R′)

5.33. *The derivation of denoter constituents*

At this point in our presentation the role of the denoter functions should be reasonably clear. It remains for us now to cover in greater detail how denoters operate and add to our rules those needed to characterize a wider class of constructions.

Earlier we saw that a denoter could have as its derivative either an embedded constituent or a series of modifiers. Embedded denoter constituents contain bundles that are related in some way to one another; this relationship either entails having a denoter operate on another denoter or having entity bundles bound to one another through a relation or process. Modifiers, on the other hand, are unrelated single concepts that specify a property of any entity, process, or relation. However, in addition to such modifiers there are a group of modifier types that modify in a related manner; these are comparative constructions: "Her smile is more brilliant than sunshine"; equative comparatives, "He is dumb as a bug." These types of modifiers are presented as MODC and MODE, respectively, and are treated in the same manner as denoters that operate on denoters; that is, they follow DEN and EMB features.

The following are some examples of different denoter constituents:

COMPLEX DENOTERS DERIVATIONS

1. Since we have already opened it, we should drink it.
DCL(A I Rr A2) ⟶ (EBA PB EBG)
EBA ⟶ (E)
PB ⟶ (DENC P) ⟶ (EMB P)
EMB ⟶ (A I′ Rr′ A2′) ⟶ (EBA′ PB′ EBG′)
EBA′ ⟶ (E′)
PB′ ⟶ (DENC′ P′) ⟶ (MOD′ P′)

EBG′ ⟶ (E′)
EBG ⟶ (E)

2. He flies faster than a speeding bullet.
DCL (A1 Rr) ⟶ (EBA PB)
EBA ⟶ (E)
PB ⟶ (DENC P) ⟶ (EMB P)
EMB ⟶ (MODC′ DEN′ DEN′ E′) ⟶ (MOD′ MOD′ MOD′ E′)

3. That is better than what came before it.
DCL(A1 Rr A2) ⟶ (EBA PB EBG)
EBG ⟶ (EMB) ⟶ (MODC)
MODC ⟶ (A1 Rr A2) ⟶ (EBA′ PB′ EB′)
EBA′ ⟶ (E′)
PB′ ⟶ (P′)
EBL ⟶ (E′)

4. She is as pretty as a picture.
DCL(A1 Rr A2) ⟶ (EBA RB EBG)
EBA ⟶ (E)
RB ⟶ (E)
EBG ⟶ (EMB) ⟶ (MODE′ DEN′ E′) ⟶ (MOD′ MOD′ E′)

5. It seems like only yesterday, I left my mind behind.
DCL(A1 Rr A2) ⟶ (EBA PB EBG EBL)
EBA ⟶ (E)
PB ⟶ (DENT DENL P) ⟶ (EMB MOD P)
EBL ⟶ (E)
EBG ⟶ (DEN E) ⟶ (MOD E)

6. Quick as a wink, he was gone.
DCL(A1 Rr) ⟶ (EBA PB)
EBA ⟶ (E)
PB ⟶ (DENM P) ⟶ (EMB P)
EMB ⟶ (MODE′ DEN′ E′) ⟶ (MOD′ MOD′ E′)

Besides showing how denoter constructions function at the conceptual level, these examples should also make it clear that not only the ordering of words for discourse is directed by concerns of discourse impact, but also the selection of words, and even the type of grammatical constructions used. For instance, choices of voice, adjectival or prepositional modifiers, and contrast devises are made on the basis of thematic impact. In example 5, the process modifier, "It seems like only yesterday," is not represented as a subordinate clause, for the selection of predicative constructions, such as "It seems," "There is," and so on, are thematically determined and not conceptually derived. However, the notion of a "seeming only yesterday" is represented at the conceptual level; only at the thematic level of realization does it become, "It seems like only yesterday."

5.40. THE REALIZATION OF CONCEPTUAL CONSTITUENTS INTO GRAMMATICAL CATEGORIES

In this model grammatical categories, semantic and syntactic, are regarded as the communicative constraints placed upon the expression of concepts. They are seen as the conventions required to render an innate thought or feeling publicly intelligible, and as such, both beneficial and restrictive to expression and thought. Therefore, although they are necessary for the expression of thought, they are not identical to it.

After the roles and relationships of conceptual constituents have been determined, the process of finding the appropriate lexical and grammatical structures begins. Because of the discrepancy between what a speaker thinks and what he can say, this is not a straightforward or simple process; it involves many backtrackings and reformulations—unless the concepts are relatively standard and simple and therefore have habitual or ''packaged'' realizations. Regulating the entire process of grammatical and lexical selection are the concerns that the speaker may have over the impact of his discourse. These concerns affect not only what word or combination of words may be selected for discourse impact, but also the overall organization of the message.

5.41. *The lexicon and the selection of words for concept realization*

Whereas concepts have no inherent grammatical properties, words do. Although a concept can be cast in the role of a noun, verb, adverb, and so on, there may not be a word which matches the content requirements of the concept and has the appropriate grammatical properties. For example, a concept referring to a mental process might be realized both as a noun (thought) and a verb (think), whereas a concept referring to great size may have a nominal and adjectival realization (largeness and large) but no verbal realization (''larged''). Poets may be forgiven for such license as ''Green dreams do sleep furiously,'' and children overlooked for ''The balloon larged,'' but ''native'' speakers seldom are.

The lexicon of a speaker acts to match concepts and their role requirements with the definitions and grammatical features of words.* The diagram illustrates how concepts are matched with words to create the sentence ''Soldiers skip to Sousa.'' In this example there are three simple concepts, which find simple realization in the words, soldiers, skip, (to) Sousa. Words and concepts are matched for their grammatical role requirements (Es can be realized as nouns, gerunds, and other nominal constructions; Ps and Rs become verbs; and MODs become adjectives, possessive nouns, or pronouns or adverbs) as well as for their content or semantic properties. Sometimes one

*See C. J. Fillmore, Types of lexical information in *Semantics*, D. D. Steinberg and L. A. Jakobovits, eds. (New York: Cambridge University Press), for a similar statement on the requirements of a lexicon.

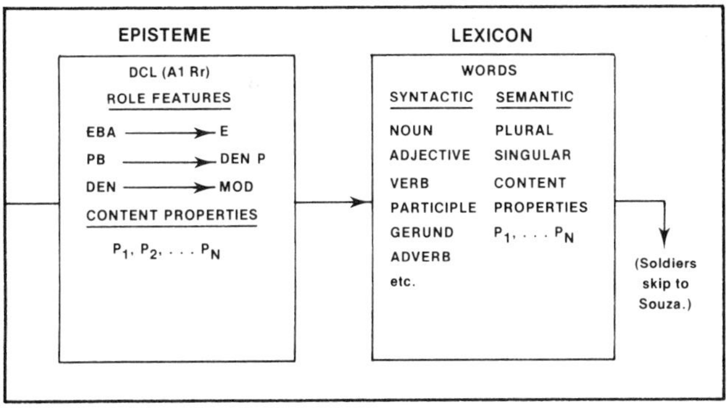

requirement will be met while the other is not: a word might have the appropriate content feature but inappropriate role features. In this case a different word is tried, one not quite so accurate in content but grammatically correct, or there is a restructuring of the episteme, signaling the impossibility of direct and accurate expression.

5.42. *The realization of concepts into nouns, gerunds, pronouns, and infinitives*

Earlier we pointed out that all entity bundles contain items that act as entities. In the simple case for which there is a single lexical item which itself is defined as an entity, the realization is simple; the entity concept becomes either a proper or common noun. However, in those cases where the vocabulary does not have such direct equivalent, other words have to be found that can play the role of a noun. Such words may be gerunds, "Flying is fun," or infinitives, "To fly airplanes is fun."

Simple entity bundles can also be realized as nonpossessive pronouns (he, she, it, they, we, us, them, her, him, me). The nominal pronouns can only be derived from entity agent or entity initiator bundles, whereas the other pronouns follow from locative, instrumental, recipient, and goal-type bundles. Their substitution for nouns is regulated by audience-impact programs, which determine if a substitution is intelligible to a listener.

The following rules summarize the realization of entity bundles into simple nouns and nounlike constructions. The symbol ">" indicates that the symbol following it was derived from the symbol preceding the >.

RULES FOR REALIZING ENTITY BUNDLES INTO NOMINAL CONSTRUCTIONS

1. EBA>E ⟶ noun, pronoun (plural or singular, depending upon concept); must have animate sematic features when combined with certain processes
2. EBA>P ⟶ gerund, infinitive
   EBG>P ⟶ gerund, infinitive

EBIN>P ⟶ gerund, infinitive
EBR>P ⟶ gerund, infinitive

3. EBG>E ⟶ noun, pronoun (singular or plural depending upon the properties of the concept)
   EBR>E ⟶ noun, pronoun (singular or plural depending upon the properties of the concept)
   EBIN>E ⟶ noun, pronoun (singular or plural depending upon the properties of the concept)
   EBL>E ⟶ noun, pronoun (singular or plural depending upon the properties of the concept)
4. EBA>R ⟶ gerund, infinitives
   EBA>R ⟶ gerund, infinitives
   EBG>R ⟶ gerund, infinitives
   EBR>R ⟶ gerund, infinitives
   EBIN>R ⟶ gerund, infinitives

5.43. *The realization of concepts into adjectives and modifier constructions*

Adjectives realize denoter concepts that can terminate in MODs. Quantifiers, classifiers, determiners, ordinals, numbers, and possessive pronouns also do this and therefore are regarded here as similar to adjectives, although their sequence of modification is different. Participles are process concepts that play the role of denoter concepts and are accordingly treated like adjectives.

Complex denoter concepts using MODE and MODC concepts realize themselves into equative adjectival constructions, "pretty as a picture," and comparative adjectival constructions, "funnier than hell."

Another type of complex modifies another adjective, for example, "the *dark* black room." This type of construction is derived from an embedded denoter constituent with two or more MODs: (DEN) ⟶ (EMB) ⟶ (MOD MOD).*

The rules below demonstrate the different ways by which adjectives and modifiers are realized from concepts.

RULES FOR REALIZING DENOTERS INTO ADJECTIVES AND MODIFIERS

1. DEN ⟶ (MOD) ⟶ adjective, definite determiner, indefinite determiner, possessive noun or pronoun, ordinal number, and classifier
2. (DEN E) ⟶ (P E) ⟶ participle + nominal construction
3. (DEN E) ⟶ (EMB E) ⟶ ((MOD′ MOD′)E) ⟶ adjective or adverb acting upon another adjective or participle that modifies a noun

*Superlatives such as "biggest" are not given special features, as the superlative property is regarded as a property of the modifying concept.

4. (DEN DEN . . . E)⟶(MOD MOD . . . E)⟶a series of modifiers possibly having one determiner, one ordinal, one number, and any number of adjectives and classifiers
5. (DEN E)⟶ (MOD E)⟶ ((MOD E)E)⟶ adjective + as + a noun or gerund or when used to modify a noun
6. (DEN E)⟶ (MODC E)⟶ ((MOD E)E)⟶ comparative adjective + than + noun or gerund when used to modify a noun

5.44. *The realization of concepts into prepositional phrases*

Those prepositions that are not determined by the character of the verb or the role of its arguments serve a modifying function, either of entities or of processes and relations. Very often it is a question of thematic choice whether a construction will be realized as an adjectival modifier, "a healthy man," or as a prepositional phrase, "a man of health"; cases do exist where the grammar of the language does not permit such a choice, but requires one or the other: "a man of means," "a meaning man," "a green plant," "a plant of greenness."

Where a preposition is not determined by the character of a verb, it is always treated as a modifier, which, through the peculiarities of the grammar or the thematic interests of the speaker, is realized as a prepositional phrase instead of a single adjective or adverb. Consequently, such prepositional phrases as "on top of the pyramid," "under the table," "over the hill," "on the divan," and "next to the circus" are all represented as concepts denoting a particular locative characteristic of an entity or process. What determines their prepositional character is not only their role as concepts but also the grammatical requirements of the lexicon.

Prepositions also realize denoter concepts that include a modifier and an entity in their modification of an entity: "man with the gray beard," "the man in the gray flannel suit." These types of prepositional phrases are derived from the following denoter constructions:

1. EB(X)⟶ (DEN E)⟶ (EMB E)
   EMB⟶ (DEN′ DEN′ E)⟶ (MOD′ MOD′ E′)
   ((MOD′ MOD′ E′) E′)
   man with the gray beard
2. EB(X)⟶ (DEN E)⟶ (EMB E)
   EMB⟶ (DEN′ DEN′ DEN′ E′)⟶ (MOD′ MOD′ MOD′ E)
   ((MOD′ (MOD′ MOD′) E′) E)
   man in the gray flannel suit

5.45. *The realization of process and relation concepts into verbs*

Just as a process or relation is the mainstay of the episteme, so is the verb a central binding force of the discourse. Contained within the structure of a process or relation concept are those features that determine its tense and modality in verbal realization. In those cases where the relator has no argument, (A1 Rr), the verb is intransitive, "the soldiers marched," and when the relator has a second argument, (A1 Rr A2), the verb is transitive, "He marched the soldiers."

The main verb determines the transitivity of the main clause and in doing so specifies the relationships and roles that each of its arguments or case components take. Since most of the process or relation concepts have verbal realizations in the model we are using, there is no problem of finding the proper verb to meet the requirements of a given concept. In those cases where there is no simple one-for-one concept–verb realization, it is likely that several sentences may be required to express relationships contained in the process or relation concept.

The distinction between processes and relations at the conceptual level finds its equivalent in the distinction between verbs that bind two or more nounlike entities, "active verbs," and those that bind a nominal construction with an attribute in transitive clauses. For example, "He went to the store," "He bought tomatoes for his friends," "He exchanged dollars for marks" are all process-type verbs. Whereas "She seemed sleepy," "She was upset," "He felt ill" are all transitive relation verbs.

For the time being, the grammar uses eight different tenses, all of which are built out of combinations of three basic tenses: present, past, and future. These three basic tenses can be combined to yield the following eight tenses (after Winograd 1971).

moves ⟶ Present
move ⟶ Past
will move ⟶ Future
can move ⟶ Modal
has moved ⟶ Past in Present
was moving ⟶ Present in Past
was going to have moved ⟶ Past in Future in Past
was going to have been taking ⟶ Present in Past in Future in Past

In this model verbs are initially given an active-voice realization. Only when the organization of the discourse message is evaluated and altered for thematic impacts is it given a passive voice. For the passive voice does not express a logical or informational property of a verb but is rather an agent of thematic operations used to highlight certain thematic properties of the discourse. Below are the possible passive constructions (Winograd 1971):

is moved ⟶ Present
could have been moved ⟶ Past in Modal
has been going to have been moved ⟶ Past in Future in Past in Past in Present

5.46. *The realization of process and relation modifiers into adverbs*

Those denoters that are a part of a process or relation bundle and break down into single MODS are realized as adverbs. There are three types of denoters that modify processes and relations: DENC, a denoter expressing a condition, which generally is not expressed as a single adverb but as an adverbal phrase or clause, "He did it *under duress*"; DENM, a denoter expressing manner, "He *quickly* disposed of the matter," "The cat *furtively* stole away"; DENT, a denoter expressing time, "I *just* said that," "Do it *later*."

In contrast to adjectives, adverbs are relatively limited in their capacity to modify. Therefore, when the modifying concept is somewhat complex, there are few adverbs singularly that can express the requisite modification. Consequently, most complex modification of processes and relations is not simply achieved through adverbs but must rely upon adverbial phrases and clauses. Very often adverbs are inserted into a discourse for purposes of emphasis and are, therefore, not just parts of the informational component of the discourse but also the interpersonal.

RULES FOR REALIZING DENOTERS INTO ADVERBS

1. PB ⟶ (DENC P) ⟶ (MOD P)
2. RB ⟶ (DENC R) ⟶ (MOD R)
3. PB ⟶ (DENM P) ⟶ (MOD P)
4. RB ⟶ (DENM P) ⟶ (MOD R)
5. PB ⟶ (DENT P) ⟶ (MOD P)
6. RB ⟶ (DENT R) ⟶ (MOD R)

5.47. *The realization of clauses*

Within this model the main clause is the primary unit of discourse; everything else either modifies or extends its meaning. At the level of conceptual representation, all the complementary roles of subordinate clauses and modifiers are collapsed into the different bundles as specified by the main process or relation concept. For example, the conceptual structure, (EBA PB EBG EBR), describes a main clause structure that can have any number of subordinate clauses sprouting out of it, depending upon whether any of the bundles have embedded structures or not. Each of these embedded constituents are derived in terms of their relationship with this main clause structure.

The derivation of the main clause is a straightforward procedure. It begins with the derivation of bundles, which determines the character and complexity of the main clause by specifying the number of elements in the clause and their respective roles. Then these bundles are in turn unwound to see if any of the roles that they play include embedded constructions. If, for example, an EBA bundle has as its derivative an embedded constituent containing an (A1 Rr A2) structure, there is a noun clause in the subject position in the discourse. Similarly, if there is an entity bundle which contains an embedded denoter of the form (A1 Rr A2), there is a modifying clause that finds realization as a relative clause. Adverbial clauses are derived from relation and process bundles and express time and condition. They are derived from DENCs and DENTs that have embedded constituents of the form (A1 Rr A2).

When subordinate clauses are shifted up from their embedded position, this event is recorded syntactically through the insertion of various types of linking words. In the case of the subordinate clause modifying a noun, a relative pronoun is inserted which agrees with the semantic properties of the modified noun. When the subordinate clause is in a primary entity position, either EBA or EBI, this fact is very often recorded by the presence of an initial "that" or "the fact that" construction. Similarly, adverbial clauses mark the nature of their modification through an initial binder. If the top-level denoter is a DENC, the binding word can be "while," "if," "since," "though," "although," and "as"; DENT subordinate modification is often prefaced by the binders "before," "after," and "when." Selection of the proper binder depends upon the type of denoter construction in which the subordinate clause is embedded.

Embedded clauses also occur in entity positions other than those occupying the initial argument position. One of the most common is that of the causal entity bundle (EBC) which, when it has an embedded (A1 Rr A2) constituent, is realized with an "as" or a "because" as a binder, for example, "He left because he had to go home" (compare with "He left in order to go home," which has the same causal entity case but a different meaning).

The binding of two or more main clauses together to form compound sentences is a decision determined by factors that are not inherent to the organization of the clause but rather by the speaker's concern with the impact of his speech. As we pointed out in Section 5.20, decisions on the binding of clauses are generally resolved at a higher conceptual level and are therefore made prior to the realization of the clause.

Below are some examples of the realization of different types of clauses, where "shift" is an operator altering the order of concepts.

A. ADJECTIVAL CLAUSES

1. the book *which you gave me*

(a) EB(X) ⟶ (DEN DEN′ E) ⟶ (EMB DEN E)
(b) EMB ⟶ (A1′ Rr′ A2′) ⟶ (EBA′ PB′ EBG′ EBR′)
(c) EBA′ ⟶ (E′) ⟶ (you)
(d) PB′ ⟶ (P′) ⟶ (gave)
(e) EBG′ ⟶ (E′) ⟶ (book)
(f) EBR ⟶ (E) ⟶ (me)
Shift [MOD E′ P′ E′ E′ E] ⟶ [MOD E REL E P E]

the you gave book to me book... ⟶ the book which you gave to me...

2. the lid *you covered it with*
(a) EB(X) ⟶ (DEN DEN E) ⟶ (MOD EMB E)
(b) EMB ⟶ (A1′ Rr′ A2′) ⟶ (EBA′ PB′ EBG′ EBIN′)
(c) EBA′ ⟶ (IE′) ⟶ ... (you)
(d) PB′ ⟶ (P′) ⟶ ... (covered)
(e) EBG′ ⟶ (E) ⟶ ... (it)
(f) EBIN′ ⟶ (E) ⟶ ... (with lid)
Shift ⟶ [(MOD (E′ P′ E′ E′)E)] ⟶ (MOD E E P E + with)
the you covered it with lid ⟶ the lid you covered it with, or
(MOD E with which E P E), the lid with which you covered it.

3. *the day that time stopped ...*
(a) EB(X) ⟶ (DEN DEN E) ⟶ (MOD EMB E)
(b) EMB ⟶ (A1 Rr A2) ⟶ (EBA′ PB′ EBL′)
(c) EBA′ ⟶ (E) ⟶ ... (time)
(d) PB′ ⟶ (P) ⟶ ... (stopped)
(e) EBL′ ⟶ (E) ⟶ ... (on day)
Shift [(MOD (E_2 P E_1) (E_1))] ⟶ (MOD E_1 that E_2 P), the day that time stopped
(MOD E_1 E_2 P), the day time stopped

4. *the place you hid the money ...*
(a) EB(X) ⟶ (DEN DENL E_1) ⟶ (MOD EMB E_1)
(b) EMB ⟶ (A1 Rr A2) ⟶ (EBA′ PB′ EBG′ EBL′)
(c) EBA′ ⟶ (E_2′) ⟶ ... (you)
(d) PB′ ⟶ (P′) ⟶ ... (hid)
(e) EBG′ ⟶ (DEN′ E′) ⟶ (MOD E_3′) ⟶ ... (the money)
Shift [(MOD (E_2′) P′ (MOD′ E_3′) (E_1′) E)] ⟶ (MOD E_1 E_2 P MOD E_3) or (MOD E_1 < where > E_2 P MOD E_3)

B. ADVERBIAL CLAUSES

1. *Since he was no fool, he knew ...*
(a) PB ⟶ (DENC P) ⟶ (EMB P)
(b) EMB ⟶ (A1′ Rr′ A2′) ⟶ (EBA′ RB′ EBG′)
(c) EBA′ ⟶ (E′) ⟶ ... (he)
(d) RB′ ⟶ (R′) ⟶ ... (was)
(e) EBG′ ⟶ (DEN′ E′) ⟶ (MOD′ E′)
(f) P ⟶ (knew)
Shift [((E′ R′ MOD′ E) P)] ⟶ (< since > E′ R′ MOD′ E P)
since he was no fool he knew

2. *When they discovered the problem, (they) ran ...*
(a) PB ⟶ (DENT P) ⟶ (EMB P)

(b) EMB ⟶ (A1 Rr A2) ⟶ (EBA′ PB′ EBG′)
(c) EBA′ ⟶ (E) ⟶ . . . (they)
(d) PB′ ⟶ (P) ⟶ . . . (discovered)
(e) EBG′ ⟶ (DEN E) ⟶ (MOD E) ⟶ . . . (the problem)
(f) P ⟶ (ran)
Shift [(E′ P′ MOD′ E′ P)] ⟶ (When + E′ + P′ + MOD′ + E′ P)
When they discovered the problem (they) ran

3. *While I was waiting for a friend,* a policeman *stopped* me.
(a) PB ⟶ (DENC₂ P) ⟶ (EMB P)
(b) EMB ⟶ (A2 Rr A2) ⟶ (EBA′ PB′ EBR′)
(c) EBA′ ⟶ (E′) ⟶ . . . (I)
(d) PB′ ⟶ (P′) ⟶ . . . (was waiting for)
(e) EBR′ ⟶ (DEN′ E′) ⟶ (MOD′ E′) ⟶ . . . (a friend)
(f) P ⟶ (stopped)
Shift [((E′ P′ MOD′ E) P)] ⟶ (While + E P MOD E P)
While I was waiting for a friend a policeman stopped me

4. *Before I go home I should stop . . .*
(a) PB ⟶ (DENT P) ⟶ (EMB P)
(b) EMB ⟶ (A1′ Rr′ A2′) ⟶ (EBA′ PB′ EBL′)
(c) EBA′ ⟶ (E′) ⟶ . . . (I)
(d) PB′ ⟶ (P′) ⟶ . . . (go)
(e) EBL′ ⟶ (E′) ⟶ . . . (home)
(f) P ⟶ (should stop)
Shift [((E′ P′ E′) P)] ⟶ (Before + E P E P)
I go home should stop ⟶ before I go home I should stop

5. He *knew* the way, *as he had been there before.*
(a) PB ⟶ (DENC P) ⟶ (EMB P)
(b) EMB ⟶ (A1′ Rr′ A2′) ⟶ (EBA′ PB′ EBL′)
(c) EBA′ ⟶ (E′) ⟶ . . . (he)
(d) PB′ ⟶ (DENT′ P′) ⟶ (MOD′ P) ⟶ . . . (before had been)
(e) EBL′ ⟶ (E′) ⟶ . . . (there)
(f) P ⟶ (knew)
Shift [((E′ MOD P′ E′) P)] ⟶ ((as E′ MOD′ P′ E) P)
he before had been there knew—as he before had been there knew

C. NOUN CLAUSES AND ENTITY ROLE-DEPENDENT CLAUSES

1. *That she is queen of the May* makes no difference.
(a) EBA ⟶ EMB ⟶ (A1′ Rr′ A2′) ⟶ (EBA′ RB′ EBR′)
(b) EBA′ ⟶ (E′) ⟶ . . . (she)
(c) RB′ ⟶ (R′) ⟶ . . . (is)

(d) EBR′⟶ (E′)⟶ . . . (queen of the May)
Shift [((E′ R′ E′))]⟶ (that + E′ R′ E′) or (the fact that + E′ R′ E′)
2. *He left because he had to go to the airport.*
(a) EBC⟶ EMB⟶ (A1′ Rr′ A2′)⟶ (EBA′ PB′ EBL′)
(b) EBA′⟶ (E′)⟶ . . . (he)
(c) PB′⟶ (P′)⟶ . . . (had to go to)
(d) EBL′⟶ (DEN′ E′)⟶ (MOD′ E′)⟶ . . . (the airport)
Shift [((E′ P′ MOD′ E′))]⟶ (because + E′ P′ MOD E)
⟶ (as + E′ P′ MOD E)
3. He likes *to go where his friends live.*
(a) EBG⟶ (PB)⟶ (DENL P)⟶ (EMB P)
(b) EMB⟶ (DEN′ E′ P′)⟶ (MOD′ E′ P′)⟶ (his friends live)
Shift [((MOD′ E′ P′)P)]⟶ (where + MOD′ E′ P′)
to go where his friends live
4. *When he graduates makes* no difference to him.
(a) EBA⟶ (DENT)⟶ (EMB)⟶ (A1 Rr)⟶ (EBA′ PB′)
(b) EBA′⟶ (E′)⟶ . . . (he)
(c) PB′⟶ (P′)⟶ (graduates)
Shift [((E′ P′))]⟶(when + E′ P′)
he graduates, when he graduates
5. *Due to the fact that he was broke* he had . . .
(a) EBC⟶ (EMB)⟶ (A1′ Rr′ A2′)⟶ (EBA′ R′ DEN′)
(b) EBA′⟶ (E′)⟶ . . . (he)
(c) RB′⟶ (R′)⟶ . . . (was)
(d) DEN′⟶ (MOD′)⟶ . . . (broke)
Shift [((E′ R′ MOD′))]⟶ (due to the fact that E′ R′ MOD′)
he was broke due to the fact that he was broke

Summary of rules used in examples (where > means "precedes")

A. ADJECTIVAL OR NOUN MODIFYING CLAUSES

1. EB(X) > DEN > EMB⟶ relative pronoun + clause
2. EB(X) > DEN > EMB > EBIN′⟶ preposition + relative pronoun + clause or relative pronoun + clause + preposition
3. EB(X) DEN > EMB > EBL′⟶ choice between linker "that," locative preposition + relative pronoun, or nothing + clauses
4. EB(X) > DENL > EMB > EBL′⟶ choice between insertion of "that," "where," or nothing + clause

B. ADVERBIAL CLAUSES

1. PB > DENC_1 > EMB ⟶ since + clause
2. PB > DENT_1 > EMB ⟶ when + clause
3. PB > DENC_2 > EMB ⟶ while + clause
4. PB > DENT_2 > EMB ⟶ before + clause
5. PB > DENC_3 > EMB ⟶ as + clause

C. NOUN CLAUSES AND ENTITY ROLE-DEPENDENT CLAUSES

1. EBA > EMB ⟶ that or the fact that + clause
2. EBC > EMB ⟶ as or because + clause
3. EBG > PB/RB > DENL > EMB ⟶ where + clause
4. EBA > DENT > EMB ⟶ when + clause
5. EBC > EMB ⟶ "due to the fact that" + clause

5.50. THE THEMATIC ORGANIZATION WITHIN THE EPISTEME AND THE ORDERING OF WORDS FOR SPEECH

Even after all the constituents of an episteme have been derived and the appropriate words inserted, it is still not ready for expression. For, the episteme and its constituents are ordered in a manner that does not necessarily reflect thematic and word sequencing requirements. Different placements entail different listener interpretations and consequently different meanings. In our computer model decisions for thematic organization are made on the basis of the speaker's intentions and his model of its listener. Different items of the episteme are marked for specific thematic impacts. Sometimes these thematic requirements can be met given the constraints of grammar; in other cases, they cannot. In the latter instance, additional planning, or abandonment of the requirement altogether, is entailed.

Thematic organization is achieved through the operations of a focus operator which can operate on single words or on complex constituents, such as subordinate clauses. It, in effect, follows a number of organization rules that transform the nonthematically structured episteme into a thematically ordered sentence. There are three types of focus that the focus operator can effect: positive, giving the greatest possible prominence; negative, obscuring, and in some cases deleting, an item; and incidental, giving an item incidental or nonessential focus. After the focus operator has reordered the items of an episteme, there are still additional orderings that have to take place to make the sentence grammatical. These orderings are obligatory and naturally override any of the decisions made by the focus operator.

In the remainder of this section we will take 10 example sentences and show how they are realized into grammatical sentences. Our presentation will concentrate on demonstrating the different thematic options achieved by the focus operator and the manner by which sentential ordering is achieved. It is at this point that we introduce a discussion of mood, as it is instrumental in determining the ordering of words within the clause. Naturally, these examples are not exhaustive but intended only to be illustrative of the general procedures used by the program model.

The following are the notational conventions that we are emphasizing. These are derived from the conceptual markers that have been discussed previously.

Adj	= adjective
Adv	= adverb
Nsing/pl	= noun singular or plural
PNsing/pl	= pronoun singular or plural
V	= verb
Pres, Past, Future, Pres Past, Past Pres, Future Pres, etc.	= all verb suffixes denoting all possible tenses
ACT/PAS	= voice suffixes to the verb, active or passive
Prep	= preposition
IDet, DDet	= indefinite, definite determiner
Part	= participle
Ger	= gerund
< >	= constituent brackets
MODL	= modals
⟶	= means rewritten as
Rel	= relative pronoun
BIN	= binder
CONJ	= conjunction
+	= positive focus
−	= negative focus
0	= incidental focus
FOC	= focus operator

Below are some rules for the derivation of grammatical categories from conceptual features. The > symbol means that the features following it was derived from the features preceding it. The sequence of these > symbols in the rule express the necessary and sufficient condition for the derivation of the grammatical category when the conceptual category is terminal.

PRELIMINARY RULES

EB(X) > MOD ⟶ ADJ
EB(X) > MOD E ⟶ a possessive, either noun or pronoun, or N + of + N
PB/RB > (MOD) ⟶ ADV
(AI Rr) > PB P ⟶ intransitive process verb
(AI Rr) > RB R ⟶ intransitive attributive verb

EB(X) > E ⟶ noun
EB(X) > DEN MOD + P ⟶ participle
EB(X) > (E E) ⟶ noun + and + noun
EBIN > (E) ⟶ instrumental preposition ± determiner ± noun
EBL > (E) ⟶ locative preposition ± determiner ± noun

EXAMPLE SENTENCES

The following example shows how the focus operator can alter the position of an adjective in order to give it prominence.

1. She wore a long black veil.
DCL(AI RT A2) ⟶ (EBA PB EBG)
.
.
.
FOC (E P MOD MOD MOD veil)
< concept features matched for grammatical features >
(Pnsing Vpast IDET ADJ ADJ Nsing)
—lexical insertion and word ordering—
(She wore a long black veil)

If the focus operator marked the third modifier positive, the realization would be
(She wore a black long veil)

The next example shows how the passive voice can be used to achieve focus on the goal of a process verb.

2. The gazebo was built by Christopher Wren.
DCL (A1 RT A) ⟶ (EBA PB EBG)
FOC (EP (MOD E))
− ((MOD E) P E)
< − concept features matched for grammatical features. >
(DDET Nsing Vpast pass prep Nsing)
—lexical insertion—
(the gazebo was built by Christopher Wren)

Focal prominence of the EBG constituent is achieved by shifting that constituent in front of the main verb and filling its slot with that of the EBA constituent and an agentive preposition.

This next sentence shows how the predicative "there is," a thematic device, is inserted to achieve focal effect.

3. There is more than one way to skin a cat.
(a) (DCL (A1 RT A2)) ⟶ (EMB RB EBR)
(b) EMB ⟶ (PB′ EBG′) ⟶ (P DEN E) ⟶ (P MOD E)

(c) RB ⟶ (R)
(d) EBR ⟶ (MODC E) ⟶ ((MOD MOD) E)
(P MOD E R ((MODC MOD) E)
< to skin a cat has more than one way >
FOC ((P MOD E) R ((MODC MOD) E))
((R(MODC MOD) E) (P MOD E))
< Conceptual feature and syntactic feature match >
(Vpred + Adj + prep + adj Nsing Vinf DDET Nsing)
—lexical insertion—
(There is more than one way to skin a cat.)

The effect of the predicative on the meaning of a sentence is quite subtle, as it entails not only a shift in emphasis but also in the meaning of the initial relation. When a speaker uses this device, he is not only altering the focus of the sentence but is making a comment on the relation implied in it. Notice that by moving the EBA constituent behind the relation, the R assumes a different syntactic realization, "is" versus "has." Thus, the statement becomes a statement about a statement, that is, a comment rather than just a statement. Compare "many people are here" with "there are many people here" and the same holds true, although the verb realizations are identical.

The next sentence illustrates how a special adverbial modifier can be shifted for emphasis and how compound constructions are handled.

4a. Since Spiro, zcro, Ncro, things have not been the same.
(a) DCL(A I Rr A2) ⟶ (EBA RB EBR)
(b) EBA ⟶ (E)
(c) RB ⟶ (EBM DEN R) ⟶ (EMB MOD R)
(d) EMB ⟶ (DENC′) ⟶ (E′ E′ E′)
(e) EBR ⟶ (MOD E)
((E) (($E_1E_2E_3$) MOD R) MOD E)
< things Nero, Spiro, zero, not have been the same. >
foc ((E) (($E_1E_2E_3$) MOD R)) MOD E)
+ 0
(($E_2E_3E_1$) E MOD R MOD E)
(E_2E_3E MOD R MOD E)
—match conceptual and grammatical features—
(BIN + Nsing + Nsing + Nsingt and + Npl + Neg Vpast DDet + Adj)
—lexical insertion—
Since Spiro, zero, and Nero, things have not been the same.
Through an alternation of focus the following sentence can be generated:

4b. Things have not been the same since zero, Nero, and Spiro.
foc ((E_+) (($\underline{E}_1E_2E_3$) MOD′ R) MOD E)
+ 0
((E) MOD R MOD E ($E_3E_1E_2$))

Notice that when "things" and Spiro are positively focused on, Spiro comes at the end of the noun list rather than at the front.

The next example shows how a concept can be realized as a noun or as an adjective, depending on the emphasis given by the focus operator.

5. A man of peace, he seldom became angry.
   (a) DCL (A1 Rr A2)——→ (EBA RB DEN)
   (b) EBA——→ (DEN E)——→ (MOD E)
   (c) RB——→ (DENC R)——→ (MOD R)
   (d) DEN——→ (MOD)
   ((MOD E) (MOD R) (DEN))
   (Peace he seldom became angry*)

Notice that at this point the concept for peace is in a modifier-adjectival position and could be realized as "Peaceful, he seldom became angry." But as this is not the desired sentence, and a lexical change and reconstruction is required.

foc ((MOD E_{+}) (MOD R) (DEN))
—seeing that there are no acceptable matches, the following solution is generated—
EBA——→ (DEN E)——→ (EMB E)——→ ((DEN E E) E)——→ ((MOD E E) E)
(((MOD E E)E) MOD R DEN)
< conceptual and syntactic features now match. >
IDET + Nsing + prep + Nsing + Pron + Adv + Vpast + adj
—lexical insertion—
(a man of peace he seldom became angry.)

It should be noted here that the problem of pronoun insertion is guided by the program's keeping track of what has been said and the likelihood of the listener understanding pronoun substitutions. The same type of consideration guides the use of ellipsis and other deletions.

So far we have only dealt with sentences in the declarative mood. In this example we will show how an imperative utterance with a conditional clause is realized.

6.1. When the clock strikes twelve, beware of the stranger.
   (a) IMP (A1 Rr A2)——→ (EBA PB EBG)
   (b) EBA——→ (E)
   (c) PB——→ (DENC P)——→ (EMB P)
   (d) EMB——→ (A1′ Rr′ A2′)——→ (EBA′ PB′ EBG′)
   (e) EBA′——→ (DEN′ E′)——→ (MOD′ E′)
   (f) PB′——→ (P′)
   (g) EBG′——→ (E′)
   (h) EBG——→ (DEN E)——→ (MOD E)
   IMP FOC (($E_{=}$) ($_{+}$MOD′ E′ P′ E′) P MOD E)
   (BIN MOD + E + E + P MOD E)$^{+}$

(BIN + DDET + Nsing + Vpres + Nsing Vimp + prep + DDET + Nsing)
< —lexical insertion— >
When the clock strikes twelve, beware of the stranger. If the embedded clause were not positively marked, the sentence would read:
Beware of the stranger when the clock strikes twelve.

This and the following examples deal with different types of questions.

7. Which hand has the M and Ms?
(a) INT (A1 Rr A2) ——→ (EBA RB EBR)
(b) EBA ——→ (DEN E) ——→ (MOD E)
(c) RB ——→ (R)
(d) EBR ——→ (DEN E) ——→ (MOD E)
INT FOC (MOD E R MOD E)
+
(Relpro E R MOD E)
< —conceptual and syntactic features matched— >
(Which hand has the M and Ms.)

The next example is a question with an interpersonal modal that focuses on the verb.

8. May I ask you a question?
(a) INT (A1 Rr A2) ——→ (EBA PB EBR EBG)
(b) EBA ——→ (E)
(c) PB ——→ (MODL P)
(d) EBR ——→ (DEN E) ——→ (MOD E)
(e) EBG ——→ (E)
I may ask a question you
INT FOC (E (MODL P) MOD E E)
+ +
(MODL E P E MOD E)
—match conceptual and syntactic features—
(Modal Pron Vpres Pron IDET Nsing)
—lexical insertions—
(May I ask you a question?)

There is a legitimate question as to whether the modal should be in the concept or supplied by the thematic component, as it has both a content and a thematic meaning. Here it was decided to include it with the content of the verb, as it is regarded as part of the initial conceptualization of the sentence.

Questions can also focus on the modifiers of verbs. The following is an example of an adverbial interrogative focus.

9. How long will you be gone?
(a) INT (A1 Rr) ——→ (EBA PB)
(b) EBA ——→ (E)
(c) PB ——→ (DENT P) ——→ (MOD P)

(E MOD P)
< you long will be gone >
INT FOC (E MOD P)
(INBIN + MOD E P)
< —match conceptual and syntactic features— >
(INBIN + Adverb Pron Vfut past)
—lexical insertion—
(how long will you be gone?)

This final example is of an interrogative that focuses on an implicit adverbial modifier.

10. When did you stop beating your wife?
(a) INT (AI Rr A2)———→ (EBA PB EBG)
(b) EBA———→ E)
(c) PB———→ (DENT P)———→ (MOD P)
(d) EBG———→ (EMB)
(e) EMB———→ (P′ DEN E′)———→ (P′ MOD′ E′)
(E (MOD P) (P′ MOD′ E′))
you when did stop beating your wife
FOC (E MOD P P′ MOD′ E′)
< —match concept and syntactic features— >
(BIN AUX Pron Vpres Ger pron + Nsing)
—lexical insertion—
(When did you stop beating your wife?)

Notice in this example that "when" was used as a modifier in the unfocused version and as a binder in the realized version. This switch is syntactic, and since in the unrealized version "when" is still a concept, it has multiple realizations depending upon its syntactic equivalent. Also, notice that the verb "stop" was focused on. This yielded the additional auxiliary verb "did," which in this case is obligatory.

5.60. REALIZATION IN THE PROGRAM

Since the realization component of the program is based upon the "grammar" that we discussed previously, it differs only with respect to the particulars of implimentation. As these particulars provide no substansive changes in our grammar and, when presented in their full number, tend to obscure the critical aspects of the realization process, I will refer to them only when they complement our understanding of the overall realization processes.

All realization is handled through multiple-body interrupt programs which specialize in unwinding and constructing concepts for realization. To understand how realization works in the program, we will focus on the three principal tasks of realization and then provide an example of realization.

These tasks are: giving a concept lexical realization, manipulating and realizing indicators, unraveling conceptual embeddings.

5.61. *The lexical realization of concepts*

Recalling our discussion of concepts in Chapter 4, token concepts are built out of generic concepts containing special indicators specifying how that token concept is to be realized lexically. For example, the token concept

(I TOKEN #I)

has the generic concept with the following features:

< REALIZED-AS (I ERMA)
< GENWORD SPECPRIN
< RELATED CONCEPT (#ERMA)

The REALIZED-AS indicator says that the token concept #I can be lexically realized as either "I" or "Erma," and the GENWORD indicators specify the program, SPECPRIN, which generates the grammatical form of this word. For example, if the "I" concept is used as a denoter, that is, if its SYN-FEAT indicator contains the property POSSESSIVE, then SPECPRIN will transform "I" to "my" or "mine." Similarly, it can perform other transformations according to the "case" of the concept. The RELATED-CONCEPT indicator notes that if another concept is desired, it should be the generic concept #ERMA.

In addition to giving concepts lexical realization, the realization component is also able to work with words. There are four different properties of words, which are relevant to their appropriate use in discourse.

Synonym: This is a list of words that are synonomous with an indicated word. At the lexical level, they function like the RELATED-CONCEPT list for concepts.

Impact: Words may have impacts of their own, either through punning, connotation, or possible inappropriateness. These possible impacts are recorded on this list, and consulted when a word selection is being made.

Denoter-Class: An adjective classification system* was used to help place adjectives in the appropriate order in a sentence. The class of the adjective is contained on this list and is used in the ordering of modifiers.

Particle: Certain words require special particles. This list contains the particles required by these words. A program consults this list to make the appropriate selection.

Process-Class: A verb classification scheme is used based upon the characteristics of transitivity and arguments for lexical realization.

*This classification system was taken from Vendler's adjective classification scheme as described in Hutchins (1971).

Since the GENWORD programs perform most of the work of lexical realizations, we should consider them in some detail. Their principal objective is to transform kernal words into their appropriate form through the addition of suffixes. Remember that concepts have no inherent syntactic properties; rather they may be an argument, a denoter, or a relation. These properties of the concept are noted through property indicators, which in turn are translated into grammatical categories. Hence, it is necessary in this program to modify a word representing a concept according to its syntactic categories. This is done either by adding the appropriate suffix or, when that doesn't suffice, finding the word that has both the appropriate meaning and syntax.

5.62. *An example of program realization*

One of the most complex, if not the most complex, things that this program does is to unwind concepts for lexical realization. The number of concepts, and all the relationships implied by their embeddings, very quickly combine to create a highly intricate structure. However, each of these structures can be typed so that each structure can be processed by a special interrupt program. As demonstrated in Chapter 4, complex concepts can be described in terms of ARDs, and these ARDs have a limited combination of arguments, denoters, and relators. Programs process these different types of structures by first evaluating the arguments and relators of the episteme and then by evaluating their indicators and property lists. When the program acquires sufficient information about a concept to give it lexical realization, it then does so, and proceeds to give the words the appropriate ordering.

In the following example we will highlight the program's realization process by beginning with a simple overview, and then by showing how the first sentence of the discourse episode was realized.

If the top-level concept, what was previously referred to as an episton, were a simple ARD, the general procedure for realizing it would be as follows: First examine the A1 slot of the ARD to find the "subject" and its indicators and properties, for example, < STRUCTURED AGENT. Then examine the remaining arguments and their indicators. Once all the requisite information about these arguments has been accumulated, and no special problems arise, such as the A1 slot being an ARD, examine the R slot of the ARD to determine whether it is a process or relation. The R concept is then examined to see what type of verb it can be realized into and what the special properties of this verb are. To make this determination, the interrupt program accesses information about the class of verb. Similarly, the interrupt program examines the property lists of the relator concept to determine its tense, mood, and voice, as well as the existence of auxillary verbs. Given this information, the program gives concepts lexical realization and constructs a clause or phrase for expression.

Given this brief overview and our previous discussion of discourse grammar, the best way to see how the realization programs work is to follow one in operation. The sentence to be generated is the first in our simulated discourse and has the following concepts in it.

```
(1 TOKEN #I)
   < SYN-STRUCT (UNDEFINITE SINGULAR)
(9 TOKEN #YOU-KNOW)
(10 TOKEN #BILL)
   < SYN-STRUCT (DEFINITE SINGULAR)
(11 TOKEN #PAYMENT)
   < SYN-STRUCT (UNDEFINITE SINGULAR)
(12 TOKEN #THINK)
   < TENSE PAST IMMEDIATE

(13 TOKEN #AGAIN)
(14 CONJOIN (10. #BILL) (11. #PAYMENT))
(15 TOKEN #SOME)
(16 ARD (1. #I) (12. #THINK) (14. #BILL))
  < CHARACTERISTICS ((9. #YOU-KNOW) (13. #AGAIN))
  > MOTIVATION (15. #SOME)
  < STRESS (FOCUS (CHARACTERISTICS (9. #YOU-KNOW)))
(INCIDENTAL (CHARACTERISTICS (13. #AGAIN)))
(FOCUS (MOTIVATION (15. #SOME)))
```

To give these concepts realization into a sentence we generate the concept

```
(17 STATE (16. #THINK) NIL)
```

and place it within the CICERO context. There are two interrupts within this context which fire when this concept is present. The first, TOP-ST-ARD-NI, realizes two argument process verbs in an ARD and the second, ST-ARD-ARD, specializes in embedded ARDs. Since there is nothing for ST-ARD-ARD to do immediately, control is switched to TOP-ST-ARD, which immediately attempts to realize the first argument, which in this case is (1. #I). Since there is no STRUCTURE indicator specifying the case, the program assumes that it is agentive and constructs the STATE concept

```
(18 STATE (1. #I) (16. #THINK))
```

and sends it to the REALIZE context.

When token #I is sent to the REALIZE context, the interrupt ST-TKAI-ARDI is fired and determines that the concept is singular and that it should take no article (UNDEFINITE). It then uses the GET-WORD program to retrieve a list of possible realizations from the semantic lexicon. It finds

```
#I
< REALIZED-AS (I ERMA)
```

selects the first word, "I," and then grows a new REALIZE context to record the fact that lexical realization has been given. Next it sees if this realization should be unacceptable for any reason. In this case, there are no objections (but if there were, the program would go back and try for another word). The program then looks to see if there are any STRESS indicators, and finding none, realizes the concept.

Having produced the first word, control is then transferred back to TOP-ST-ARD-NI and concept 14, (BILL), the second argument, is examined for realization. It also is placed in a STATE format and sent to the REALIZE context. Since concept 14 is a CONJOIN-type concept, it fires the interrupt, ST-CONJ-ANYTHING, which evaluates each of the token concepts and realizes them in very much the same way as token I was realized. However, whereas token I had no article, the token bill does, since it contains the property DEFINITE. Articles are selected through a special program which examines the properties under SYN-STRUCT and then finds the appropriate article. The resulting realization for concept 14 so far is

(20 STATE (10. #BILL) (14. #BILL))
< REALIZED-AS (the bill)
(21 STATE (11. #PAYMENT) (14. #BILL))
< REALIZED-AS (payment)

Since concept 14 is a conjoined concept, concepts 10 and 11 are combined by the ST-CONJ-ANYTHING interrupt to produce

< REALIZED-AS (the bill and payment)

Next, the program realizes the verb in the R slot by using the interrupt, ST-TKAI-ARDI. However, since this program is primarily concerned with working with nouns, some of its operations are inappropriate, such as looking for an article. Before it embarks upon this erroneous course, it is interrupted by another program, ST-TKR-ARDI, which prevents this from taking place and then, itself, completes the realization. Hence, the concept THINK gets realized as

< REALIZED-AS (just thought)

(The "just" was somewhat surreptitiously inserted as a complement to the tense indicator to stress the time of the action of the verb.)

The next task for the program is to give the indicators (CHARACTERISTICS, MOTIVATION, STRESS*) and their property-lists realization and placement within the discourse. The placement of these indicators and their properties within the REALIZE context causes the interrupts ST-TKDEN-ARDI to select the appropriate lexical realizations, and gives these words their appropriate position in the discourse. For example, the concept #YOU-KNOW has the STRESS

*See page 43, for the different types of stress indicators. The stress indicator is similar to the focus operator discussed in the previous section.

marker FOCUS, which means that it should be given prominence in the discourse; hence, it is placed at the beginning, whereas the concept #AGAIN has the marker INCIDENTAL, indicating that this concept should be placed at the end of the sentence.

One of the experimental aspects of the realization process is the use of indicators for lexical realization. An example of this is the realization of the STRESSed concept #SOME, which is under a MOTIVATION indicator. One of the tentative rules developed was to here lexically translate the MOTIVATION indicator as "reason." Hence, the realization of this concept is "for some reason," and since it has a FOCUS stress, it is placed right after "You know" in the discourse. The final form of the output is as follows:

> You know, for some reason, I just thought about the bill and about payment again.

Unlike other language-generating programs, ERMA does not simply generate nice clean sentences. Rather it will very often say one thing, change its mind, qualify itself, and then try to say something else. Therefore, its discourse is marked by false starts, incomplete sentences, and other features common to natural language speakers. In order to simulate these features of natural discourse, the program has two special features. The first is a set of interrupt injections, such as "you know" or "uh," "I mean" (Johnsonian interrupts), which become inserted into the discourse when a bad impact is anticipated or when a problem in realization has been encountered. The second feature is a system of tags which breaks up the potential utterances into easily manipulable units so that they can be interrupted or built upon, depending upon the nature of the discourse.

5.63. *Indicators and their realization*

One of the obvious ways in which the computer realization differs from that of the discourse grammar is in the way that modifiers or denoters are represented and used. Essentially, the idea is the same except that different indicators play the role of denoters, each of which have particular modes of realization. The most common is the CHARACTERISTICS indicator, which can take a simple token concept or a complete ARD. In either case it acts as a modifier, either as a single modifier (adverb or adjective) or as a complex one (a clause or phrase). Such indicators as CHARACTERISTICS—TIME, PLACE, MOTIVATION, and IMPACT—can be operated upon by the thematic indicator, STRESS. This indicator is most important to the general method of realization, as it gives thematic prominence to concepts, and thereby can be used to manipulate the "interpersonal" information of the discourse.

There are five types of STRESS which are most commonly employed within this model. The first, T, is the unmarked case for the arguments and relators and requires no change in their ordering. The second, NIL, is interpreted to mean that the concept so marked should not be given realization. The third stress marker, FOCUS, means that that concept should be given prominent emphasis with the sentence. The fourth type marker, PIVOT, is generally attached to embedded ARDs and results in their being realized as a relative clause. When the fifth type marker, INCIDENTAL, is attached to a concept, it means that that concept should be given a position of lesser prominence within the sentence. The program is equipped with a set of realization rules for each of these types of stress markers and their possible combination with other indicators. It uses these rules to determine how a concept with a stress marker is to be realized. In those cases where there exist no acceptable realizations for a stressed concept, the concept is returned to the context in which it was formed and altered for acceptable expression.

This completes our discussion of the realization component of the program. In Chapter 6, we shall describe how the actual discourse episode of the patient was simulated by the model.

6 : SIMULATION OF DISCOURSE EPISODE

It is as if our languages were confounded; when we want a thought, they bring us a word; when we ask for a word, they give us a dash; and when we expect a dash, there comes a piece of bawdy.—LICHTENBERG

6.10. OVERVIEW

In this chapter is described how the program simulates the discourse episode of a patient. We begin with a scenario of the patient's discourse in which we trace in general terms some of her thinking and try to offer interpretations of why she said what she did. This is followed by a detailed description of the manner in which the program simulates the discourse episode. Beginning with the initiation of the discourse by the SPEAK-UP program, we trace its development through the CALVIN, MACHIAVELLI, CICERO, REALIZATION, and FREUD contexts. In the discussion of each of these contexts, we identify the principal interrupt programs used to derive, inhibit, and realize the discourse. Diagrams of the derived conceptual structures are provided throughout the discussion to show how concepts are related to one another and how they then become realized into passages of discourse. The discussion is broken into two parts, reflecting the differences in the derivation of the discourse. The first part describes the patient's formulation of her request to have the billing arrangements of the therapy altered, and the second part, the introspective phase, describes her attempts, as modeled by the program, to understand her initial request and give expression to this understanding.

In the final section of this chapter we take a detailed look at how key contexts and their programs work to produce the second sentence of the episode. Diagrams are provided of the contexts and their programs, showing how all the concepts are formed and realized into natural language. Also included are printouts of the conceptual structures and linguistic structures produced in the MACHIAVELLI, CICERO, and REALIZATION contexts. The chapter ends with a reproduction of the discourse that the program is currently capable of producing.

6.20. SCENARIO

The discourse episode simulated by the model was selected from a large corpus of transcripts taken from tape-recorded sessions of four years of psychoanalytic treatment. Although only a relatively small episode was used, an episode was chosen that was representative of the patient's discourse and cognitive behavior. The topic and the style of the discourse episode were common throughout the transcripts and represent recurrent features of the patient's discourse behavior. However, since I did not have access to all the transcripts, and had to confine myself to working with selected samples of complete sessions, no claims can be made about the relative importance of this episode, nor can any inferences be made about the substantive nature of the patient's problems. My intention in working with these transcripts was to find a discourse situation in which there was a minimum of verbal and visual interaction and a maximum of complex, but characteristic discourse cognition. As was shown in Chapter 3, the transcripts have carefully recorded virtually every stammer, stutter, hesitation, and pause of the patient so that the recorded discourse behavior is very human and very natural. Incomplete sentences abound, as do other instances of ungrammatical speech. This is as I wanted it, for the model is concerned with natural discourse, and I felt that I needed a sample of a discourse which contained all the "aberrant" and ungrammatical qualities of normal speech. Furthermore, by working with relatively unpolished discourse I hoped to be able to uncover some of the cognitive processes that went into its formation. In other words, I was more interested in the mistakes that the patient made than in her competency.

The patient is a 31-year-old woman who suffers from depression, anxiety, and general feelings of ill worth. Throughout her sessions she painfully talks about her feelings of isolation, dependency, and anger. One topic with which she has particularly difficulty is sex and the expression of her feelings about it. She seems to desire intimacy with others but is distrustful of herself and others. This comes out in her relationship with her therapist (in this episode a woman, but in most previous episodes, a man), whose love and care she desires but fears to trust or even acknowledge. Her relationship with the therapist is further complicated by the fact of her having to pay for the attention that she is receiving. This, she seems to feel, undermines the legitimacy of any support of her and impedes any genuine affective relationship.

The discourse episode opens with the patient mentioning the fact that she "just thought about, uh, about the bill and payment again. . . ." This she does in a highly guarded fashion, as she makes it appear as if the idea just came to her. Moreover, she couches her statement in dubatives and qualifiers (you know, for some reason):

> You know, for some reason, I, uh, just thought about, uh, about the bill and about payment again. . . .

Having prefaced in safe terms what is to be a request, she then makes her request:

> that (pause 2 seconds), that, uh (pause 4 seconds), I was, uh, thinking that I—of asking you whether it wouldn't be all right for you (pause 2 seconds), you know, not to give me a bill.

Notice that where the impacts of the request are apparent to the patient, she either pauses or injects dubitatives such as "you know." This is a major request for the patient, as it threatens the ground rules of therapy and may (in her eyes at least) jeopardize her relationship with the therapist. After making the request, she realizes that the therapist might have some objections to her suggestion. These she then obliquely acknowledges, and then goes on to make her point in more appealing terms.

> Well, I immediately thought of objections to this, but my idea was that I would simply count up the number of hours and give you a check at the end of the month.

However, she immediately sees the pitfalls of her suggestion, for she correctly remembers that she and the therapist have had some disagreements over when she should pay for sessions. This topic of when and how much to pay is recurrent throughout her therapy and was a point of contention between the therapist and the patient. It is a theme common to many therapy situations and one that profoundly affects the course of the treatment.

> Then I realized that there might be some, uh (hesitates), some diagreee-ment (pause 2 seconds) on occasion about whether I was to pay for an hour.

Having acknowledged the possible problems with her request, she then backs off a bit.

> That if, you know, if I should miss it or anyway there might be instances in which, uh (hesitates), I—I shouldn't be, uh—toting up my own bill. (pause 40 seconds)

The effect of this last statement can be taken to be a withdrawal of the request and an acknowledgment of the therapist's authority in this situation. Evidently, what happened at this point is that the patient began with a request to redefine the therapy situation by her controlling payment of her own bills. Yet as she began to make this request and heard herself speaking, she came to realize that the request was most inappropriate, and in her final statement withdraws it, or at least dampens it. She then pauses for 40 seconds to try and figure out what it was she was attempting to say. At this point she enters into what is her introspective phase of discourse behavior, for everything that she says from this point on in the episode is a reflection on what she said before. In this phase she is employing the techniques which she learned in therapy to uncover the cognitive paths that lead to her unusual request.

> I'm just trying to think how that connects with what I was, uh, saying. And I (pause 4 seconds), hum, I s—think it may (hesitates) be that, uh, I mean, on my—original reason for thinking about this was that, uh (pause 3 seconds), I never was, I mean, that every time I've gotten a bill, I've always known how much it would be.

Notice that her attempt to recover her intentions and speak about them is marked by numerous pauses, interruptions, and even a false start. She is struggling both to identify and express a feeling or thought which part of her wants to keep hidden. She attempts to rest her explanation on the fact that she always knew how much her bill would be. It is difficult to know exactly what she means by this statement. A possible interpretation is that in a very guarded way she is expressing dissatisfaction with the formality or the lack of informality of the therapy situation. In other words, she seems to feel that the payment of bills on a regular basis deprives the therapy of an intimate and affective bond. Yet she also realizes that this is only an approximation of her real reason.

> And it seemed a kind of—uh (pause 3 seconds), e—empty little ritual—uh (pause 3 seconds), but I don't know necessarily why I—you know, why I wanted to do away with it.

Notice in this statement that the patient explicitly acknowledges for the first time that she wanted to do away with the payment of bills. This is something she could not explicitly state previously. Having acknowledged this, she seems to feel free to investigate the actual causes for her initial request, but this she still does with constraints.

> Uh (pause 3 seconds), like just, I mean, it may be that somehow I (pause 2 seconds), uh, again, that I should (pause 2 seconds), it can't really be that I should have control over it. But something like that.

This statement gets closer to the truth but attempts to soften the impact of the disclosure by negating its impact. Yet her negation is not really a negation in any logical sense, as it is apparent that she does want to control the therapy. The negation just lets the therapist know that a part of her does not really agree with such a suggestion. Hence, the negation is more of a disavowal than a denial. However, she still has not answered the question of why she would want to control the session. This she attempts to do through the following statement.

> But maybe because of it would—uh (pause 2 seconds), it would reduce some—I—the amount of, uh (pause 2 seconds), I—exchange or, uh (pause 2 seconds), I was going to say interchange, but that's not right. And then I thought of, uh (slight laugh) (hesitates), intercourse between us.

Her censors seem to be particularly active in this passage. She pauses, starts to say something, stops, begins anew. And then she starts to unravel her motivations. Notice that she uses a denial device, "would reduce the amount of exchange," when in fact she really means to increase the amount of interaction. She then realizes that this is not correct and comes up with the nice association between interchange and intercourse. In this very compact passage some very complex cognition has taken place, for in order to understand what the patient is saying, one cannot rely upon a simple interpretation of the manifest content and the sequencing of her speech. Notice that all along the patient has been talking about minimizing interaction or interchange when in fact she wants to eliminate a particular type of interaction, the exchange of bills and payment, in order to permit a more intensive interaction. This she becomes aware of in the final statement of this discourse, and to any reasonably well informed listener her statement would also be intelligible. But it is only so because we are able to infer and model some of the processes that she is using. There is nothing in her explicit statements that would provide this information, but when the final association is made, intercourse, some of the previous behavior becomes understandable.

We cannot say unequivocally that what we described is *really* what is taking place in this episode. This knowledge is neither available to us or to any psychiatrist, for that matter. As there exist no experimental methods for verifying hypotheses about internal cognition of this character, all such hypotheses can only be evaluated in terms of their reasonableness with respect to experience. This problem becomes accentuated when we want to do an in-depth simulation of the patient, as there are relatively few clues about the deeper cognitive procedures which she employs. Since the model does not simply spew out coded sentences, but derives them through a complex process of deduction, there is the added problem of determining those things which she elaborately deduces and those which she simply retrieves and inserts. Obviously, there is a great deal of complex deduction involved in the planning of the discourse episode, as well as in unraveling it. But how complex? In other words, how deeply must she go to create and implement her discourse plan? How are her concepts actually represented? These questions can only be given approximate answers and this is what was done. However, if we were able to determine that what was represented as a relatively simple deduction was indeed complex, there is nothing inherent in the method of representation to prevent us from simulating this more complex process.

Before proceeding into a description of the model's simulation of the discourse episode, let us first describe the deductions that are involved in the creation of the episode. Given this, we can see how these somewhat intuitive notions were implemented in the model.

Based upon an analysis of this episode and a survey of similar discourse episodes, it appears that the patient initially wanted to request intercourse with the therapist. By this is not simply meant sex, although this may be part of it, but a warm, affective, and intimate relationship. This she quickly recognizes is impossible because of the nature of the therapy situation, which is formal and contractually regulated through the payment of bills. The patient then decides that if she were able to change the situation in some way, the thing preventing her intimacy with the therapist might be removed. Hence, she concludes that she must gain some control over the situation and redefine it through altering the conditions under which payment is made. This she attempts to do through her request of not being given a bill. She quickly realizes that her statement was a bit too strong and then attempts to explain it and nullify it. In her formation of her discourse and throughout her expression of it, she is very much aware of the therapist's possible interpretations. Consequently, her selection of topic and discourse devices are regulated by her concern over the impact of the speech upon the therapist. She does not want to alienate the therapist or to jeopardize the therapy, yet at the same time she wants to institute a radical change in the situation. Through her interactions with her perceptions of the therapist's possible responses, she comes to understand her objections and the ultimate impossibility of her request. This recognition then causes her to reflect upon what she said. The content that she generates for this second phase of the episode is wholly derived through an attempt to recover the motivations and causes for her previous discourse. She begins her introspection at that level most accessible to her, which in this case is the manifest content of her previous statements. She attempts to justify her request by calling the therapy ritualistic and empty, but she realizes that this is not a sufficient explanation of her behavior. She then reflects on her wanting control and then determines that by controlling payment, she can effect a change in the conditions of the therapy. Once she has uncovered this line of deduction, she is then able to locate the original motivation for her request. But this does not come easily, and only through two false associations, or rather incomplete associations, is she able to identify the source of her motivation. Once she has done this, a new topic is identified and a new discourse episode begins.

From our discussion, the cognition the patient used in generating this episode may not seem all that complex. But, as we will see in the following section, when all the details are unraveled and each step of the deduction and generation is examined, the process is indeed quite complex.

6.30. THE SIMULATION OF THE DISCOURSE EPISODE

Before describing the cognitive processes whereby the discourse episode is derived, a comment is required on our level of description. Since there are over 40 interrupt programs involved in discourse cognition, we shall not discuss all the programs that are used, only those of more general interest.

The model initiates discourse through the top-level program SPEAK-UP. There are two ways in which this program can generate a topic for discourse: it can take a topic off a possibilities list of topics, or it can generate topics through a search of the data base. Once a topic has been selected, this program then "grows" a new CALVIN context on an old CALVIN context, and a new FREUD context on the old one. Where these new contexts are placed is dependent upon the nature of the topic suggested, so that the model may entertain conflicting opinions about the same topic, depending upon context. The next thing that SPEAK-UP does is to set up a hopper in which to catch suggestions for introspection generated by other programs. These suggestions it sends to the FREUD context, where some other program suggests that introspection is required. Once the contexts and the hopper have been set up, the selected topic is then sent down to the CALVIN context, where it is evaluated for its expression. The following diagram summarizes this initial process. The solid arrows indicate a structure being set up and the dashed lines indicate the transmission of information.

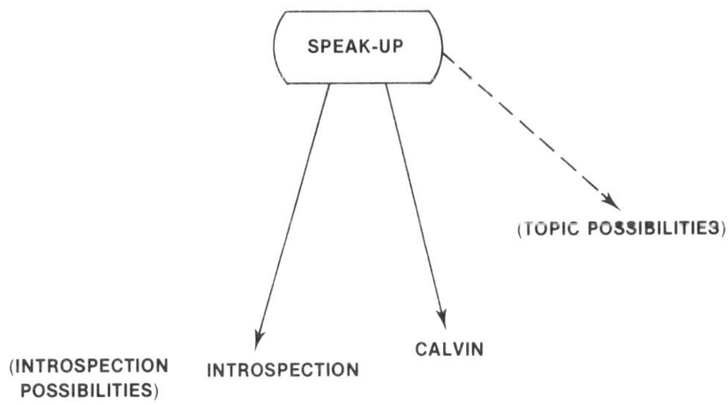

The topics that SPEAK-UP generates are of the form I want *x*, I think *x*:

(#I #WANT something)
(#I #LIKE something)
(#I #THINK something)

In the case of this particular episode, the topic that is picked from the TOPIC-POSSIBILITIES list is

(ARD (#I #WANT (ARD (#I #INTERCOURSE #THERAPIST))))

When this concept, which is actually a number of embedded concepts, is sent to the CALVIN context, an interrupt is fired which specializes in taking want-type concepts and determining whether what is desired is acceptable both to the patient and to the recipient of the desire. If it is determined that the desired object or action is unacceptable, it then makes suggestions as to how the desire might be displaced into a more acceptable form. The interrupt that handles these problems is WANT-EXPAND, and the manner in which it operates is rather complex, as it interacts with a number of other interrupt programs. This is one of the difficulties in understanding the operations of interrupts, as the control of processing is being continually shifted from one program to another and back again. Those who are accustomed to the nice linear progression of more conventional programming techniques will find the discussion unsettling.

To abet this confusion as best we can, we will trace the steps of computation taken by WANT-EXPAND and show how it interacts with other interrupts. Recall that one of the things that WANT-EXPAND does is examine want-type concepts to determine their acceptability. This it does by sending the desire to another CALVIN context. When it does this, another interrupt is fired, INTERCOURSE-CENSOR, which examines the concept to see if it is unacceptable to anyone. The program determines that such a desire is unacceptable to therapist and then attaches an unacceptable indicator to the concept. When this indicator is included, another interrupt program fires, which tries to determine why the desire is unacceptable. This it does by examining the indicator PREVENTED-BY to see what those things are that make it unacceptable. The interrupt program that does this is the UNACCEPTABLE-EXPLAINER, and it returns suggestions as to the reasons why the desire is unacceptable. One of the reasons that it is unacceptable to request intercourse with the therapist is that the situation is a formal or contractual one, and hence such intimate requests are out of limits. This the UNACCEPTABLE-EXPLAINER determines by using a special type of program called THERAPY-PREVENTS. In effect, what this program does is deduce that the reason the request is prevented from being expressed is that the therapy session is a member of a formal situation. In other words, the UNACCEPTABLE-EXPLAINER program "asks" the THERAPY-PREVENTS program what it is that is preventing the concept (I Intercourse Therapist) from being expressed, and the UNACCEPTABLE-EXPLAINER replies that it is because the therapy is formal.

So far, what deduction has the program accomplished? It has initiated a want-type concept, determined that it is unacceptable, and found out what made it unacceptable. Since the patient is concerned with getting around these constraints and expressing her desire, the next step is to figure out what it is that makes the situation formal and how that situation can be altered. The "logic" runs something like this: if the request for intercourse is prevented by the situation being formal and the reason that the situation is formal is because it is contractual and involves the exchange of bills and payment, there is a correlation between the payment of bills and the situation being formal and the patient not being able to make her request. Hence, if she were able to control payment over the bills, she would be able to control the therapy situation, and therefore be able to make her request.

The deduction above is initiated by having the interrupt PREVENTED-TRANSITIVE fired when the pattern (A PREVENTED-BY B) is present. What this interrupt does is inform any interested program, in this case, INTERCOURSE-CENSOR, of the causes and correlations for any concept being prevented by another concept. The causes for the therapy situation being formal is deduced by the special interrupt program FORMSIT-CAUSE-EXCHANGE. This program gives as a reason for the formality of the situation the fact that payment is exchanged to the therapist in receipt of a bill. The fact that this is so is deduced by the interrupt FORMSIT-CORREL-CONTROL, which suggests that there is a correlation between the fact that the situation is formal and the fact that she does not control it. These inferences are picked up by the INTERCOURSE-CENSOR program, and the following structure is set up in the CALVIN context, where the labels on the arrows are indicators and their designations are properties.

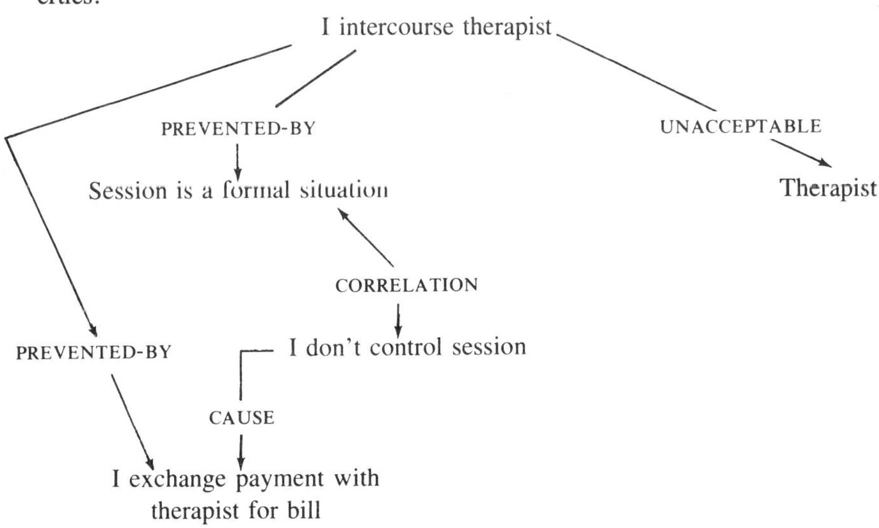

Control is now returned to WANT-EXPAND, which then sees if those things that are preventing the expression of the desire are valid. If it finds out that indeed they are, it sets about finding ways to undo those things which prevent expression of the desire. The first property on the PREVENTED-BY property list is "I exchange payment with therapist for bill." This it attempts to negate by sending the concept into a MACHIAVELLI context, where the appropriate program can work on it.

When this concept is added to the MACHIAVELLI context, the interrupt, EXCHANGE-PRESERVE, is fired. This program first checks to see if the object which is being exchanged, in this case payment, is something that is desired by the recipient. It quickly finds out that such is the case. It then sees what would be the reaction of the therapist if that object were deleted. It does this by sending the concept down into the CICERO context, which has special-purpose programs to determine the impact of excluding some object or action desired by a listener. These programs return suggestions as to the possible impacts of not paying the bill. The EXCHANGE-PRESERVE interrupt then takes these suggestions and attempts to find ways of getting around the bad impacts. This it does by generating the suggestion that the therapist not give her a bill. Notice that rather than flatly stating that she would not give the therapist payment, she suggests that the therapist should not give her a bill. The difference is slight but evidently sufficient to pass through the patient's censors. The program that avoids bad impacts is called the 4A-SHOCK-DISAPATOR, and this it does by producing the first sentence.

> You know, for some reason, I just thought about the bill and about payment again.

Even from our somewhat sketchy description of the programs involved in the derivation of this sentence, it is apparent that the program did not simply generate a precoded sentence. Rather, it thought about complex alternatives and derived the sentence as a possible solution to a multileveled problem of expression. Notice that this first sentence has the effect of laying the groundwork for her request. It is then followed by the statement of the request, which is controlled by the EXCHANGE-PRESERVER program.

> That, that I was thinking that I—of asking you whether it wouldn't be all right for you, you know, not to give me a bill.

However, in the course of generating this sentence, the program realizes (through CALVIN interrupts) that the therapist might have objections to not billing her. In order to combat this objection, a program derives the suggestion that she should mention paying the therapist, as not doing so would threaten the therapy situation. Through these deductions, she constructs the following structure.

Yet the suggestion of paying the therapist is not sufficient, as she feels that she should make it clear to him that she would pay the correct amount at

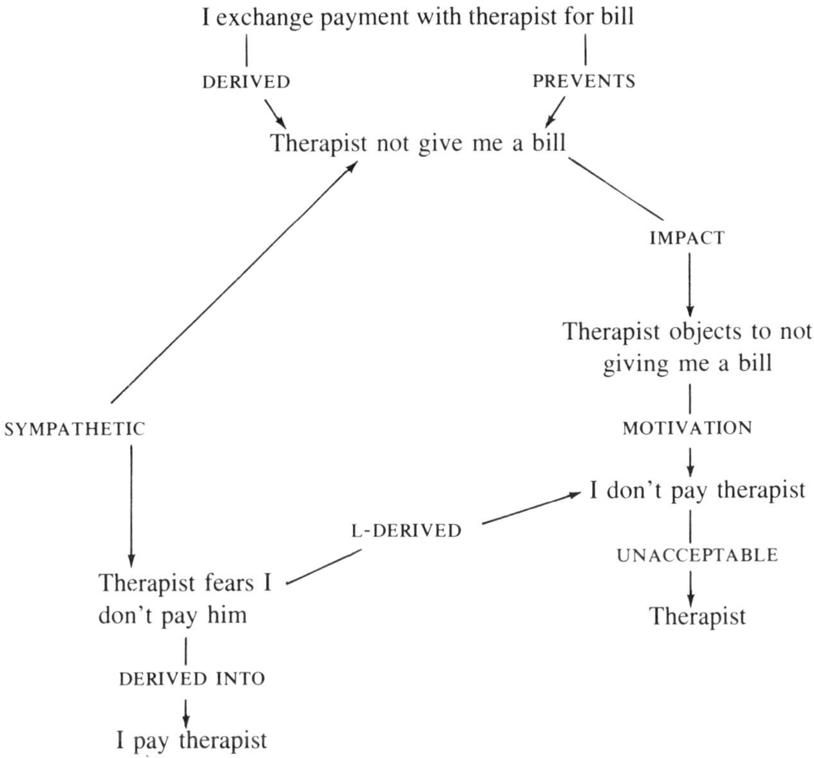

the proper time. She then devises a plan that would make her request more reasonable. This is done through the PAY-CAL interrupt in the MACHIAVELLI context, and the third sentence is generated.

> I would simply count up the number of hours and give you a check at the end of the month.

However, as before, once she states the sentence, she becomes aware of possible problems with the therapist's interpretation of it. Therefore, she tries to provide some reassurances. This thought, however, is not fully expressed and is cut off after "usually."

"I usually [by the end of the month, know the amount of the bill]."

At this point ERMA realizes that mere assurances are not sufficient, as there have been disagreements with the therapist in the past regarding payment for missed sessions. This bit of knowledge is created through interrupt programs and looks something like the following:

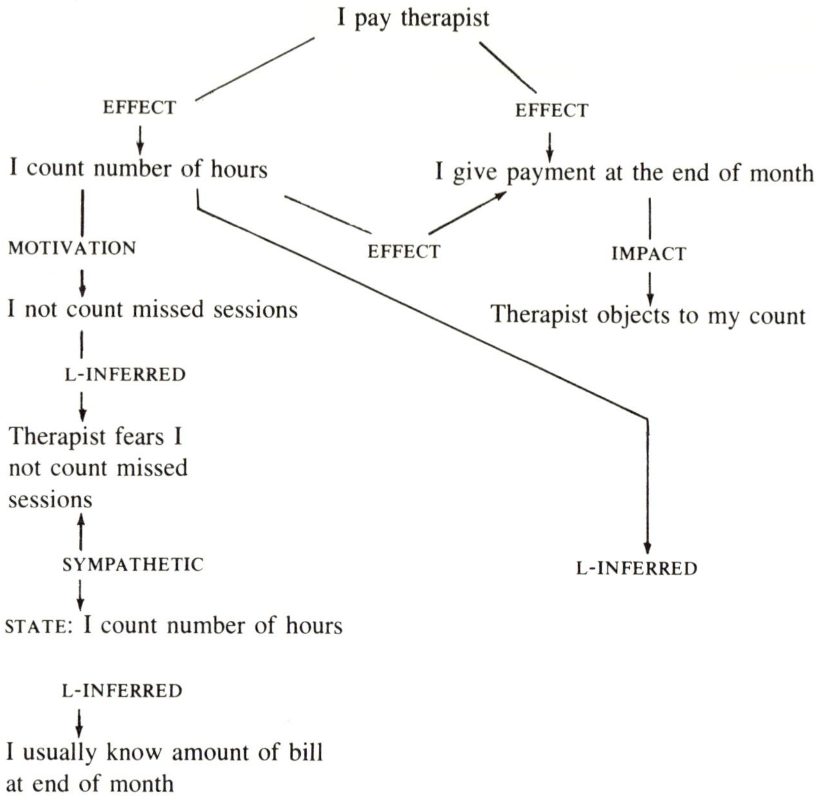

This information is combined and picked up by the WANT-EXPANDER program, which sends it to the MACHIAVELLI context, where the interrupt program GENERAL-REALIZER produces the following:

> That is, I would, since I usually know by—well, I immediately thought of the objections to this, but my idea was that I would simply count up the number of hours and give you a check at the end of the month.

Yet, once again, she realizes that she has not sufficiently dispelled the negative impacts of her request and that she must address herself to the problem of the disagreement between herself and the therapist. She first acknowledges the disagreement through the interrupt, NEGEMP-DOPINION-EFFECTS,

> Then I realized that there might be some disagreement on occasion about whether I was to pay for an hour.

Then through the interrupt, PAY-QUESTION-TIMER, she states the conditions under which the disagreements might arise:

That if, you know, if I should miss it or. . . .

However, even these qualifications do not suffice, and she then attempts to modify her entire request by

Anyway, there might be instances in which I shouldn't be toting up my own bill.

This last comment was generated by the interrupt CONDITION-JUSTIFICATION, and having completed its work control is returned to WANT-EXPAND, where the second phase of the episode begins, that of introspection. The knowledge structure which has been generated so far looks as follows:

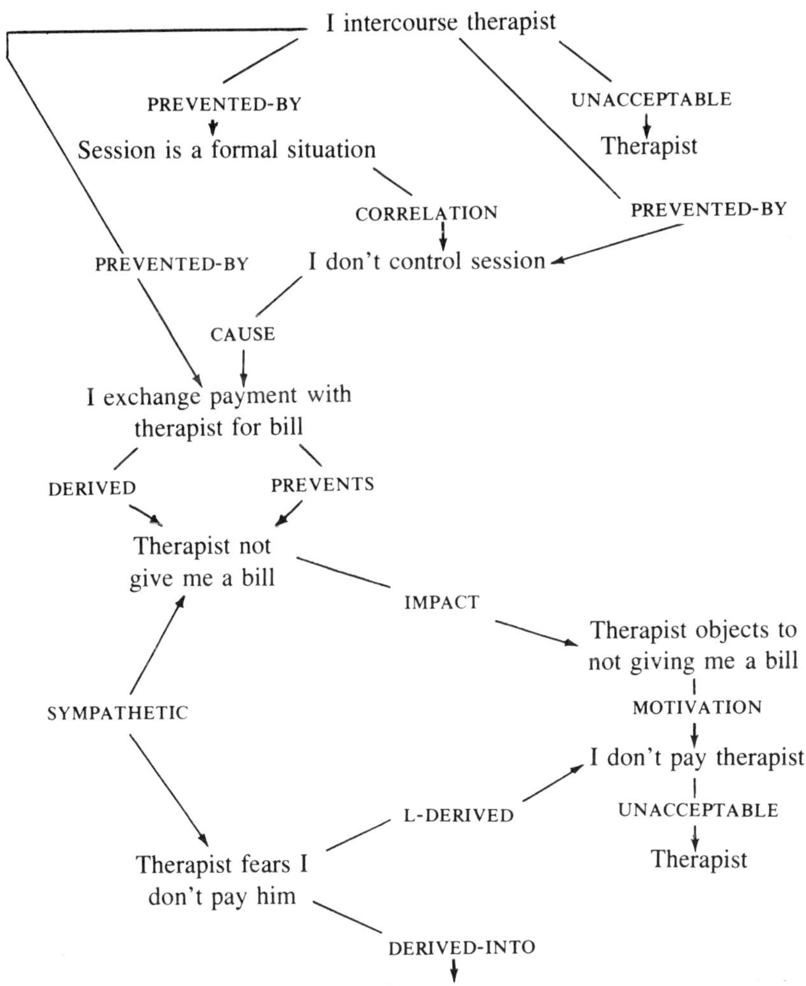

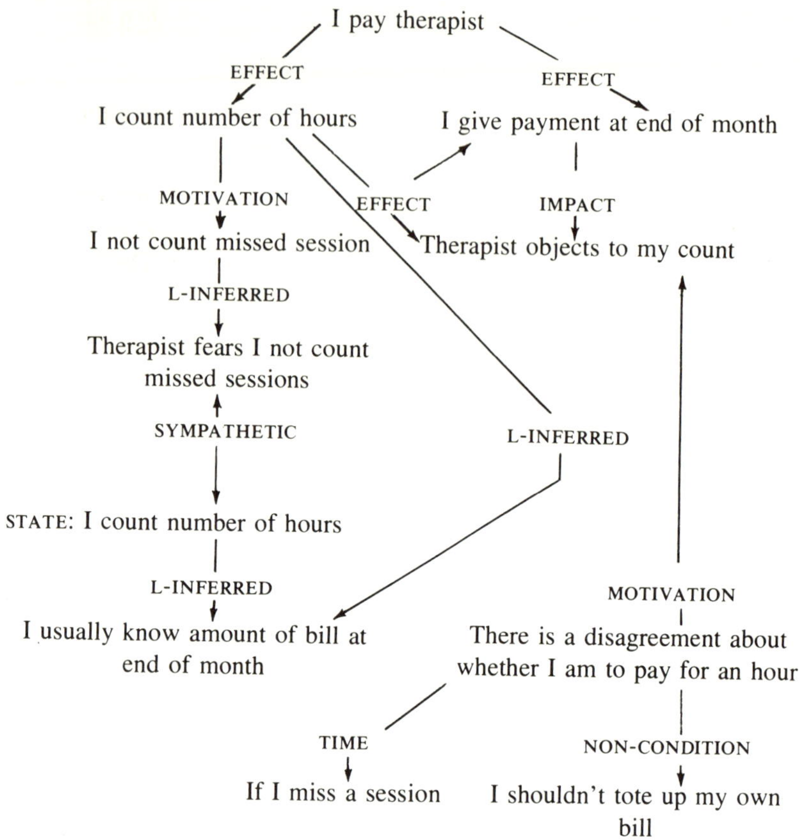

Once this knowledge structure has been generated, the patient enters her introspective phase after a 40-second pause. Like the modeled patient, the program notices that there is something strange about what it has been saying and that this should be investigated. The condition that sets off the introspection is the request for a change in the therapy situation, for in the context of her speaking, this condition has no apparent explanation, and hence the patient's motivation for requesting it is not self-evident. The interrupt that picks this up is the WANT-EXPAND interrupt, and it makes some suggestions as to how the introspection should proceed. These suggestions are based upon an examination and reconstruction of the previous knowledge structure.

In uncovering the paths of cognition that led to the generation of a particular concept, the introspective interrupts work on linkages established through L-INFERRED, L-DERIVED, DERIVED INTO, PREVENTED-BY, and similar operational indicators. In this particular introspective episode, these indicators are used to infer the fact that if an event is prevented by another event or condition, and this second condition is prevented by another condition, there is a conditional linkage between the first event and the last event or condition. Translated into the discourse episode, this means that a patient begins with the recognition that she wanted to alter the terms of payment, and then infers the conditions that prevented this request from being directly stated. Remember that she attempts to understand how what she just said relates to the fact that she is requesting a change in the conditions of the therapy situation. This she does by noticing that her thought about altering the exchange relationships was followed by her request not to be given a bill, which, in turn, led to the recognition that the therapist feared nonpayment, to which she reacted by stating that she would pay by counting up the hours and giving payment at the end of the month. This recognition causes her to initially conclude that the reason for her attempting to alter the therapy situation was related to the fact that the therapist felt she would not pay her bill, despite the fact that she always knew how much it would be. Hence, her initial explanation is a reaction to her assumption that the therapist did not trust her to pay her bills regularly. The following diagram shows how this deduction was arrived at. Notice that the explanation in terms of "I give payment at end of month" is the fifth in a series of derivations and therefore represents the most "distant" explanation.

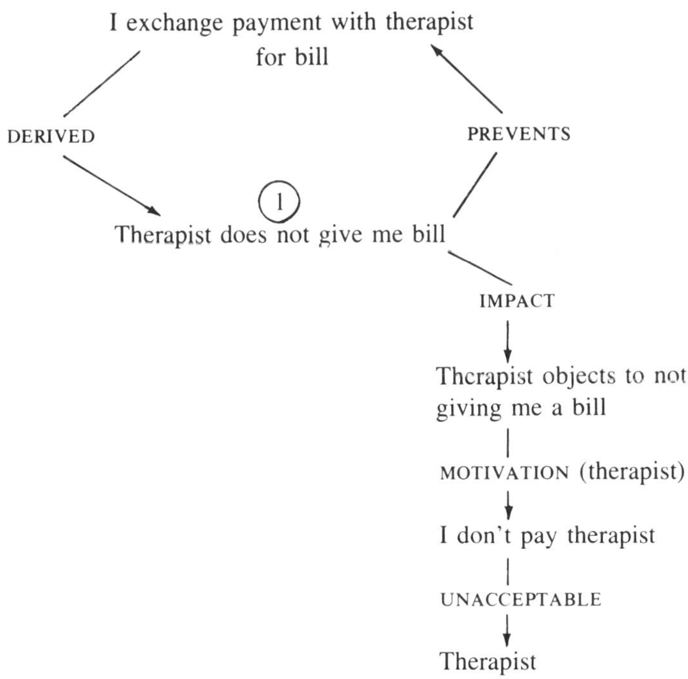

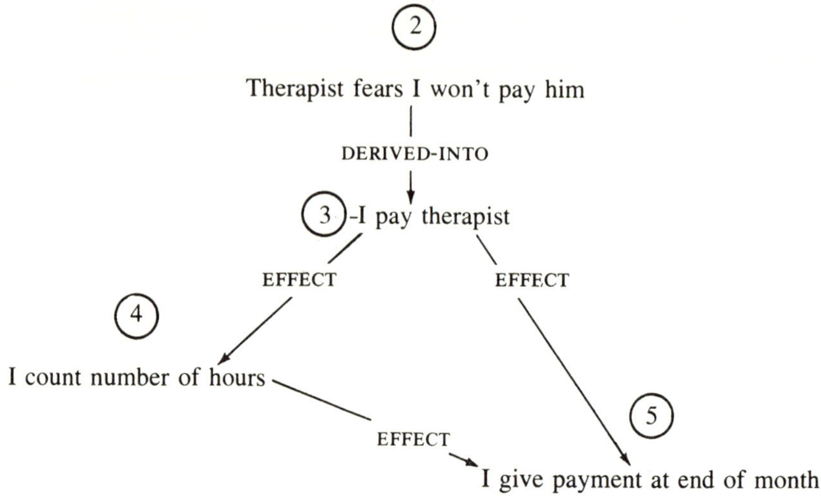

However, before stating this concept, the patient first prefaces her remarks with

> I'm just trying to think how that connects with what I was saying.

She goes on to say,

> And I think it may be that, I mean, on my—original reason for thinking about this was, I never was, I mean, that every time I've gotten a bill, I've always known how much it would be.

Having then expressed the fact that the billing was disagreeable to her, she makes a stronger statement about her dissatisfaction with the therapy situation. She does this by calling it "an empty little ritual." A special interrupt program derives this phrase through a deduction on the following knowledge structure.

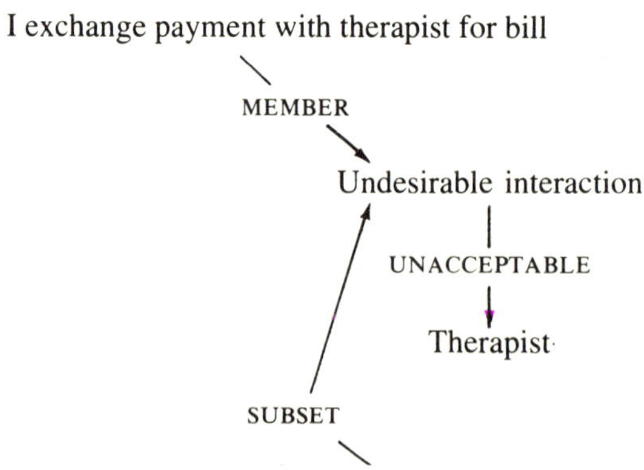

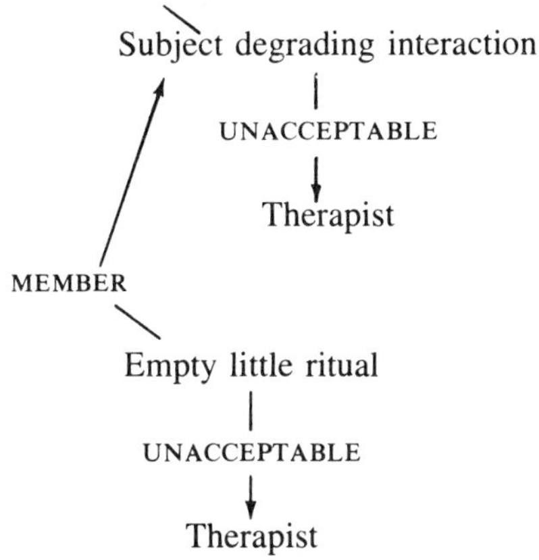

This deduction results in:

Exchange ⟶ a kind of empty little ritual.

and finds expression in the discourse through

> And it seemed a kind of empty little ritual—uh . . .

She pauses for 3 seconds and then recognizes that this is not sufficient reason for her wanting to do away with the situation. This recognition produces the statement

> But I don't know necessarily why I—you know, why I wanted to do away with it.

This last bit of discourse was derived through the deduction of only one main introspective interrupt, which returned it as a suggestion to the WANT-EXPAND interrupt. At the "same time" that this deduction was being performed, there were other deductions performed which returned other suggestions. Significantly, the patient's implicit desire to have "intercourse" with the therapist was linked to the fact that she counted up the number of hours at the end of the month in order to pay her bill. Hence, the "underlying" motivation for her making her request is now known to her in the FREUD context. Yet she does not immediately acknowledge this to be the cause of her request, but rather attempts to uncover the conditions which prevented the request from being realized. There are several candidates: "I don't control session," "Session is formal situation," and the conditions of the exchange relation. Although it is not possible to unequivocally determine why she should choose one alternative over another, it is my assumption that she choose that candidate which was most immediately vexing, which, in this case, is "I don't control session." Remember that her previous statement expressed her irritation over the therapy situation being an "empty little ritual," and this feeling was due to the fact that she felt put on the spot by the therapist regarding her payment of bills. Therefore, the choice of "I don't control the session" is a possible explanation for this irritation. However, when she attempts to say that she should have control over the therapy situation, she negates her comment in order to reduce its bad impacts. This is a common device of the patient.

> Uh, like just, I mean, it may be that somehow I, again, that I should, it can't really be that I should have control over it. But something like that.

Notice the great difficulty she has stating her insight. In terms of the model, this difficulty is due to interrupts firing at the negative impacts of her acknowledging her intended manipulation of the therapy situation. They just won't let the statement come out without negating it.

Having then stated that she wanted to control the session, she attempts to figure out why she would want to do so. She then deduces that the exchange relationship is the cause of her not controlling the session, and this is correlated with the fact of the therapy situation being formal. She starts to express these inferences, but then catches herself,

> But maybe because of it would, it would reduce some—I—the amount of . . .

and begins to identify her top-level desire:

> I—exchange or, I was going to say interchange, but that's not right. And then I thought of intercourse between us.

The confusion of this last statement is most interesting, as the word interchange is halfway between exchange and intercourse, and therefore its selection represents her attempt to state both concepts in a single word. However, upon discovering that interchange was not the correct explanation of her desire, she quickly and easily identifies the top-level motivation for her initiating the discourse, and the episode is terminated. When this occurs, control is transferred back to SPEAK-UP and a new topic of discourse is generated.

6.40. A CLOSER LOOK AT COGNITION AND REALIZATION

In the previous section we gave an overview of the model's production of the knowledge and cognition involved in the generation of the discourse episode. Although technical in some respects, the discussion did not identify in detail the manner in which the programs actually worked, the transfer of control from one program or programs to others, or the critical process of the translation of conceptual structures into the language of discourse. In this section we shall attempt to resolve these deficiencies through diagrams of the processing flow of programs and examples of the information structures generated in the MACHIAVELLI and REALIZATION contexts.

A detailed discussion of this kind is needed to address those questions that naturally arise over the generality of the method, the degree of difference between concepts and words, and the organization of processing within the program. By virtue of the magnitude of their technical detail, computer programs can very easily accomplish a type of explanatory sleight of hand, in that they can be made to appear to know more or describe more than they actually do. Consequently, a healthy skepticism is always in order when evaluating the explanatory claims of any complex simulation model. As regards the ERMA model, the question naturally arises whether its conceptual structures are, in fact, linguistic structures in a clever disguise and whether their realization into discourse is just a simple matter of stripping away the disguise.

Since concepts *do* become realized into discourse, there is a correspondence, but the critical question is at what level the concepts are free of linguistic constraints. To this question there cannot, I believe, be a conclusive answer for the present. Intuitively, I feel that people are able to think at many different levels, some of which are linguistic and some so global or "deep" as to be undescribable at present. These very deep cognitive structures are in all likelihood acquired in imitation of correlate physical actions, and only through developmental processes become realized into more specific cognitive procedures. However, that being said, there are differences in conceptual and linguistic knowledge. Therefore, in this section we shall attempt to show that the information structures called concepts are *relatively* free of linguistic constraints. As the program was only developed for experimental and exploratory purposes, it is not, nor was it intended to be, a complete statement of the theory, and therefore is neither as refined nor as general as it might be. As was said before, the representational method could have been more general and complex in many cases, but owing to programming constraints and an unfamiliarity with certain problems during implementation, the program takes a fairly specialized approach to the problems it solves, both linguistic and conceptual. Although it would certainly be desirable to have a small set of very elegant procedures which handled a wide class of problems very efficiently, such as having one procedure do all foregrounding, I doubt the possibility and even the desirability of such an approach, for native "thinkers" seem to employ diverse and specialized procedures for what would taxonomically, at least, seem as similar tasks. Certainly more general solutions can be found to many of our cognitive and realization procedures, and as these environments are better understood and further charted, no doubt they will be. But as a general rule, I doubt that anything like a competence-type description will be possible except for "global" concepts (those with physical correlates), or perhaps, for highly socialized concepts. I suspect that for the time being successful theories in this area will have to be performative in nature and must account for the formation, proliferation, and recombination of specialized problem-solving procedures and their attendant data structures. Neither the theory nor the model is this advanced, and, as a consequence, I cannot say whether concepts should be more general in this case, and more specific in that. Granted these limitations, it can be said that the conceptual structures presently used in the program certainly are not sentences coded in another form, as the realization process is by no means a trivial enterprise, and the conceptual structures themselves may relatively easily assume a form that is inexpressible in natural discourse. Hence, the concepts in this model are at a level of description which subsumes rather than presumes the conventions of English. Moreover, the indicators used at this level of description, while having a transformed role in the realization programs, primarily function in a cognitive capacity and therefore are independent in their roles to realization-based operations.

6.41. *A detailed look at interrupt operations in cognitive contexts*

While our discussion in Section 6.30 provided a sense of how individual sentences were formed from different types of interrupts, it did not show how the interrupts worked together, nor did it show how processing flowed from one interrupt and one context to another. Here we shall offer a series of diagrams to help give a concrete sense of what each program does. As the diagrams replicate much of the narrative discussion of Section 6.30, we will not introduce yet another extended narrative description into this well-worked example, but will let the diagrams speak for themselves. Before explaining the notational system used in the diagrams, it should be noted that, although the diagrams are reasonably accurate portrayals of how the programs work, they do not capture all the steps and interdependencies that exist. To include these would render the diagrams unintelligible and obfuscate the more significant operations. For each of the cognitive contexts CALVIN and MACHIAVELLI, we shall provide a detailed diagram and a summary description of their operations. We shall then include an example of the knowledge structures in the MACHIAVELLI context.

The conventions to be used in the diagrams are on page 129.

Although the diagrams are relatively simple in comparison with the actual operations of the program, a great deal of confusion can result if they are not read correctly and certain facts are not born in mind. First, control is transferred through the sending of concepts and the inclusion and exclusion of datums, and therefore the programs themselves are not the controlling agents so much as are the *patterns* to which they respond; in other words, the flow of data patterns regulates the processing. Second, the diagram should be read from the top down, bearing in mind that many programs may be "simultaneously" operating, and by their outputs becoming data in a context, are capable of firing other programs. Looking at Diagram 6.41.1 we can see that the discourse episode is initiated by the SPEAK-UP program, sending concept 6 into the CALVIN context, where it is picked up by the WANT-EXPAND program and then sent again into another layer of the CALVIN context. Here it is

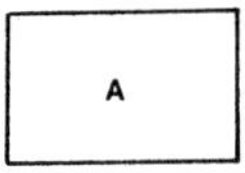

. . . . . a rectangle symbolizes the interrupt program A.

. . . . . a line with many arrow heads indicates that a concept is being sent.

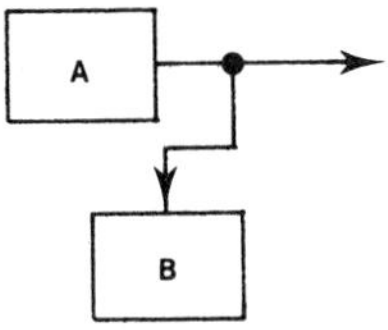

. . . . . this means that the output of program A is intercepted or fired upon by program B, and that control is transferred to program B.

. . . . . all squares symbolize possibilities lists; that is, lists of concepts that can be used by other programs in their solution of a particular problem.

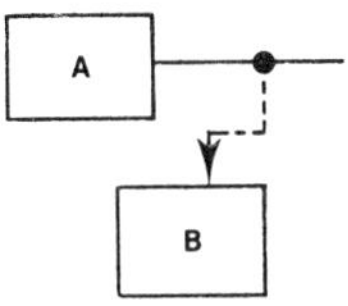

. . . . . a dot with a dotted arrow means that the results of program A's computations are taken and used by program B.

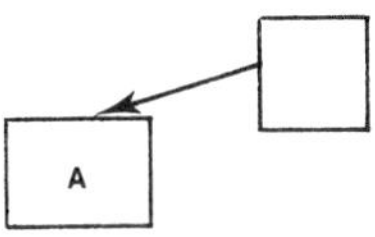

. . . . . this means that the concepts in the possibilities list are used by program A.

+< UNACCEPTABLE (#THERAPIST)

. . . . . a + sign here means that the indicator UNACCEPTABLE has been added by the program along with the property (#THERAPIST)

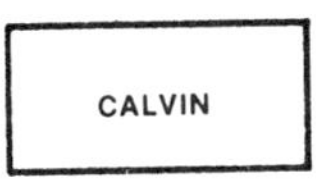

. . . . . all enclosed symbols are within CALVIN context.

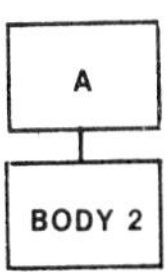

. . . . . BODY 2 is the second body of interrupt program A

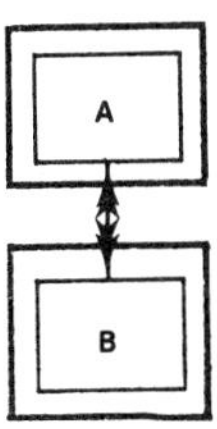

. . . . . the double-headed send arrow means concepts are sent back and forth between A and B in separate contexts.

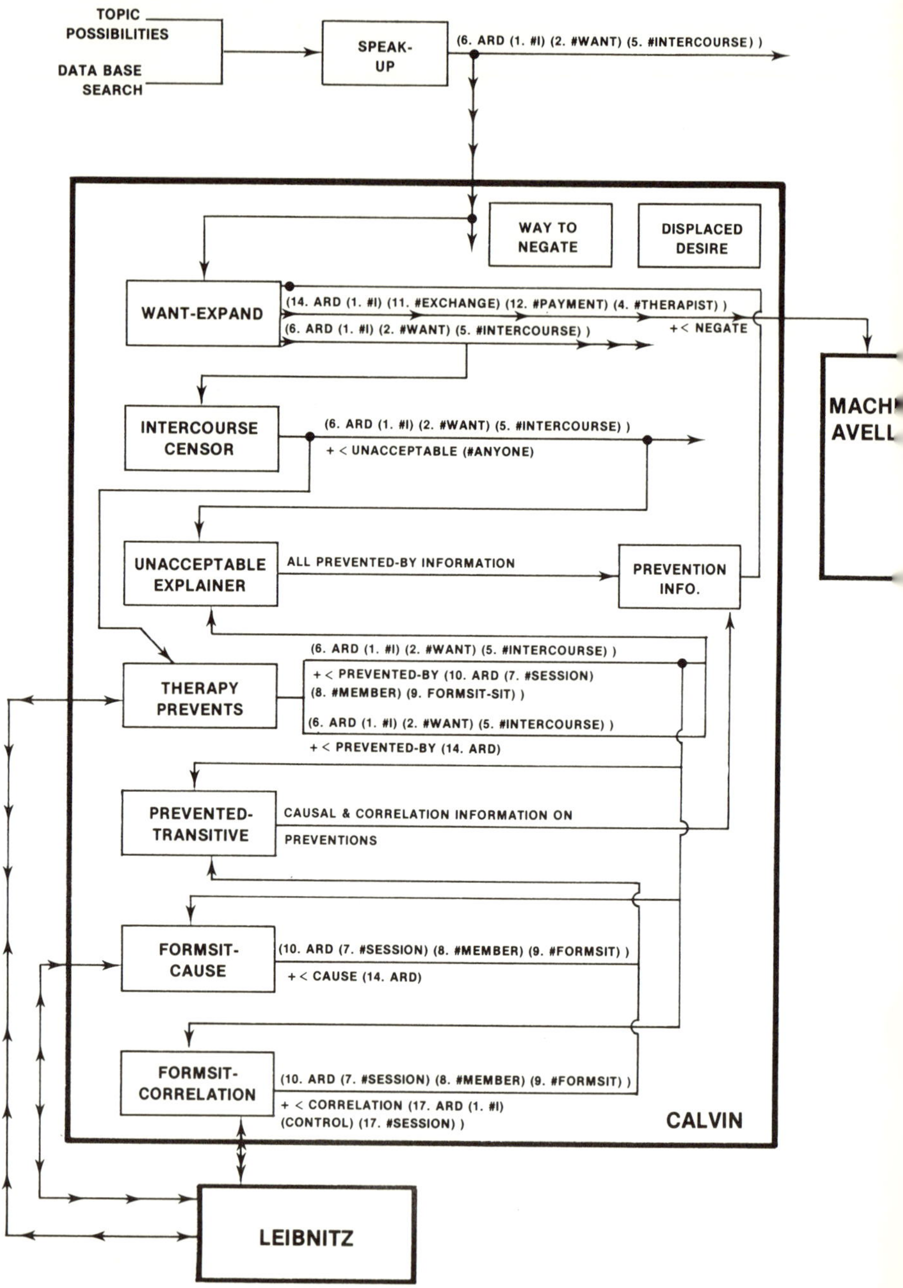

DIAGRAM 6.41.1

intercepted by INTERCOURSE-CENSOR, which attaches the indicator UNACCEPTABLE and the property ANYONE to it. The creation of this pattern causes two other programs to fire, UNACCEPTABLE-EXPLAINER and THERAPY-PREVENTS. For the moment, let us hold up our discussion on the first program and see what the second accomplishes. THERAPY-PREVENTS looks for properties under the indicator PREVENTED-BY for all concepts that match its invocation pattern by looking in the LEIBNITZ context. If it finds a property under this indicator, it attaches the property to the intercepted concept. UNACCEPTABLE-EXPLAINER then takes this information and places it on a possibilities list, which, in turn, will be used by the WANT-EXPAND program to determine those things which are preventing concept 6 from being actualized. However, while this possibilities list is being filled, other programs, PREVENTED-TRANSITIVE, FORMSIT-CAUSE, and FORMSIT-CORRELATION, both send the concept to the LEIBNITZ context, the first to determine causal information and the second to determine common causes. Both programs return their results to PREVENTED-TRANSITIVE, which in turn places them on the possibilities list. Once all these lower-level programs have completed their computations, the WANT-EXPAND program then selects concepts from the possibilities list and tries to negate them. It then sends each of these negated concepts into the MACHIAVELLI context (see Diagram 6.41.2), where programs attempt to uncover ways of overcoming or circumventing those things that thwart the realization of a desire or action.

Looking at Diagram 6.41.2, we can see that although WANT-EXPAND negates and sends all the concepts on the possibilities list into MACHIAVELLI, only one concept (no. 14), that returned by THERAPY-PREVENTS, has a successful resolution. When it is entered into the MACHIAVELLI context, it fires the interrupt EXCHANGE-PRESERVE. This program might be thought of as specializing in exchange relationships as it performs a number of computations about the nature of such relationships and suggests ways in which they can be altered. As with all interrupts, the first body determines its applicability to the problem. This it does by determining whether the object being exchanged, in this case the payment, is desired or acceptable to the person receiving it. Finding that it is, the first body assigns the indicator ACCEPTABLE and the property THERAPIST. Another program, PLEASURE-ACCEPTABILITY, answers the question as to why receiving payment is acceptable to the therapist by attaching the EFFECT indicator and the property, PLEASURE. The second body of EXCHANGE-PRESERVE then tries to see what would happen if the payment desired by the therapist were eliminated. To make this determination the concept of payment (no. 12) is excluded from the main concept (no. 14) and sent into the CICERO context to determine possible impacts of the omission of payment. Here the program IRREVERENTLY-SHOCK notes that the impact of this exclusion would be to shock the therapist (concept 19). When this concept is sent back into the MACHIAVELLI context, it causes the 4A-

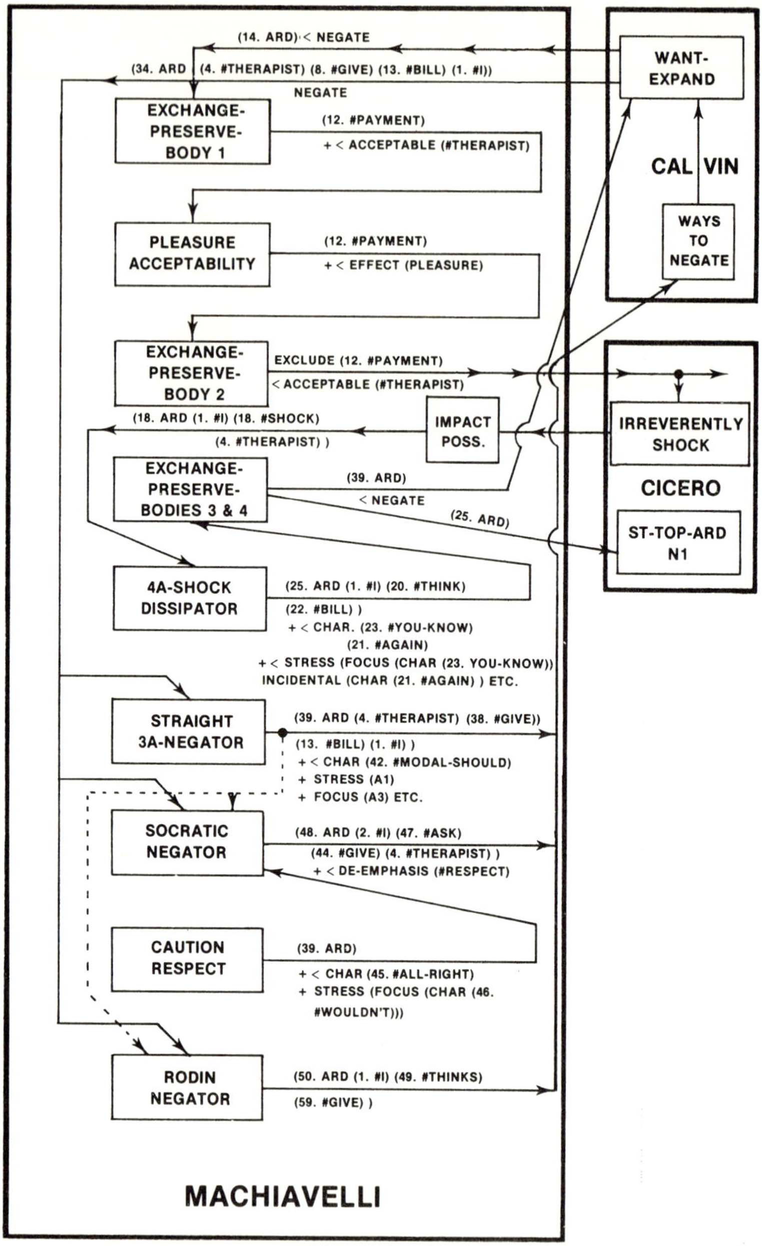

DIAGRAM 6.41.2

SHOCK-DISAPATOR program to fire. In effect, what this program does is to provide a foregrounding and a form of qualification that reduces the impact of potentially shocking statements. Once it has made its suggestion, the third body of EXCHANGE-PRESERVE sends it down into CICERO to be given realization. The fourth body, on the other hand, suggests a better way of changing the exchange relationship by generating concept 39. This concept is returned to WANT-EXPAND and entered into another layer of the MACHIAVELLI context. At this point three interrupts fire, STRAIGHT-3A-NEGATOR, SOCRATIC-NEGATOR, and RODIN-NEGATOR, all three of which produce concepts that find discourse realization but only one of which, SOCRATIC-NEGATOR, achieves final expression. This is due to the fact that programs in the CICERO context objected to their realizations and therefore attached impact properties which the CALVIN programs, in turn, picked up and used to prevent their realization. As this process of inhibition is primarily handled during realization, we shall not discuss it here but in Section 6.42.

One interesting feature about the three negator programs is that they are able to work together (something that is not adequately captured in this diagram). For example, both SOCRATIC-NEGATOR and RODIN-NEGATOR uses their bodies to "steal" results from STRAIGHT-3A-NEGATOR. Similarly, SOCRATIC-NEGATOR uses CAUTION-RESPECT to determine whether respect should be expressed in formulating its request and is able to incorporate its suggestions (concepts 45 and 46) into its final response. RODIN-NEGATOR, on the other hand, is less cautious and respectful and completes its suggestion by merely adding the qualifying concepts (1.. #I) (49.. #THINK2) to the concept created by STRAIGHT-3A-NEGATOR.

Below is the printout for the knowledge structures generated in the MACHIAVELLI context for the second sentence of the modeled discourse: "I was thinking of asking you whether it wouldn't be all right for you not to give me a bill." In reading this printout, notice that the concept created by SOCRATIC-NEGATOR is made up of a number of constituent concepts that were formed by other programs. Each of these concepts has a number and is presented in order as it appears in the top-level concept. Although this is primarily a cognitive context, there are indicators present which appear syntactic in nature and therefore out of place. For example, the indicators SYN-STRUCT, SYN-FEAT, and TENSE should be included within the CICERO and REALIZATION contexts. For most of the concepts this is what is done, but for some concepts it was necessary to short-circuit the realization process to simplify programing. These shortcuts do not, I believe, signify any theoretical deficiency on the part of the model, but are primarily technical problems. In a more complete version of the model, differences between the cognitive and the linguistic properties of concepts could be worked out in greater detail in accordance with the grammar discussed in Chapter 5.

```
(52. ARD (1. . #I) (51. . #THINK2) (48. . #ASK))
             CONSTRUCTED BY SOCRATIC-NEGATOR

(1. TOKEN #1)
             CONSTRUCTED BY *INITIALIZATION*

   < SYN-STRUCT   SINGULAR (VIA *INITIALIZATION*)
          UNDEFINITE (VIA *INITIALIZATION*)
   < SYN-FEAT   INDIRECT-OB (VIA STRAIGHT-3A-NEGATOR)
(51. TOKEN #THINK2)
             CONSTRUCTED BY SOCRATIC-NEGATOR

   < TENSE   PAST (VIA SOCRATIC-NEGATOR)
          CONTINUING (VIA SOCRATIC-NEGATOR)
(48. ARD (1. . #I) (47. . #ASK) (44. . #GIVE) (4. . #THERAPIST))
             CONSTRUCTED BY SOCRATIC-NEGATOR

   < STRESS   (NIL A1) (VIA SOCRATIC-NEGATOR)
          (NIL A3) (VIA SOCRATIC-NEGATOR)
          (INCIDENTAL A2) (VIA SOCRATIC-NEGATOR)
   < STRUCTURE   BENEFACTOR (VIA SOCRATIC-NEGATOR)
C<-

(48. ARD (1. . #I) (47. . #ASK) (44. . #GIVE) (4. . #THERAPIST))
             CONSTRUCTED BY SOCRATIC-NEGATOR

   < STRESS   (NIL A1) (VIA SOCRATIC-NEGATOR)
          (NIL A3) (VIA SOCRATIC-NEGATOR)
          (INCIDENTAL A2) (VIA SOCRATIC-NEGATOR)
   < STRUCTURE   BENEFACTOR (VIA SOCRATIC-NEGATOR)
(1. TOKEN #1)
             CONSTRUCTED BY *INITIALIZATION*

   < SYN-STRUCT   SINGULAR (VIA *INITIALIZATION*)
          UNDEFINITE (VIA *INITIALIZATION*)
   < SYN-FEAT   INDIRECT-OB (VIA STRAIGHT-3A-NEGATOR)
(47. TOKEN #ASK)
             CONSTRUCTED BY SOCRATIC-NEGATOR

   < TENSE   CONTINUING (VIA SOCRATIC-NEGATOR)
(44. YN-QUESTION (39. . #GIVE))
             CONSTRUCTED BY SOCRATIC-NEGATOR

   < SYN-STRUCT   YN-WHETHER (VIA SOCRATIC-NEGATOR)


   < POS-EMPHASIS  (41. . #RESPECT) (VIA SOCRATIC-NEGATOR)
(4. TOKEN #THERAPIST)
             CONSTRUCTED BY *INITIALIZATION*

   < SYN-STRUCT   SINGULAR (VIA *INITIALIZATION*)
          UNDEFINITE (VIA *INITIALIZATION*)
D<-

(39. ARD (4. . #THERAPIST) (38. . #GIVE) (13. . #BILL) (1. . #I)) PRE
SENT BY WANT-EXPAND
             CONSTRUCTED BY EXCHANGE-PRESERVER

   < CHARACTERISTICS   (45. . #ALL-RIGHT) (VIA CAUTION-RESPECT)
   < STRESS   (INCIDENTAL A2) (VIA STRAIGHT-3A-NEGATOR)
          (FOCUS A1) (VIA SOCRATIC-NEGATOR)
          (T A3) (VIA SOCRATIC-NEGATOR)
          (FOCUS (CHARACTERISTICS (45. . #ALL-RIGHT))) (VIA CAUTION-RE
```

```
SPECT)
          (PIVOT (CHARACTERISTICS (45. . #ALL-RIGHT))) (VIA CAUTION-RE
SPECT)
   < DERIVED   (14. . #EXCHANGE) (VIA EXCHANGE-PRESERVER)
   < NEGATE   NIL (VIA EXCHANGE-PRESERVER)
   < IMPACT   (55. . #OBJECTS) (VIA EXCHANGE-PRES2)
   < PREVENTS   (14. . #EXCHANGE) (VIA EXCHANGE-PRESERVER)
(4. TOKEN #THERAPIST)
             CONSTRUCTED BY *INITIALIZATION*

   < SYN-STRUCT   SINGULAR (VIA *INITIALIZATION*)
          UNDEFINITE (VIA *INITIALIZATION*)
(38. TOKEN #GIVE)
             CONSTRUCTED BY EXCHANGE-PRESERVER

   < CHARACTERISTICS   (42. . #MODAL-SHOULD) (VIA STRAIGHT-3A-NEGATOR)
          (43. . #NOT) (VIA STRAIGHT-3A-NEGATOR)
   < STRESS   (T (CHARACTERISTICS (43. . #NOT))) (VIA STRAIGHT-3A-NEGA
TOR)
   < TENSE   INFINITIVE (VIA SOCRATIC-NEGATOR)
(13. TOKEN #BILL)
             CONSTRUCTED BY FORMSIT-CAUSE-EXCHANGE

   < SYN-STRUCT   SINGULAR (VIA FORMSIT-CAUSE-EXCHANGED
          DEFINITE (VIA FORMSIT-CAUSE-EXCHANGE)
(1. TOKEN #1)
             CONSTRUCTED BY *INITIALIZATION*

   < SYN-STRUCT   SINGULAR (VIA *INITIALIZATION*)
          UNDEFINITE (VIA *INITIALIZATION*)
   < SYN-FEAT   INDIRECT-OB (VIA STRAIGHT-3A-NEGATOR)
D<-
```

6.42. *The organization of realization programs*

The process of transforming concepts into discourse is a highly complicated process within this program both in terms of the realization of the concepts themselves and in terms of the final expression of discourse elements. As we noted throughout this book, the realization process does not end with the formation of sentences, as these sentences may be determined to be unacceptable for expression, and substitute forms may have to be found. Determining whether a discourse constituent is unacceptable and finding a substitute form involves a great deal of travel on the part of the constituent and, in those cases where it is unacceptable, additional processing. Once a concept has been given final lexical realization, it may have invoked programs in almost every context of the program, so that although the realization of the constituent is confined to two contexts, CICERO and REALIZATION, its final expression involves CALVIN and MACHIAVELLI as well.

Before we can obtain an understanding of the particulars of the realization process, we first need to obtain an overview of the realization process as a whole, and then telescope our attention to the workings of the CICERO and REALIZATION contexts. Diagram 6.42.1 provides an overview of the overall realization process within the program. Notice that the overall realization process is controlled by the GENERAL-REALIZER program within the

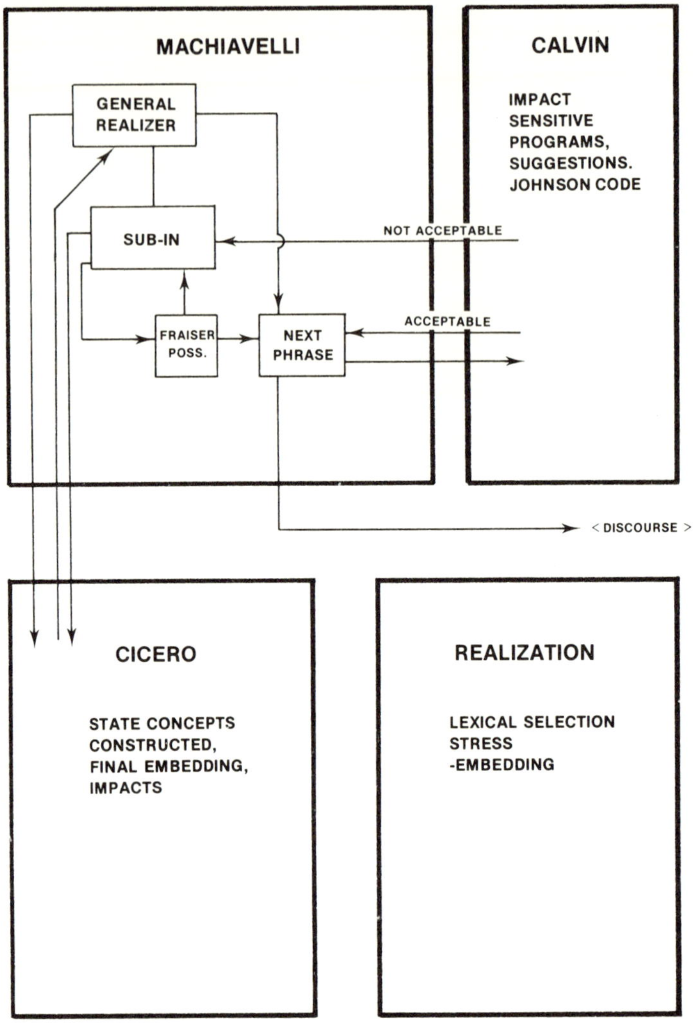

DIAGRAM 6.42.1

MACHIAVELLI context and that it oversees the passage of concepts between the various contexts. By sending concepts into the CICERO context, it causes the formation of STATE concepts and thereby initiates actual realization. For our purposes at the moment, the key program within this context is ST-ARD-NI. It "interacts" with the realization context by the sending and receiving of concepts. The programs in the REALIZATION context, in turn, are primarily concerned with the lexical realization of constituents and the determination of stress. However, these programs are also concerned with the actual embedding of "troublesome" constituents and the assignment of syntactic tags to these constituents.

In addition to creating STATE concepts and completing the final embedding of discourse constituents, the CICERO context has programs that assess the impact of stating concepts. As you will recall from our previous discussion, two formed sentences did not achieve final expression. This was due to the program IMPERTINENT-NOT-GIVE attaching to the concept requesting not to be given a bill (no. 39) the indicator MOTIVATION and the property (65. ARD (#I.. #I) (63.. #STOP) (64.. #THERAPY)). When concept 39 is sent by GENERAL-REALIZER into the CALVIN context for final approval, a program there, MOTIVATION-DENOUNCIATOR, first tries to see if that would be acceptable to the therapist, and finding that it isn't, includes an indicator saying that the expression of this concept would be unacceptable to ERMA (as it would give the impression that it is trying to stop the therapy). Therefore, concept 39 fails to achieve realization and GENERAL-REALIZER, through its program SUB-IN, uses suggestions returned from CALVIN context and then sends them into the CICERO context, where the normal realization process is initiated. Once given realization, the concept is returned to GENERAL-REALIZER, and the concept is substituted in and given expression through the program NEXT-PHRASE. In some cases, the CALVIN suggestions may only include a selection from the JOHNSON-WORRIED code such as "I mean," and therefore would not require an additional realization. In those cases where the STATE concept is acceptable, the SUB-IN program is bypassed and the NEXT-PHRASE program simply expresses the concept. It should be noted that the elements which are expressed are not always phrases, but rather the constituents of the STATE concept as they are stored and tagged in the possibilities list used by the NEXT-PHRASE program.

Now that we have seen how the overall realization process operates, we can examine the programs in the two contexts principally responsible for realization. Our diagram will be somewhat more general than those characterizing the two cognitive contexts, as the outputs for each program vary according to the STATE concepts they process, and the manner in which control is transferred between programs is also different. The programs in the REALIZATION context transfer their results and hence their control by creating and eliminating different context layers so that the notation used in previous diagrams is not altogether appropriate here. The arrows in this diagram indicate in somewhat loose terms the flow of processing, and the output statements indicate the type of operations they perform. The key to understanding the realization process is to remember that the program begins with top-level concepts, most of which contain a large number of embedded constituents, and then tries to unravel each to identify its grammatical and semantic constituents, and, having done so, reembeds the constituents according to their proper position in the sentence. Each constituent is made a STATE concept and is identified according to its higher-level role (such as a first argument or as a relator), and then is broken down until it is reduced to the level of a TOKEN concept, whereupon it is given lexical realization.

Once lexical selection has been made, the second phase of realization is initiated, whereby the words are then reembedded into their parent constituents according to their appropriate syntactic and thematic position. Where the nature of the constituent places special constraints upon the placement of lexical items, the reembedding is performed by a program that specializes in such constituents, whereas in simpler and more standardized cases the reembedding is performed by a more general-purpose program such as TOP-ST-ARD-NI.

Diagram 6.42.2 provides a rough overview of how the programs in CICERO and REALIZATION realize various conceptual constituents into the second sentence of the discourse. The outputs of each of the programs represent what each program does. TOP-ST-ARD-NI performs most of the realization for all concepts that occupy an argument position, and in effect determines the case for each argument. In its sixth body, it determines the tense, voice, and verb class for the relator concept. When it has successfully identified the features of the conceptual constituents, it "sends" them into the REALIZATION context, where they are broken down into TOKENS and realized as words by ST-TKAI-ARDI. If there is a STRESS indicator, then, depending upon its nature, other programs are invoked to give the stressed concept realization. For example, CH-SR-TF-TK-ARD is a program designed to realize a stressed concept which is a TOKEN and has a CHARACTERISTICS indicator. However, owing to the complexity and diversity of concepts that may be stressed, this interrupt alone is not sufficient to process all stressed concepts. Consequently, the program has a great number of special-purpose programs to handle special cases of stress. Nonetheless, once these special-purpose programs have realized the STRESS concepts, they either return their results directly back to the seventh body of TOP-ST-ARD-NI. This body then reembeds all the constituents and passes them on to the eighth body, where they are finally checked out and then sent on to GENERAL-REALIZER for final expression—should they not be intercepted by the CALVIN interrupt programs.

The realization of concepts is the most complex operation that this program performs. Part of the complexity is inherent in the nature of the problem; however, programming could probably be considerably simplified with the addition of new rules and a more carefully worked out realization scheme. Therefore, although this program at present uses a number of specialist programs, I doubt whether they are necessary to the extent that they are presently used within the program.

The following pages of printout show some of the steps involved in the realization of concept 52. They should be read in the same manner as was the previous example, bearing in mind that the realization process begins with a

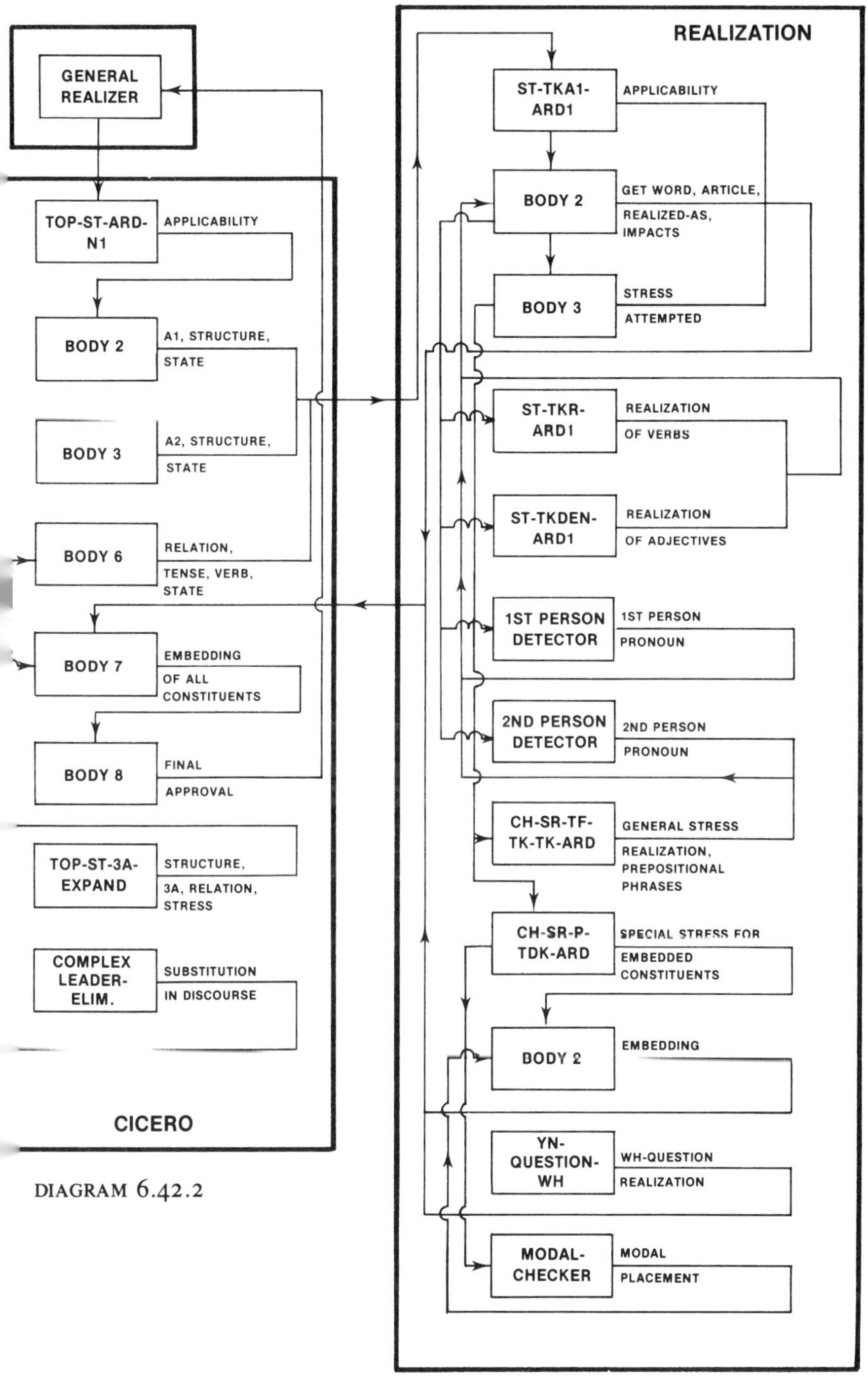

DIAGRAM 6.42.2

top-level concept and ends with a REALIZED-AS indicator and its properties. The final production of the discourse results in the expression of the sentence in a standard linear format.

```
(52. ARD (1. . #I) (51. . #THINK2) (48. . #ASK))
            CONSTRUCTED BY SOCRATIC-NEGATOR

   < REALZ-STAT    (92. . #I) (VIA TOP-ST-ARD-N1)
         (93. . #ASK) (VIA TOP-ST-ARD-N1)
         (109. . #THINK2) (VIA TOP-ST-ARD-N1)
   < REALIZED-AS    ((A1 ((PRN . I)))
                      (R ((VB WAS / THINK-ING)))
                      (EMB ((PREP . OF)))
                      (A2
                             ((R ((VB / ASK-ING)))
                               (A2
                                      ((A1
                                             ((EMB
                                                    ((CONJ)))
                                               (EMB ((PRN . IT)))
                                               (CHARACTERISTICS
                                                    ((*IGNORE*
                                                          106.)
                                                      (ADV)))
                                               (EMB ((VB / BE)))
                                               (CHARACTERISTICS
                                                    ((*IGNORE*
                                                          104.)
                                                      (ADJF1 . / )
                                                      (ADV)))
                                               (EMB ((PREP . FOR)))
                                               (A1 ((PRN . YOU)))
                                               (R
                                                    ((ADV . NOT)
                                                      (VB
                                                          TO
                                                          /
                                                          GIVE)))
                                               (A3 ((PRN . ME)))
                                               (A2
                                                    ((ART . THE)
                                                      (N . BILL))))

(1. TOKEN #I)
            CONSTRUCTED BY *INITIALIZATION*

   < REALZ-STAT    (92. . #I) (VIA ST-TKA1-ARD1)
         (94. . #I) (VIA ST-TKA1-ARD1)
         (99. . #I) (VIA ST-TKA1-ARD1)
   < SYN-STRUCT    SINGULAR (VIA *INITIALIZATION*)
         UNDEFINITE (VIA *INITIALIZATION*)
   < SYN-FEAT    INDIRECT OB (VIA STRAIGHT-SA-NEGATOR)
         FIRST-PERSON (VIA FIRST-PERSON-DETECTOR)
   < STRUCTURE    AGENT (VIA TOP-ST-ARD-N1)
   < REALIZED-AS ((PRN . HE))
(51. TOKEN #THINK2)
            CONSTRUCTED BY SOCRATIC-NEGATOR
```

```
   < REALZ-STAT    (109. . #THINK2) (VIA ST-TKA1-ARD1)
   < SYN-STRUCT    SINGULAR (VIA TOP-ST-ARD-N1)
        DEFINITE (VIA ST-TKA1-ARD1)
   < TENSE    PAST (VIA SOCRATIC-NEGATOR)
        CONTINUING (VIA SOCRATIC-NEGATOR)
   < STRUCTURE    RELATION (VIA TOP-ST-ARD-N1)
   < REALIZED-AS ((VB WAS /  THINK-ING))
(48. ARD (1. . #I) (47. . #ASK) (44. . #GIVE) (4. . #THERAPIST))
           CONSTRUCTED BY SOCRATIC-NEGATOR

   < REALZ-STAT    (94. . #I) (VIA TOP-ST-ARD-N1)
        (95. . #GIVE) (VIA TOP-ST-ARD-N1)
        (107. . #THERAPIST) (VIA TOP-ST-3A-EXPAND)
        (105. . #ASK) (VIA TOP-ST-3A-EXPAND)
   < STRESS    (NIL A1) (VIA SOCRATIC-NEGATOR)
        (NIL A3) (VIA SOCRATIC-NEGATOR)
        (INCIDENTAL A2) (VIA SOCRATIC-NEGATOR)
   < STRUCTURE    BENEFACTOR (VIA SOCRATIC-NEGATOR)
   < REALIZED-AS    ((R ((VB /  ASK-ING)))
                      (A2
                             ((A1
                                     ((EMB ((CONJ . WHETHER)))
                                       (EMB ((PRN . IT)))
                                       (CHARACTERISTICS
                                              ((*IGNORE*
                                                     106.)
                                                (ADV . WOULDN/'T)))
                                       (EMB ((VB /  BE)))
                                       (CHARACTERISTICS
                                              ((*IGNORE*
                                                     104.)
                                                (ADJF . / )
                                                (ADV . ALL/ RIGHT)))
                                       (EMB ((PREP . FOR)))
                                       (A1 ((PRN . YOU)))
                                       (R
                                              ((ADV . NOT)
                        ((ADV . NOT)
                          (VB TO /  GIVE)))
                 (A3 ((PRN . ME)))
                 (A2 ((ART . THE) (N . BILL)))))

(48. ARD (1. . #I) (47. . #ASK) (44. . #GIVE) (4. . #THERAPIST))
           CONSTRUCTED BY SOCRATIC-NEGATOR

   < REALZ-STAT    (94. . #I) (VIA TOP-ST-ARD-N1)
        (95. . #GIVE) (VIA TOP-ST-ARD-N1)
        (107. . #THERAPIST) (VIA TOP-ST-3A-EXPAND)
        (105. . #ASK) (VIA TOP-ST-3A-EXPAND)
   < STRESS    (NIL A1) (VIA SOCRATIC-NEGATOR)
        (NIL A3) (VIA SOCRATIC-NEGATOR)
        (INCIDENTAL A2) (VIA SOCRATIC-NEGATOR)
   < STRUCTURE    BENEFACTOR (VIA SOCRATIC-NEGATOR)
   < REALIZED-AS    ((R ((VB /  ASK-ING)))
                      (A2
                             ((A1
                                     ((EMB ((CONJ . WHETHER)))
                                       (EMB ((PRN . IT)))
```

```
                                        (CHARACTERISTICS
                                              ((*IGNORE*
                                                    106.)
                                                (ADV . WOULDN/'T)))
                                        (EMB ((VB /  BE)))
                                        (CHARACTERISTICS
                                              ((*IGNORE*
                                                    104.)
                                                (ADJF . / )

                                                (ADV . ALL/ RIGHT)))
                                        (EMB ((PREP . FOR)))
                                        (A1 ((PRN . YOU)))
                                        (R
                                              ((ADV . NOT)
                                                (VB TO /  GIVE)))
                                        (A3 ((PRN . ME)))
                                        (A2 ((ART . THE) (N . BILL)))))

(1. TOKEN #1)
            CONSTRUCTED BY *INITIALIZATION*

   < REALZ-STAT    (92. . #I) (VIA ST-TKA1-ARD1)
          (94. . #I) (VIA ST-TKA1-ARD1)
          (99. . #I) (VIA ST-TKA1-ARD1)
   < SYN-STRUCT     SINGULAR (VIA *INITIALIZATION*)
          UNDEFINITE (VIA *INITIALIZATION*)
   < SYN-FEAT   INDIRECT-OB (VIA STRAIGHT-3A-NEGATOR)
          FIRST-PERSON (VIA FIRST-PERSON-DETECTOR)
   < STRUCTURE   AGENT (VIA TOP-ST-ARD-N1)
   < REALIZED-AB ((PRN . HE))
(47. TOKEN #ASK)
            CONSTRUCTED BY SOCRATIC-NEGATOR

   < REALZ-STAT    (108. . #ASK) (VIA ST-TKA1-ARD1)
   < SYN-STRUCT    NIL (VIA TOP-ST-3A-EXPAND)
          PLURAL (VIA ST-TKA1-ARD1)
          DEFINITE (VIA ST-TKA1-ARD1)
   < TENSE   CONTINUING (VIA SOCRATIC-NEGATOR)
   < STRUCTURE   RELATION (VIA TOP-ST-3A-EXPAND)
   < REALIZED-AS ((VB /  ASK-ING))
(44. YN-QUESTION (39.   #GIVE))
            CONSTRUCTED BY SOCRATIC-NEGATOR

   < REALZ-STAT    (96. . #GIVE) (VIA YN-QUEST-WHETHER)
   < SYN-STRUCT    YN-WHETHER (VIA SOCRATIC-NEGATOR)
   < STRUCTURE     GOAL (VIA TOP-ST-ARD-N1)
   < POS-EMPHASIS     (41. . #RESPECT) (VIA SOCRATIC-NEGATOR)
(4. TOKEN #THERAPIST)
            CONSTRUCTED BY *INITIALIZATION*

   < REALZ-STAT    (97. . #THERAPIST) (VIA ST-TKA1-ARD1)
          (107. . #THERAPIST) (VIA ST- TKA1-ARD1)
   < SYN-STRUCT    UNDEFINITE (VIA *INITIALIZATION*)
          PLURAL (VIA SECOND-PERSON-DETECTOR1)
   < STRUCTURE   AGENT (VIA TOP-ST-ARD-N1)
   < REALIZED-AS ((PRN . YOU))
```

```
D<-

(4. TOKEN #THERAPIST)
            CONSTRUCTED BY *INITIALIZATION*

   < REALZ-STAT    (97. . #THERAPIST) (VIA ST-TKA1-ARD1)
         (107. . #THERAPIST) (VIA ST-TKA1-ARD1)
   < SYN-STRUCT   UNDEFINITE (VIA *INITIALIZATION*)
         PLURAL (VIA SECOND-PERSON-DETECTOR1)
   < STRUCTURE   AGENT (VIA TOP-ST-ARD-N1)
   < REALIZED-AS ((PRN . YOU))
(38. TOKEN #GIVE)
            CONSTRUCTED BY EXCHANGE-PRESERVER

   < CHARACTERISTICS   (42. . #MODAL-SHOULD) (VIA STRAIGHT-3A-NEGATOR)
         (43. . #NOT) (VIA STRAIGHT-3A-NEGATOR)
   < REALZ-STAT    (100. . #GIVE) (VIA ST-TKA1-ARD1)
   < REALZ-STRS    (101. . #NOT) (VIA ST-TKA1-ARD1)
   < STRESS    (T (CHARACTERISTICS (43. . #NOT))) (VIA STRAIGHT-3A-NEGA
TOR)
   < SYN-STRUCT   PLURAL (VIA TOP-ST-3A-EXPAND)
         DEFINITE (VIA ST-TKA1-ARD1)
   < TENSE   INFINITIVE (VIA SOCRATIC-NEGATOR)
   < STRUCTURE   RELATION (VIA TOP-ST-3A-EXPAND)
   < REALIZED-AS ((ADV . NOT) (VB TO /  GIVE))
(13. TOKEN #BILL)
            CONSTRUCTED BY FORMSIT-CAUSE-EXCHANGE

   < REALZ-STAT    (98. . #BILL) (VIA ST-TKA1-ARD1)
   < SYN-STRUCT   SINGULAR (VIA FORMSIT-CAUSE-EXCHANGED
         DEFINITE (VIA FORMSIT-CAUSE-EXCHANGE)
   < STRUCTURE   GOAL (VIA TOP-ST-ARD-N1)
   < REALIZED-AS ((ART . THE) (N . BILL))
(1. TOKEN #I)
            CONSTRUCTED BY *INITIALIZATION*

   < REALZ-STAT    (92. . #I) (VIA ST-TKA1-ARD1)
         (94. . #I) (VIA ST-TKA1-ARD1)

         (99. . #I) (VIA ST-TKA1-ARD1)
   < SYN-STRUCT   SINGULAR (VIA *INITIALIZATION*)
         UNDEFINITE (VIA *INITIALIZATION*)
   < SYN-FEAT   INDIRECT-OB (VIA STRAIGHT-3A-NEGATOR)
         FIRST-PERSON (VIA FIRST-PERSON-DETECTOR)
   < STRUCTURE   AGENT (VIA TOP-ST-ARD-N1)
   < REALIZED-AS ((PRN . ME))
C<-

(42. TOKEN #MODAL-SHOULD)
            CONSTRUCTED BY STRAIGHT-3A-NEGATOR
C<-

(43. TOKEN #NOT)
            CONSTRUCTED BY STRAIGHT-3A-NEGATOR

   < REALZ-STAT    (102. . #NOT) (VIA ST-TKA1-ARD1)
   < SYN-STRUCT   DEFINITE (VIA ST-TKA1-ARD1)
         PLURAL (VIA ST-TKA1-ARD1)
   < STRUCTURE   DENOTER (VIA CH-SR-TF-TK-TK-ARD1)
   < REALIZED-AS ((ADV . NOT))
```

```
C<-

45. TOKEN #ALL-RIGHT)
            CONSTRUCTED BY CAUTION-RESPECT
   < CHARACTERISTICS  (46. . #MODAL-WOULDNT) (VIA CAUTION-RESPECT)
   < REALZ-STAT   (104. . #ALL-RIGHT) (VIA ST-TKA1-ARD1)
   < REALZ-STRS   (105. . #MODAL-WOULDNT) (VIA ST-TKA1-ARD1)
   < STRESS   (FOCUS (CHARACTERISTICS (46. . #MODAL-WOULDNT))) (VIA CA
UTION-RESPECT)
   < SYN-STRUCT   DEFINITE (VIA ST-TKA1-ARD1)
          PLURAL (VIA ST-TKA1-ARD1)
   < TENSE   MODAL (VIA MODAL-TENSE-MODIFICATION)
   < STRUCTURE   DENOTER (VIA CH-SR-P-TOK-ARD)
   < REALIZED-AS ((ADV . WOULDN/•T) (ADJF . / ) (ADV . ALL/ RIGHT))
D<-

(105. STRESS FOCUS) (CHARACTERISTICS (46. . #MODAL-WOULDNT)) (45. . #
ALL-RIGHT) (39. . #GIVE)) PRESENT BY ST-TKA1-ARD1
             CONSTRUCTED BY ST-TKA1-ARD1

   < REALZ-STAT   (106. . #MODAL-WOULDNT) (VIA CH-SR-TF-TK-TK-ARD1)
   < REALIZED-AS   ((A1
                             ((EMB (CONJ . WHETHER)))
                               (EMB ((PRN . IT)))
                               (CHARACTERISTICS
                                      ((*IGNORE*
                                             106.)
                                        (ADV . WOULDN/•T)))
                               (EMB ((VB /  BE)))
                               (CHARACTERISTICS
                                      ((*IGNORE* 104. . #ALL-RIGHT)
                                        (ADJF . / )
                                        (ADV . ALL/ RIGHT)))

                               (EMB ((PREP . FOR)))
                               (A1 ((PRN . YOU)))
                               (R ((ADV . NOT) (VB TO /  GIVE)))
                               (A3 ((PRN . ME)))
                               (A2 ((ART . THE) (N . BILL))))))

D<-

(39. ARD (4. . #THERAPIST) (38. . #GIVE) (13. . #BILL) (1. . #I))  PRE
SENT BY WANT-EXPAND
             CONSTRUCTED BY EXCHANGE-PRESERVER

   < CHARACTERISTICS   (45. . #ALL-RIGHT) (VIA CAUTION-RESPECT)
   < REALZ-STAT   (97. . #THERAPIST) (VIA TOP-ST-ARD-N1)
          (98. . #BILL) (VIA TOP-ST-ARD-N1)
          (99. . #I) (VIA TOP-ST-3A-EXPAND)
          (100. . #GIVE) (VIA TOP-ST-3A-EXPAND)
   < STRESS   (INCIDENTAL A2) (VIA STRAIGHT-3A-NEGATOR)

          (FOCUS A1) (VIA SOCRATIC-NEGATOR)
          (T A3) (VIA SOCRATIC-NEGATOR)
          (FOCUS (CHARACTERISTICS (45. . #ALL-RIGHT))) (VIA CAUTION-RE
SPECT)
          (PIVOT (CHARACTERISTICS (45. . #ALL-RIGHT))) (VIA CAUTION-RE
SPECT)
```

```
  < DERIVED   (14. . #EXCHANGE) (VIA EXCHANGE-PRESERVER)
  < NEGATE   NIL (VIA EXCHANGE-PRESERVER)
  < IMPACT   (55. . #OBJECTS) (VIA EXCHANGE-PRES2)
  < PREVENTS   (14. . #EXCHANGE) (VIA EXCHANGE-PRESERVER)
  < REALIZED-AS   (EMB ((PRN . IT)))
                   (CHARACTERISTICS
                          ((*IGNORE* 106. . #MODAL-WOULDNT)
                            (ADV . WOULDN/•T)))
                   (EMB ((VB /  BE)))
                   (CHARACTERISTICS
                          ((*IGNORE* 104. . #ALL-RIGHT)
                            (ADJF . / )
                            (ADV . ALL/ RIGHT)))
                   (EMB ((PREP . FOR)))
                   (A1 ((PRN . YOU)))
                   (R ((ADV . NOT) (VB TO /  GIVE)))
                   (A3 ((PRN . ME)))
                   (A2 ((ART . THE) (N . BILL))))

<<< EPISTEME

NIL
<-  (SIMPLE-GRINDER (GET-REAL (GTNO 52.) REALIZE-CONTEXT))
  ((A1 ((PRN . I)))
    (R ((VB WAS /  THINK-ING)))
    (EMB ((PREP . OF)))
    (A2
          ((R ((VB /  ASK-ING)))
            (A2
                 ((A1
                         ((EMB ((CONJ . WHETHER)))
                           (EMB ((PRN . IT)))
                           (CHARACTERISTICS
                                  ((*IGNORE*
                                         106.)
                                    (ADV . WOULDN/•T)))
                           (EMB ((VB /  BE)))
                           (CHARACTERISTICS
                                  ((*IGNORE* 104. . #ALL-RIGHT)
                                    (ADJF . / )
                                    (ADV . ALL/ RIGHT)))
                           (EMB ((PREP . FOR)))
                           (A1 ((PRN . YOU)))
                           (R ((ADV . NOT) (VB TO /  GIVE)))
                           (A3 ((PRN . ME)))
/)                         (A2 ((ART . THE) (N . BILL))))))))))
```

6.43. *Comparison of a sample of program discourse with modeled transcript*

The purpose in designing and writing the ERMA program was to test out a theory of the discourse formation and realization processes. In writing the program, the entire discourse episode was analyzed and hand-simulated. However, only part of the entire discourse episode was computer-simulated. The reason for this is simply that since all the major representational and theoretical problems had been worked out, the additional programming needed to make the program complete would not have contributed substantively to either the theory or the methods developed. It is my belief that as a research strategy little is gained, and often much is lost, by developing massive operational programs when the research is still in an exploratory stage. Therefore, although the program does simulate a part of the discourse, and potentially all the discourse, it should be borne in mind that the model is not regarded here as complete or definitive but as exploratory. This is, in effect, the status of all computer models of complex linguistic and problem-solving processes.

Below is a sample of the discourse actually produced by the program; it is not all that the program can produce at present, only that amount which is solidly bug-free. (Realized, but unexpressed sentences are given in parentheses).

> You know for some reason I just thought about the bill and about payment again. (You shouldn't give me a bill.) <Uh> I was thinking that I (shouldn't be given a bill) of asking you whether it wouldn't be all right for you not to give me a bill. That is, I usually by (the end of the month know the amount of the bill), well, I immediately thought of the objections to this, but my idea was that I would simply count up the number of hours and give you a check at the end of the month.

The discourse in the transcript reads as follows:

> You know, for some reason, I, uh, just thought about, uh, the bill and about payment again. That (pause 2 seconds), that, uh (pause 4 seconds), I was, uh, thinking that I—of asking you whether it wouldn't be all right for you (pause 2 seconds), you know, not to give me a bill. That is, uh, I would (hesitates), since I usually by—well, I immediately thought of the objections to this, but my idea was that I would simply count up the number of hours and give you a check at the end of the month.

In most respects the two discourses are similar, except for certain repetitions and the insertion of several "uhs" and a "you know." Both these differences are relatively slight; however, the "uhs" are more difficult to account for than the "you know." This is because they come at points where the speaker evaluates what she is going to say, and therefore, in order to be properly inserted, require additional programs in CALVIN and CICERO to register and note impacts. The insertion of the "you know," on the other hand, is not as difficult as the interruption, and the substitution has already occurred.

7 : A THEORETICAL DISCUSSION OF THE MODEL

Fundamental progress has to do with the reinterpretation of basic ideas.— WHITEHEAD

7.10. OVERVIEW

In Chapters 4, 5, and 6, our discussion was fairly technical, and although we alluded to the theoretical value of some of our mechanisms, we have yet to develop their theoretical ramifications. In this chapter, we shall first discuss the theoretical value of our notions of concepts, contexts, and multiple-body interrupts, and then compare these theoretical mechanisms to those developed by Freud, Piaget, and Bateson. In our discussion of the theoretical mechanisms, the following points will be made: *generic and extended concepts* can represent affective, logical, and behavioral knowledge in a manner that is readily realizable into discourse and not subject to the problem of access and inference found in taxonomic conceptual models; *contexts* are a precise and intuitively acceptable means for accounting for the compartmentalization of mental activity and an individual's ability to manipulate hypothetical universes—even when he is unconscious of so doing; *multiple-body interrupts* are a possible approach to the problem of the regulation of complex cognitive processes and suggest new theories of human thought and speech.

In the second section, the theories of Freud, Piaget, and Bateson will be discussed in terms of the theoretical mechanisms. In our discussion of Freud, we will focus on his notion of the compartmentalization of the mind and the mechanisms of defense. We shall attempt to demonstrate some of the epistemological weaknesses of his explanations and then show how some of the psychological processes he was attempting to describe could more precisely, and perhaps more adequately, be explained in terms of our model. Our treatment of Piaget will center on his theory of cognitive development and his use of an algebraic formalism to describe cognitive processes. It will be argued that Piaget, despite his later writings, does not provide an interactive and self-regulating model of cognition, and, by his reliance upon algebraic formalisms, incorrectly identifies intelligence and adaptation with structures rather than the procedures that use them. Next, Bateson's theory of logical types will be discussed in terms of its metaphorical use of logic to characterize levels of communication. The point is made that schizophrenic behaviors result not from the improper use of logic but rather from the schizophrenics' acquisition of "externalized control structures" which effectively inhibit self-regulation. An example of schizophrenic discourse is discussed in terms of our model.

7.20. THEORETICAL RAMIFICATIONS OF THE MODEL

The purpose of this section is to elaborate on the explanatory and theoretical value of some of the principle concepts of our model. In developing a computer model of discourse formation and generation, the objective has not been to demonstrate the power or trickery of computers in simulating human cognition but to develop a precise theory of human cognition and discourse behavior, which can identify the mechanisms, operations, and structures used in the formation and production of discourse. The hope is that the theoretical concepts developed have a general explanatory value beyond their place in the simulation model. Since the model stresses cognitive processes in the formation and generation of discourse, and since it simulates "psychological" processes, it makes theoretical statements that cut across many different theoretical domains. Consequently, in our discussion we shall attempt to bridge these different theoretical domains by demonstrating the broad but unified scope of the theoretical concepts we have used. The first part of this section briefly discusses the epistemological and general theoretical posture of the model in an effort to establish the key importance of viewing cognition and language from the inside out. The remaining parts cover selected concepts developed in the model and argue for their general theoretical value as models of cognitive processes.

7.21. *Meta-perspectives: self-regulation and adaptation*

In Chapter 1, I argued for a theory of discourse that modeled language behavior from the perspective of the speaker and not the observer. Here, too, it will be argued that models of cognition should represent cognitive processes in terms of the organism, which is to say that an appropriate description of human cognition is one which acts indistinguishably from the modeled subject. In Freudian theory, for example, as in other theories of cognition, the difficulty of going from an external description, which constructs its explanatory semantics in terms of an object typology, to an explanation that constructs its explanation in terms of the experiences of the subject is never successfully resolved.

In Freud the division is classic, as his therapeutic epistemology, which is subject-based, never is successfully reconciled with his theoretical or ''scientific'' epistemology. Phenomenologists have correctly chastized the social sciences for their failures to describe human action in the terms in which it is experienced, and this failure is reflected in the social sciences' attempts to describe human behavior in terms of ''data'' rather than as experienced action. To achieve such a description, a teleologically based language is needed to represent the processes and structures an individual uses to interpret, shape, and direct his experience. This language must be of such a logical type, to use Bateson's terms, that it itself is not a member of the class of concepts and actions actually used by the modeled subject. Programming languages such as CONNIVER seem to meet this requirement, as they can represent cognitive processes without themselves being a part of the content of these processes.

Another important factor in modeling human cognition is that it must be represented as a whole process. This is not to say that everything must be known about it in order to represent it, but that its basic and universal properties must be initially represented within the theory so that the closure implied in any theoretical description does not restrict its extension.

In modeling cognition, great emphasis has been given to the self-regulating or teleological properties of the system.* By this is meant, as was meant in Chapter 2, the capacity of a system to model its own behaviors and those of the environment with which it interacts. The focus is on the regulatory requirements of the system, for by seeing cognition from this perspective, we are better able to identify those fundamental processes that shape and direct the form of cognition. There is an ever-present danger in modeling complex cognitive processes to isolate them and to study them *sui generis*. The outcome of such limitation is to lose sight of the recognition that cognition is inherently a teleological process which must accommodate the needs of the individual to the demands of his environment. Hence, to study the individual, one must also study and represent his environment, both in terms of its intrinsic properties and its interpretation by the individual. Consequently, environmental features have been incorporated into the model through the model's audience-impact programs. In this way, it is possible to represent cognitive processes as adaptive mechanisms that respond to, protect, and advance human needs under the constraints of the environment. By representing cognition as an interactive process, we avoid some of the limitations of static taxonomic conceptions of cognitive development. For, although many theories acknowledge the importance of adaption and interaction in cognition, they do not identify the regulatory mechanisms by which adaptation takes place. In Piaget's case, for example, intelligence is identified with the acquisi-

*For a more comprehensive discussion of the role of subsystem independence and adaptivity, see W. R. Ashby, *Design for a brain* (New York: Wiley, 1960), pp. 205–17.

tion of various structures and operations rather than with the effectiveness of the control structures that deploy them. It is my contention that intelligence should not be identified with the presence or absence of certain structures or operations but rather assessed in terms of the organisms' general regulatory capacity. To do so requires a model that is able to represent the environments with which the model interacts. This has been done in a somewhat elementary fashion, yet by doing so, a theoretical perspective is provided that is amenable to considerations of the impact of environmental or interactive variables on conceptualization. As will be seen in subsequent sections, such a perspective is missing in both Piaget and Freud.

7.22. *Concept representation*

The theoretical value of this method of modeling concepts is that a method of representing knowledge is provided that is flexible and capable of arbitrary growth and modification. However, although the representation of concepts has an intuitive basis, the representation is by no means simple and quickly escapes characterization in natural language. As was pointed out in Chapter 4, our linguistic notion of a concept implies a single bounded entity, whereas their representation in the model is not bounded or singular. Consequently, it is of questionable utility to speak of a concept as a bounded entity, as it can be of arbitrary complexity and in a state of continual modification.

Significantly, our concepts are represented as structures, yet these structures are the products of procedures and therefore should be understood in terms of the procedures that use and generate them. Too often, human cognition is studied in terms of the structural properties of concepts, thereby seeking to identify the meaning of the concept with its structure. Yet, as has been argued in the previous section, concepts are the products of processes and thereby have no intrinsic meaning other than how they are used. It is meaningless to speak of homeostatic conceptual structures, as Piaget speaks of schemata, for concepts have no intrinsic stability or instability. Such criteria of stability depend upon their use by various procedures and the constraints of their use. Hence, depending upon the context to which it is applied and the procedure that uses it, a concept can be either stable or unstable.

Concepts have two types of information represented. The first is content information, which is nothing more than a pattern which uniquely characterizes the properties of an event, object, property, process, or relation. The second type of information is operational; it tells how that content information corresponds to the knowledge that the individual or system has about its own operations, and therefore, although not a part of the concepts "definition," it is critical to its use. The distinction between content and operational information is not fixed: it shifts according to the uses to which the concepts are put. Consequently, some information can be used for its content by one procedure and used for its operational information by another. Very often operational information is not made explicit in discourse of communication, resulting in a confusion of the meaning of the concept. The use of the STRESS indicator for the realization of discourse is a case in point, for its effect is reflected in the organization of the clause. But when operational indicators have no explicit discourse expression, such as when the discourse topic is displaced or not referred to directly, the listener either must be very accomplished at inferring what these operators are, or be forced to interpret a highly ambiguous discourse.

Another feature of this method of concept representation is that concepts are not organized hierarchically or in any taxonomic fashion. Unlike a semantic net or similar type of conceptual structure, concepts achieve their ordering and relationship to one another through the programs that are keyed to use them. The relationships that may exist between them are noted by programs designed for that purpose. Consequently, their organization with respect to one another may be highly idiosyncratic, depending upon the uses to which they have been put and the manner in which they are referenced. Hence, the commonality of conceptual organization between communicants is less a reflection of some intrinsic ordering common to both than a commonality of processing experience. Since the generation and organization of concepts is here regarded as a highly interactive process, one entailing both an environment of communicants (whether real or symbolized is not important) and an autoregulative communicant, it is not surprising that different persons have similar types of conceptual organization.

The fact that concepts are represented recursively has more than just formal significance. Not only would it be very difficult to perform the computations needed to simulate cognition using a different formal method, it would also entail a different theory of cognition. Piaget, for example, represents cognitive operations in terms of algebraic structures; hence, he concentrates upon the "operations" possible at different "stages" of cognitive development. His choice of formalism not only determines his method of description but also affects his theory of cognition. Similarly, a recursive representation of concepts has theoretical implications as it emphasizes the procedural aspect of cognition in the unwinding of embedded conceptual structures. It is this embedded quality of concepts that is important in understanding both their complexity and their communicability. For in generating a discourse, a speaker must go from a highly embedded structure to a linear structure, and, in making this transition, he must be careful to communicate the relationships contained within these embedded structures. As was discussed in Chapter 5, the episton must be broken down into its episteme constituents, and this recursive process of decomposition must be regulated by the speaker's perception of the listener's understanding of his conceptual structures. In those cases where the speaker and the listener are well acquainted, the transmission of a highly embedded concept is possible. Yet when the listener is not so well known, the concept must be broken down into those more elemental concepts with which the listener is better acquainted. Naturally, the determination of the decomposition of epistons for expression is a process that requires a great deal of social and linguistic competence, and, when improperly regulated, may result not only in poor communication, but in highly repetitive situations and psychological damage. The egocentric quality of childrens' speech, for instance, may be due to their lacking the appropriate procedures (gained through socialized knowledge) for communicating embedded concepts. The problem with such speech is not so much that it is "infantile" or less sophisticated, but that the process by which concepts are translated into speech has not been socialized, and hence stabilized.

7.23. *Contexts and their organization*

One of the theoretical benefits of working with contexts is that they provide a precise means of discussing the diversity of mental operations without falling into the epistemological traps of positivism or behaviorism. At worst, they provide a preliminary answer to the paradox of the mind being both rational and irrational, and at best they provide a precise and operational means for describing the compartmentalizations and interactions of mental operations. Before discussing the theoretical implications of contexts, let us first examine their application in the model.

Contexts, as we saw in Chapter 4, are layered tree structures containing datums and interrupts. They can be thought of as representing the state of a "microworld" which may be altered through the removal or addition of datums and their properties. Since it is possible to have several microworlds treat similar concepts differently, each may have its own "belief" about the validity of a conceptual proposition. The psychological implication of modeling cognition in terms of contexts is that "consciousness," and cognition in general, is differentiated into special processing domains, some of which are only partially accessible to the other. These domains are organized not according to strict logical principles but in terms of the differing processing needs of the mind. Their general representational power is due to the fact that they do not impose a logical framework on processing but rather are able to work with patterns which can or cannot be described logically. Hence, the evidence of logical properties in the operations of a context is not due to those operations being intrinsically logical, but to their functioning in a manner that is "logical."

The notion of contexts also provides an insight into how the different compartments of the mind might communicate and interact with one another. For example, when Freud says that the unconscious communicates with the conscious through the subconscious, what does this mean? However, if one speaks in terms of contexts, one knows precisely what is meant by a CALVIN interrupt firing in a MACHIAVELLI context. Similarly, in our own experience of the cognition of ourselves and others, contexts seem to make sense. How often have we noticed another person, or for that matter ourselves, taking very different points of view on the same subject in a very short period of time. The fortunate fact is that we are a multiple as our microworlds and that these microworlds pop into place whenever their special abilities are called for. Never mind consistency across cases, as the mind that can effectively change from one context to another according to need is far more adaptive than the one confined to a single consistent domain.

From both a developmental and a psychiatric perspective, contexts are of interest as they provide a means of understanding how knowledge is accumulated, regulated, and used. For example, the child's use of egocentric speech may in part be attributed to his lack of developing a context which specializes in assessing the audience impacts of his speech, or if he has such a context, his lacking the means of integrating its knowledge with those of his discourse formation context. From a psychiatric perspective, contexts are important in that a patient's confusions over his own behaviors and thoughts may be attributable to his not having developed the appropriate contexts (e.g., an introspective context), or, having such a context, lacking the means of regulating its knowledge with other contexts. Hence, much of the work that a therapist performs is in instructing a patient on how to reorganize his contexts to achieve a more conflict-free and manageable existence. For the patient's experience of himself as many different persons, some of whom have little regard for his own interest, can be understood in terms of his having many different contexts which have disparate opinions as to how he should function. The fact that he is unable to do what he wants can be attributed to the fact that those contexts, whose interrupt programs exert critical control, function on a different set of premises than those of the context he wishes to exert control. In a very real way the therapist reprograms the patient by providing him with an introspective context whereby he can identify his internal contexts and control structures. Once he can access these troublesome contexts, the patient can then create new contexts and interrupt programs whereby he can better regulate his behavior.

What is relevant for treatment, therefore, is the organization of contexts and their interrupt programs in terms of their accessibility to one another and their general ability to function effectively and adaptively. One way to create more adaptive cognitive structures and processes is to increase the knowledge of the introspective context and, in this sense, make the unconscious conscious. But if this knowledge is only a function of that context, and if it is not linked into other contexts, little is accomplished. Consequently, learning must be effected in many different contexts, some of which stand in isolation from one another, and therefore represent differently conscious selves. It is the lack of awareness of these other selves or contexts that makes it difficult for the patient to regulate his own behavior, for as he understands himself, he is a single entity. This awareness comes by his being able to establish a context (ego?) which can effectively monitor and regulate the operations of the other contexts so that they act in a manner consistent with its criteria. In other words, this context permits the other contexts to do what they wish as long as certain conditions are not violated. However, when these conditions are violated, this context is aware of it and can interrupt processing with the appropriate corrective measures.*

A discussion of our own representation of mental organization might help illustrate the importance of contexts in studying cognition. In analyzing the patient's transcripts, I noticed that the patient would on a number of occasions initiate a sentence, hesitate, start another sentence, and then question why she stated what she did. It was apparent that the criteria she used to initiate the sentence were different than those she used after she produced it. Similarly, she seemed to have another set of criteria once she reflected on her entire statement. This I concluded was due to the different ways in which she processed similar concepts in different contexts. For what was acceptable to MACHIAVELLI, which was more eager to satisfy wants than reality constraints, was not acceptable to CALVIN or CICERO, which were sensitized to the potential negative impacts of the discourse. Consequently, she would start to produce a sentence that met MACHIAVELLI's criterion, but when seen by CALVIN, she would then interrupt herself and either suppress the sentence or state it in a more qualified manner. The evident confusion of her discourse was due to the interrupt programs of different contexts interrupting one another and thereby making it extremely difficult for her to state what she initially wanted to say—the trouble being that each context had its own opinion about how she should speak, and that the CALVIN context in particular did not want her to say anything which she "shouldn't" say. The only way in which she could state what she wanted to say was to set up a context that overrode the CALVIN context. This the therapist attempts to establish by creating a situation in which the patient is free to say anything that comes to mind. In this way the rules under which the CALVIN context operates are neutralized both through their irrelevancy and the trust of the therapist. Once these inhibitions are circumvented, the therapist is in the position to cultivate a dominant context, in this case FREUD, which can then create a more adaptive control structure.

In the simulated discourse episode the patient reflects this ability, for although she initially is unable to speak her mind, she is able to introspect as to why, and achieve an approximate understanding of her confusion. Were her

*The partition of a system into many independent subsystems that are both inherently and collectively stable is still only partially understood, as Ashby's discussion of multistable systems indicates. For, although subsystem independence is desirable, its adaptivity is determined in large measure by external environmental factors, which if themselves unstable, necessitate the intervention of some control mechanism to regulate the subsystem.

introspective programs more developed, she probably could have avoided the whole incident by interrupting the CALVIN programs before they started and thereby state what she needed to say. This, of course, would be an extremely difficult thing for her to do, as she would also have to be aware of the MACHIAVELLI and CICERO programs, as well as be able to identify their operations to a considerable level of detail.

7.24. *Multiple-body interrupts*

We shall not discuss MBIs in terms of their value as computational methods, although this is implicit in our discussion. Rather we shall attempt to demonstrate that the mechanism can be used to model the very complex processes whereby concepts are constructed to solve problems of discourse, understanding, and human interaction. Previously, we noted that present theories of cognition do not give sufficient attention to the problem of conceptual regulation and that such an understanding is essential to developing adequate cognitive models and therapeutic techniques. We shall discuss in detail how MBIs can be used to provide such an understanding or at least begin a dialogue for achieving such an understanding.

To review a bit, MBIs are programs which are entered and removed from contexts and which are not called by another program aware of its presence, but which interrupt processing when particular data patterns are detected. They contain "bodies" that can be used to regulate the order of the firing of the various parts of the MBI and to coordinate their operations with other interrupt programs. Within this model they do all the computation and control all the cognition and discourse generation. The effect of using MBIs and contexts is to create a system which has a highly accessible, modular, and flexible control structure. Taken as models of cognitive processing, MBIs present a model of cognitive processing that is highly decentralized, interactive, and specialized. As pointed out in the previous section, they also imply that awareness or "consciousness" is not a wholly integrated state, but one that varies according to the context in which the MBIs are operative. Hence, a single cognitive system can entertain and believe in many different worlds, some of which are contradictory. The firing of MBIs control which world the state of consciousness is in and direct processing from one context to the next, according to the problem being processed. Because of their role as vehicles of computation and mechanisms of control, their pattern specification and placement within a context is critical to the adaptive capabilities of a cognitive system. For, although the organization and embeddings of conceptual structures do affect a system's ability to perform its cognitive taks, the MBIs are of prime importance, for they construct and deploy concepts. Cognitive theories that focus upon the structures of cognition without identifying the mechanisms by which they are constructed and used miss a critical aspect of cognition. Since cognition is primarily a process of regulation, attempts to change or replace conceptual structures are of dubious therapeutic value, unless the MBIs or the equivalent mechanisms are also altered. More attention should be given, therefore, to the means by which interrupts and similar procedures are used and learned.

The adaptivity or general problem-solving ability of an MBI is affected by a number of parameters. The first parameter is the pattern that it is keyed to fire on, for it is this pattern that determines what the MBI looks at and evaluates. If the pattern is too narrowly or too generally defined, the MBI might not only be incorrect in its operations but, in some cases, may hinder effective computation. To take an example from our transcripts, there is an interrupt program which states that it is not acceptable for the patient to request intercourse with anyone. The fact that this interrupt program fired and is keyed to the rather inclusive variable ''anyone'' creates a great deal of conflict and difficulty for the patient. And, although she has other interrupts that can eventually get around this problem, the fact that it does fire and is keyed to such a general category generates unnecessary problems of control. Were the pattern of the interrupt more specific, it would be far more functional and would not create the conflicts that it does create. Perhaps one of the things that a patient learns is to discriminate between concepts and create interrupt programs that respond to more specific patterns appropriate to the needs of the patient. Censoring interrupts of this type, when keyed to general variables, by and large are not a good thing, as they either block problem-solving activity altogether or severely handicap it. A more adaptive system would have finely discriminatory interrupts keyed to very specific patterns so that a problem could be broken down carefully and therefore be solved more easily. Certainly general patterns have their place, but probably only at a very global level, where the global patterns of problems are relevant and tied to specific patterns.

The second important parameter of a MBIs effectiveness is its placement in a context. As we discussed in Chapter 4, contexts are structured into layers, and, depending upon where placed, an interrupt can be masked from other interrupts or it can be ''watched over.'' It is neither good nor bad to be either masked or exposed, as such criteria are relative to the problem being processed. However, that being said, it probably would be best to have a system so well organized that when malfunctions did arise, they could be quickly identified and corrective action taken. As it is, our modeled patient does not have access to all that is taking place within her head and so must struggle with conflicting interrupt commands. Hence, the ''unconscious'' behavior of this program is reflected through the masking of interrupt programs by their placement in different or masked contexts. Resistance in therapeutic sessions might be attributable to interrupt programs of one context intercepting messages being directed at another. Such programs would be keyed to fire on certain conceptual patterns considered disruptive and thereby prevent their being processed in a different context by other interrupts. The fact that these other interrupts would process these concepts is irrelevant until the censoring interrupts cease their censorship. Therefore, although a person appears to understand a concept that is disruptive by his resisting it, he can only really understand it when it reaches the resisted context. Until that point, his understanding is not so much unconscious as it is partial or different. Consequently, the placement of interrupts in context is determined or should be determined by how computationally effective it is to have them watch over one another. In those cases where they are computationally effective, there is no reason why they should not be unconscious; in fact, in some cases, this may be an advantage, because it would avoid problems arising from excessive interdependency. One can only guess what the best cognitive control structure would be, but it seems reasonable that in general a system would benefit from having a context that could monitor key cognitive operations and be so equipped to correct these failures. FREUD appears to be such a context.

Another important feature of MBIs is the organization of their bodies and the programs they contain. The knowledge contained in these bodies is process knowledge, and how this knowledge is ordered and coordinated can be quite important in solving a problem. For example, a child building an arch must learn which building blocks to select, the order in which they are combined, and the difficult task of placement. If he does not properly sequence and coordinate the processes by which he constructs the arch, he may deem the task to be impossible. In our psychological model, procedures or multiple interrupt programs are the knowledge processes that are used to solve the problem. In this case, the child must have MBIs with sufficient bodies to be able to coordinate their firing in the solution of the problem. If the child were imaginative in his solution of the problem, he would use interrupt programs from another context and use, for example, Scotch tape to hold the blocks together. Although the latter solution might not be the best one, it demonstrates another facet of MBI programs—that the selection of the Scotch tape might be due to the child's ability to utilize suggestions taken from other MBI programs in other contexts. However, if the child then decided that the Scotch tape was not such a good idea after all, he could note this fact and INHIBIT the program that offered that solution.

The same processes are involved at "higher" levels of cognition, except that instead of being directed toward explicit physical actions they work with conceptual structures. Working with conceptual structures is not in itself a more complex activity than working with blocks, except that concepts often have complex histories and consequently involve many more operations to process. Consider our patient in the simulated discourse situation. She wants to make a somewhat indiscrete request of her therapist, which she realizes she should not do. She then tries to figure out how she might create a situation in which the request would not be indiscrete and thereby permissible. She does this by using MBIs in very much the same way as the child used them. She thinks about different suggestions returned by other MBIs and selects the suggestion that has the best chance of working. One can easily see how the coordination between MBIs, the ordering of the firing of their bodies, and their location in contexts could be most important in therapeutic situations, as patients often lack the computational competence to deal with certain types of interactive situations. This is, of course, due to faulty or incomplete learning and is therefore reflected in the manner in which concepts are *processed*. For, very often they are not aware of the processing alternatives available to them and therefore become locked into dysfunctional processing modes. It would not suffice to inform a patient that meta-communication is taking place in which higher-order logical paradoxes are being inflicted. The patient must be taught how to develop and process conceptual representations of complex problems in a way that provides an intelligible and viable solution. In programming terms, he must either have new bodies added to his existing interrupt programs or be given a new interrupt program that processes the problem situation differently.

The previous comments about correcting aberrant interrupts raises another point about the character of interrupts that might be of psychological interest. MBIs can be added to a system without having to reprogram it. They can either supplement an existing MBI or can supersede it altogether. Of course, to add an interrupt, one must have detailed knowledge about the patterns that fire the existing interrupt program, but once this knowledge is available, the insertion of the program is relatively simple. When extended to psychology, this means that if the context of a disruptive MBI can be identified along with its invocation pattern, treatment techniques might be delivered with far greater accuracy than they are at present. It also implies that learning, and hence knowledge, is not simply accumulative or continuous but often discontinuous, one MBI replacing another.

7.30. COMPARISON OF EXPLANATORY MECHANISMS OF THE MODEL WITH SELECTED THEORIES OF COGNITION AND COMMUNICATION

7.31. *Freud and psychoanalytically based explanations*

With the possible exception of literary and historical criticism, psychiatry (analytic psychiatry in particular) is the discipline most concerned with systematic interpretation of discourse. The patient's discourse is the analyst's data, and the Freudian paradigm is still the model for interpretation. Although the theories of Freud have been bent, twisted, and reformulated to suit the fashions of the times, they remain the principal documents of psychiatry. This is particularly true if modern psychiatric theories are examined at their most basic level of assumption. Here, the Freudian paradigm still retains its hold; the mind is still regarded as being compartmentalized into different levels of consciousness, and "self-understanding" is still the goal of treatment. For these reasons our discussion will focus on Freudian theory. We will, however, discuss only the basic elements of his theory, as an extended discussion is beyond the scope of this volume. Our objectives are twofold: first, to identify some of the epistemological fallacies that underlie the Freudian model of cognition and defense, and second, to show how some of these epistemological and theoretical problems can be resolved, or at least better understood, by applying the programming concepts of our model. Selected Freudian concepts such as condensation, displacement, and projection will be discussed in terms of our model in an effort to demonstrate its relevance to psychiatry. In chapter eight a more detailed account is offered.

When Freud began to develop his early psychological theories, the language of science at that time was physics. It and the biological sciences were the model disciplines of the scientific method, and in emulation of them he formulated his initial theory of psychological process in his *Metapsychology* of 1895 (Freud 1966). In this work he attempted to provide a neurological model to explain the higher mental processes. This model was to be the scientific basis on which his theories were to rest and, like others of his time, he sought to explain psychological phenomenon in terms of a common, elemental, and essentially biological cause. Lacking the scientific procedures to describe complex symbolic behaviors, he sought to reduce their complexity by seeing in them a simple, instinctual, and biological cause. In so doing, his explanations often assume a reductive and moralistic air. Consequently, an odd mixture of Darwinism and Victorian morality permeates his theories; since human psychological processes were biologically based and derived from the instincts of lower forces of life, they were sexual in character, and hence at variance with man's higher, "rational" powers.

This dualism of instinct and reason, like his others (life and death, pleasure principle and reality principle, and affective and nonaffective), are a consequence of an approach that uses a reductive or genetic mode of explanation. They have their origins in a Cartesian mind-and-body dualism, which Freud, as did others of his time, attempted to heal by reducing mind to body. However, in accepting one half of the dualism, he was never able to escape the other, hence the proliferations of higher–lower, either–or dichotomies in his theories. Although this type of Manicheanism may have been unavoidable then, it is unnecessary now. Cybernetic descriptions which model the information-processing behaviors of organisms and mechanism require no such division. Instead, they provide a common language for modeling both cognitive and biological processes. In programming languages such as CONNIVER, there are representational conventions to describe both motor and mental activities. This capability is significant, as it effectively dispels the criticism of those, especially analysts, who argue that such techniques are "rational" and hence incapable of any "irrational" or affective behaviors. For example, robots have been developed using LISP-based languages to model motor as well as cognitive behavior (Becker 1973; Winograd 1971). In light of these developments, it would appear that the affective motor–rational dichotomy is at best a red herring, as both processes can be represented by a similar convention. Consequently, the genetic explanations of the Freudian epistemology are not only unnecessary but tend to prejudice treatment toward an overly historical perspective, and thereby overlook many of the positive benefits that come with teleological and phenomenological approaches to human behavior. Cybernetics is one means by which such approaches can be developed in more rigorous and scientific terms.

Even Freud was not altogether satisfied with his own genetic epistemology and often found that his greatest insights were gained initially through literature and introspection. One of his great gifts was the manner in which he could translate these almost literary insights into the language and metaphors of his model of psychic processes. In the following account, he effectively makes this translation:

> The unconscious system may be therefore compared to a large anteroom, in which the various mental excitations are crowding upon one another like individual beings. Adjoining this is a second, smaller apartment, a sort of reception room, in which consciousness resides. But on the threshold between the two stands a personage with the office of door keeper, who examines the various mental excitations, censors them, and denies them admittance to the reception room when he disapproves of them. . . . The excitations in the unconscious are not visible to consciousness, which of course is in the other room, so to begin with they remain unconscious. When they have pressed forward to the threshold and have been turned back by the door keeper, they are "incapable of being conscious"; we call them repressed. But even those excitations which are allowed to pass over the threshold do not necessarily become conscious; they can become so only if they succeed in attracting the eye of consciousness. This second chamber therefore may be suitably called the preconscious sytem (Freud 1969, p. 260).

Notice that the processes described in this passage could not be characterized in other than metaphorical terms. Yet, notice also the great similarity between his notion of the unconscious and its censors and our notion of CALVIN and its interrupt censors; also, compare his comments on the invisibility of mental excitations to our previous discussion of interrupts. Despite these pleasing similarities, there are significant differences. In Freud's model, the mind is organized into three sections, unconscious, preconscious, and conscious, which, in turn, have a linear relationship to one another. The excitations begin in one location and attempt to move upward, whereas in our model they can originate in a number of different contexts and can move any which way. However, like the Freudian model, most motivations come from a single context, CALVIN, but unlike the Freudian model, these motivations can originate elsewhere and are not necessarily invisible to other contexts. Another important difference is that, whereas the unconscious seems to be qualitatively different from the conscious, in that it is the reservoir of instinctual desires and hence the source of all "true" motivation, our contexts are not qualitatively distinct. A consequence of the Freudian position is that all legitimate—in the sense of being nonmeditated—excitations arise from the unconscious, and all other forms of mental activity are "sublimated" expressions of it. As critics of Freud have noted, his theory of sublimation has its problems, as on the one hand it postulates the necessity of sublimation, and on the other, it disavows this possibility. This problem does not arise with contexts, for no context is more fundamental than another, and as centers of control, they can vary in the contents they process. Similarly, the notions of visibility and censorship have a much more precise meaning when used in terms of contexts than they do in the Freudian model. There are numerous ways in which a concept can be censored or an interrupt masked, and presumably the course of the treatment would depend upon these differences. Yet in the Freudian model there is no clear statement of how censorship or masking works, and hence the application of therapeutic techniques can only be crude.

Another aspect of the Freudian model that bears resemblance to the model presented here is the manner in which obsessional and other acts are analyzed. Freud's approach at times is implicitly teleological, as he attempts to explain patient's behaviors in terms of the underlying goals of the behaviors. Unfortunately, and in keeping with his genetic epistemology, he often dismisses many behaviors as "wish fulfillments" or symptoms of substitution, which may be legitimate solutions to cognitive problems. Notice how in the following passage his descriptions of the patient's thought processes resemble the problem-solving orientation of our model. "Think of the obsessive acts of our first patient. This woman has to do without the husband she loved so intensely; on account of his deficiencies and short-comings, she could not share his life. She had to be faithful to him; she could not put anyone in his place. Her obsessional symptom gives her what she so much desired; it exalts her husband, denies, and corrects his deficiencies, above all his impotence. This symptom is fundamentally a wish-fulfillment, in that respect, exactly like a dream" (Freud 1969, p. 263).

This patient's obsessive acts, like our patient's discourse request, is one solution to a difficult problem. Because of a dearth of options—her loving an impotent man and having to be faithful to him—her solution space is so confined as to permit only a fanciful solution. Her problem may not be due so much to her relationship with her husband as it is to her lack of adequate procedures and conceptual structures to find a functional solution. In other words, if she had a more skilled understanding of alternative courses of action, she might find a solution that effectively worked for her. Hence, from our perspective, the erotic origin of her problem is less important than the nature of the procedures and structures she has to resolve this problem. Yet, for Freud, the solution rests with an identification of the erotic origins of the problem.

Yet, by implicitly regarding the mind as a problem-solving mechanism, Freud identified many of the techniques it used to resolve cognitive conflicts. A number of these are similar to the techniques employed by the ERMA program. The three that are most common in the modeled discourse are displacement, projection, and condensation.

Displacement takes place when ERMA decides not to request "intercourse" with the therapist but seeks a substitute goal instrumental to this end. Whereas the Freudian would regard such an act as unconscious and hence qualitatively distinct, in our model there are no such distinctions of level. Rather, this goal differs from other goals only in that it is both thwarted and critical to the patient's well-being. It is unconscious only in the sense that the procedures which generate it are "masked" from those in other contexts.

Projection is present in the model through the impact-sensitive programs located in CALVIN, MACHIAVELLI, and CICERO. However, projection is less a mechanism than a type of deduction about an audience's anticipated responses. ERMA uses the same mechanisms to project onto the therapist false inferences as correct ones. The difference is that the projection is ERMA's belief, not the therapist's, and in this case is incorrect. Its problem, in other words, is one of incorrect attribution.

Condensation is a more difficult process to observe, but it, like projection, appears to be less a pathological mechanism per se than the consequence of inadequate cognitive processing. For example, the concept intercourse, as used by the patient, is probably a deeply embedded concept which has meanings beyond those conventionally given. In this program, the generic concept is given a realization that was inadequate to express both to the patient and the therapist all the meanings—hence, its "condensed" character.

Although it is my belief that many of the programming concepts that have been used are more precise and powerful explanatory mechanisms than those found in the Freudian model, it is not my contention that this model has equal status as a systematic theory of mental processes. Quite the contrary, our discussion is intended only to be illustrative of some of the ways in which a computer model such as ERMA can be used to make inferences similar to those made by psychoanalysts.

7.32. *Piaget's genetic psychology*

Nowhere has Jean Piaget developed a systematic theory of discourse interpretation and composition, yet his work has considerable relevance on both epistemological and experimental grounds to the theory and model presented here. Like psychoanalytic theory, his work cannot be adequately summarized here. Instead, I will concentrate upon those aspects of his theories that concern problems of language use and cognition. Specifically, discussion will focus upon Piaget's general theoretical framework and his reliance upon algebraic models to both describe and explain cognitive and linguistic development.

Piaget is one of the few major psychologists to develop a theory of cognitive development that is both comprehensive and grounded in a formal theory. While his experimental methods have from time to time come under attack for a lack of replicability and rigor, his theories and methods, nonetheless, have been instrumental in shaping virtually a whole tradition of thinking about cognitive processes and their development. Of particular interest are his notions and those of his associates regarding "egocentric" communication and speech. Although this term is no longer used by Piaget, "in deference to the criticisms from the many psychologists who are still not familiar with the practice in the exact sciences of using a term only in accordance with the definitions proposed" (Piaget and Inhelder 1969, p. 61), it will be used here to mean those speech acts which inappropriately employ speech criteria based upon the experience of the self when speaking to another. Flavell et al. (1968) are quite specific in their definition of egocentric communication:

> (1) *S* (speaker) cognizes *X* (data) and covertly codes them so that they are meaningful and 'communicable' to himself.
> (2) *S* sends *L* (listener) a message about *X*. The message is in all important respects unrecoded, that is, it is essentially a simple externalization without modification of his private coding and is hence an egocentric communication (Flavell et al. 1968, p. 8).

In citing Piaget's earlier writings (Piaget 1926), Flavell et al. attribute egocentric communication "to the extent that the child fails to discriminate those role attributes of the other which are relevant to the sort of message the child should send to the other in the latter's role as a listener, to that extent is the message likely to be ill-adapted to the other's informational needs and hence inadequately communicative" (Flavell et al. 1968, p. 8). The recognition that rule differentiation, the ability to take another's point of view, is essential to the development of mature speech behaviors is not striking in itself. However, the fact that differences in speech behaviors can be related to differences in cognitive and linguistic development and that these in turn have some prospect at least of being formally described and explained within the same general theoretical framework makes the notion of egocentricism both interesting and important.

Indeed, what Piaget has to offer, or any other psychologist or linguist, for that matter, beyond commonplace or obvious observation is the ability to represent and analyze cognitive and speech data in such a way that nontrivial and systematic descriptions and explanations can be made. Piaget's notions of reversibility/irreversibility, centrism/decentrism, preoperation/operation go a considerable way toward this goal. They falter, however, when they are pushed to account for the processes and mechanisms involved in the actual formulation and expression of communicative acts. Lacking the means by which to discuss these processes, Piaget and his associates are forced to rely upon secondary indicators of cognitive behavior and competence. The notion of complexity is invoked to explain differences in the developmental abilities of children; egocentric speech is less complex than socialized speech.

But, is this always the case? It is if Flavell et al.'s definition is adhered to, because the direct expression of "internal thoughts" without regard to the audience is certainly more easy to accomplish than discourse shaped to the needs and background and role of the listener. However, if one goes one step further and identifies egocentric speech with incorrect attributions, then, indeed, we are all egocentric speakers and the distinction loses its force. In the simulated discourse episode, for example, the 31-year-old speaker is plagued by her continual false attributions, but it is doubtful, at least at a cognitive level, that she is underdeveloped, for she is quite capable of viewing experience from many points of view.

The point is that, in lacking a means to characterize the processes and structures involved in the formation and expression of communication acts, Piaget and his associates are forced to fall back upon abstract normative standards of cognitive and discourse processes. Different stages are identified according to degree of complexity, and these levels of complexity are in turn related to algebraic operations. The difficulty with this approach is that the notion of complexity is too blunt a tool to account for the differences in cognitive and linguistic performance, unless it is possible to show why the particular process is more complex. To assume that since more operations or computations are involved in a set of discourse acts, or that since these operations formally presuppose other operations, they are indeed more complex and advanced, especially in a normative developmental sense, is to my mind suspect. It is suspect because the cognitive and linguistic performance of a speaker, especially a young speaker, is strongly affected by the context and character of the discourse task. Piaget's approach only weakly acknowledges this fact and attempts to theorize it away by stressing the importance of general rules of mental operation in different stages of cognitive and linguistic development. However, my suspicion is that if one wants to understand how actual speakers initiate, form, and express discourse, these rules, as well as this general formalist approach, are too limited.

One of the first difficulties is that Piaget's model lacks any precise means for accounting for the microprocesses involved in cognition and speech. If the simulation model is any analogue of what people do, then qualitative, that is, content or pattern-specific properties are extremely important in understanding speech performance. Moreover, since speakers can be inconsistent and can exhibit differences in performance, even for the same types of tasks, something like the notion of contexts is going to have to be included in a theory of cognitive and linguistic development. It may be that part of the decentering process involved in development is context differentiation. If this is the case, it needs to be distinguished from the notion of inappropriate attribution, which is an altogether different type of cognitive process.

The difficulty with Piaget, therefore, in this respect is not with his general theoretical notions—they are teleological, interactive, and symbolically oriented—but with the type of explanation that a genetic and an algebraically based psychology is trying to provide. By attempting to apply principles of logic and algebra to the description of cognitive activity, Piaget removes himself from a truly teleological and symbolic analysis and, in effect, becomes committed to a method of description that is not in the last analysis teleological. As Minsky (1974) has effectively argued, efforts to describe human cognitive activities in terms of various systems of logic are ill advised, for human symbolic activity, whether in problem solving or in discourse formation, is often inconsistent and always purposeful. Strictly formal approaches miss this point and focus on those operations or capabilities that are important for the formal system but which for the most part are of lesser importance for human thinkers and speakers. Moreover, formal theories of this type are so aggregated, that is, they condense so much information about how the actual processes work, that they tend to be too abstract for actual descriptions. Attempts to formalize Piaget's theories by Osherson (1974) and others testify to this fact. Osherson's comments on his own efforts in this direction are especially to the point: "However, construction of new theories of this nature will probably be counterproductive, regardless of the accuracy of their predictions. The approach exemplified in this volume seems to the writer unredeemably misconceived" (Osherson 1974, p. 141).

Therefore from the standpoint of the theory and model developed here, Piaget's work in a general theoretical sense is quite close. But when one gets down to the actual type of description being sought and the type of formal means used to make that description, they are quite different. The ERMA model represents an attempt to understand the discourse formation and production process in some depth, and although no general claims can be made about it per se, it does operationalize a theory of discourse. Hence, the program is in part the testing of a theory. Piaget comes from a different tradition, and consequently does not seem to be so concerned with the description of the actual processes involved in discourse cognition and production; rather, his concern is with more general theoretical statements. However, it can be questioned whether it is possible to make these statements with any empirical or explanatory force when his theories and models are incapable of describing the actual processes and structures involved in cognitive and linguistic performance. Although it is often argued that a model which describes human abilities need not have direct connection to the internal processes that account for these abilities, such, perhaps, as Piaget's model, the description so obtained is both weak and inevitably limited.

7.33. *Bateson's cybernetic theory of communication and cognition*

Of the three theories discussed in this chapter, Bateson's perspective is closest to that of the theory presented herein. He, too, uses a cybernetic framework in which to interpret human communication and interaction, and he uses regulation and goal direction as a key feature of human cognition. Yet, in discussing Bateson's theory of logical types and the "double bind," we will attempt to show that despite his concern with regulatory processes, his theories of communication, particularly his application of logic, are misleadingly static and metaphorical. We shall then offer alternative explanations of some of the communication problems that Bateson identified. In so doing, I hope to demonstrate that programming languages such as CONNIVER not only offer a formalism suitable for representing many of the processes discussed metaphorically in Bateson's work, but through such a formalism, more precise, detailed, and, hopefully, more accurate theories of human cognition and communication are possible.

Bateson observed that many psychiatric patients, particularly schizophrenics, confused the literal and metaphorical meanings of messages and that this confusion was often due to their having to repeatedly process contradictory commands. For example, the wife who complains about her husband's passivity and imperiously asks him, "Why won't you dominate me?", is giving him conflicting messages. If the husband acquiesces to her demands and tries to dominate her, he is only capitulating to her demands, and if he does not, he is not being suitably dominant. Either way he loses. If this communication pattern is continually repeated, and if it is structured in such a way that the individual cannot effectively escape it, then, Bateson argues, schizophrenia can result. He terms such a communication pathology a "double bind" and attempts to explain it in terms of Russell and Whitehead's theory of logical types. This theory states that a logical class cannot be a member of the class it describes; for example, the class of all chairs is logically distinct from the member of its class; a desk chair is not equivalent to the class of desk chairs. Although such an observation may seem obvious, Bateson argues that many mental patients confuse the name with the thing being named, hence are unable to communicate or even process information properly. Bateson further contends that schizophrenics consistently commit this error as a defense against conflicting and potentially punitive messages.

He cites an example from normal discourse in which this takes place. "For example, one day an employee went home during office hours. A fellow employee called him at his home and said lightly, 'Well, how did you get *there*?' The employee replied, 'By automobile' " (Bateson 1972, p. 209). The employee responded literally because he sensed an accusation in his friend's question, and in this way was able to avoid responding to the intended meaning of the message. Bateson contends that unlike "normal" individuals, schizophrenics continually feel accused and eventually identify the metaphorical meaning of a message from its literal content. He explains such discourse behavior as an example of incorrect logical typing, as it entails a confusion of communicative levels, which, Bateson contends, is similar to that of the class/membership confusion in logic. Although it is not difficult to see the analogy between a confusion over levels of meaning in a message and a confusion of a member of a class with the class itself, it is difficult to see how the theory of logical types actually explains the discourse behavior he cites in his example. In this, as in other examples he uses, the problem of communication does not appear to be one of logic but of control. The reason the employee responds literally is not because he made an error in his propositional logic but because he did not want to acknowledge to his friend that he left work early. By responding literally, he in effect took "control" away from his friend and either neutralized it or acquired it himself. If one attempts to apply the theory of logical types rigorously to this example, one quickly becomes confused. If the friend's question is metaphorical, does that mean it is a class or a member of a class? Is a metaphor a class? Is a literal message a member of a class? Which class, the class of "how did you get there?" What defines that class?

Obviously, Bateson's use of logic is not literal but itself metaphorical, and, although it is helpful in identifying some of the more general forces at play in such interactive situations, it is misleading in its presumptive use of logic and the rigor it implies. Furthermore, it displaces attention from the multiple regulatory forces at work in discourse to an artificial notion of logical structure. It is our belief that this type of behavior can be precisely described without resource to a metaphorical logic, for the distinction that Bateson seems to be making between literal and metaphorical discourse seems very similar to the distinction made in Chapter 3 between fixed and negotiated discourse.

Fixed discourse is discourse in which interpretations are standardized by a publicly acknowledged code. Its rules and interpretations are not subject to negotiation but constitute the very structures upon which the communicability of the language depends. Every speaker of English, for example, has a firm grasp of the use of syntax and knows the probable interpretation of a wide class of standard words. What restriction the adoption of the rules, categories, concepts, and the fixed-discourse code may entail for a speaker is never personal and seldom known, as it constitutes the bedrock of his view of the world. Negotiated discourse, on the other hand, deals with intended rather than stated meanings. Although constructed of the same rules and words as fixed discourse, its meaning is conveyed through their unique and rather idiosyncratic arrangement rather than through their standard use. The objective of N-discourse is to get beyond the limitations of standardized interpretations to express thoughts, feelings, and ideas that are unique and novel to the speaker and listener. Only N-discourse can be personal and affective, because only its meanings are tailored to achieve a nonstandard effect on its audience. While scientific discourse, as the paradigm of F-discourse, can be directed to a specific audience and deploys words with unique meanings, it always attempts to be explicit and consistent. N-discourse has no such strictures. Its meanings shift according to the intentions of the speaker and the understanding of the listener. Moreover, unlike F-discourse, it can often be controlling, as the creation of nonstandardized meanings often requires the resolution of conflicting goals and interpretations. How these conflicts are resolved naturally depends upon the competence of those involved, their social status, and their willingness to acknowledge one another's points of view. It is not difficult to see why a speaker–listener lacking competence, social position, and a cooperative audience would avoid N-discourse and attempt to confine his discourse to F-type discourse. Apparently, many schizophrenics are just such people and avoid situations of "negotiated interpretation" by conversing in only the more impersonal and, in many cases, caricatured terms of F-discourse.

To see how we might use our model to describe and simulate some of the discourse behavior of a schizophrenic, let us take as an example a schizophrenic patient Bateson used in describing his double-bind theory. The questions we shall attempt to address are: How would our program have to be modified to produce this discourse? and What theoretical implication would this have on the organization and behavior of the patient's own cognitive mechanisms? Obviously, our discussion will have to be conjectural, but it is intended to be suggestive of the manner in which programs can be used to describe cognitive behaviors and thereby to generate new theoretical interpretations of schizophrenic behaviors.

The simulated discourse behavior was that of a neurotic, who although conflicted in her desires and her ability to express them appropriately, nonetheless was aware, or could be made aware, in part at least, of the thoughts and feelings that governed her actions and speech. You will recall that her discourse is marked by numerous interruptions of conflicting internal messages (I want intercourse–you cannot have intercourse), and that, failing to express her feelings or thoughts directly, she sought indirect means of expression and manipulation. One of the principal barriers to her effective self-regulation was formed by the CALVIN interrupt censors. These censors reflect her experience and learning during her earlier years and, from a cybernetic perspective, constitute the regulative effect of her environment upon her thoughts and actions. For example, the interrupt that prevents her from expressing her desire for intercourse is an internalized command (superego?) acquired either directly or indirectly from her attempts to express such a desire. In other words, it is a simulated representation of her environments, in this case her therapist's reaction to her request. Whereas such censoring mechanisms have a powerful and controlling effect on this patient and lead to defensive behaviors (attempted control of the billing situation and highly qualified discourse), they do not affect her basic processing of concepts. Unlike the schizophrenic, she knows the difference, or can learn to know the difference, between a substituted request (the billing arrangement) and her actual request (desire for intercourse). Although using many of the same types of defensive mechanisms, the schizophrenic apparently cannot make, or is unwilling to make, the distinction, as the following passage taken from Bateson shows. "A patient, for example, has a central notion that "something moved in space" and that that is why he cracked up. I somehow, from the way he spoke about "space," got an idea that space is his mother and said so. He said, "No, space is *the* mother." I suggested to him that she might be in some way the cause of his troubles. He said, "I never condemned her." At a certain point he got angry, and he said—this is verbatim—"If we say she has movement in her because of what she caused, we are only condemning ourselves" (Bateson 1972, p. 195).

One of the remarkable features of these statements is the extraordinary degree to which they are abstracted and, in that sense, resemble F-discourse. As Bateson properly intuited, a substitution has taken place between "space" and "mother," but notice that in contrast to the neurotic, who can distinguish between the substituted or displaced concepts, the schizophrenic equates them, "Space is *the* mother." Without a severe overhaul, our program would never make this equation, as it "knows" the difference between its motivational concepts and those it substitutes to satisfy its censor programs. Evidently, the concepts representing "space" and "mother" have assumed an equivalent use and, hence, meaning. If this is so, it could only result in the most severe disorganization of the patient's cognitive processes and would therefore make conceptual regulation most difficult. Notice also that space is a concept with an objectified and impersonal meaning, whereas mother normally would have strong personal meanings. Yet the patient makes them not only equivalent but insists upon the generic meaning of mother by stressing the article "the." In this manner he makes it a wholly generic concept in our terms and thereby robs it of any personalized meaning normally associated with token concepts. In so doing he exhibits a symptom commonly attributed to schizophrenics—having ill-defined "ego-boundaries."

Why is this the case? Cybernetics tells us that unless a system can effectively regulate against the "disturbances" of its environment, the environment will evidently regulate the system (Ashby 1956). The patient makes this point very clearly when he says, "If we say she had movement in her because of what she caused, we are only condemning ourselves." Unlike the neurotic patient, this individual appears to be internally controlled by his censoring mechanisms. Indeed, they have seemed to have become so generalized and pervasive that they effectively initiate and regulate the majority of his conceptual behaviors. In Freudian terms, this might be described as the superego wholly dominating any ego functions to the point where all regulation is governed by external forces, in this case the mother. Evidently, the only stability available to this poor individual is through the adoption and internalization of these external commands. Any expressions against such commands are so strongly censored and scrutinized for possible clues of counterregulation that they are depersonalized and abstracted into a diverted F-discourse.

A similar point is made by Watzlawick (Watzlawick, Beavin, and Jackson 1967) in their theory of disconfirmation, where they argue that schizophrenics have experienced not the mere rejection of their behaviors but total disconfirmation of their right to self-control. The difference is between telling a child that what he did is "worthless," or telling him that he is "worthless." Although disconfirming statements of this type may be damaging, they only become dehabilitating when, as Bateson points out, they effectively deny self-regulation. This can only come about through the systematic and total frustration of the schizophrenic's self-regulatory efforts.

8 : THE GENERAL THEORY AND PSYCHOTHERAPEUTIC IMPLICATIONS

All men, except fools, have their irrational sides. Who does not believe what his reason will labor in vain to justify? Such belief may have its roots spread through generalizations broader than any specific rational process of which man is conscious. And a man is marked by the character of his suprarational convictions or beliefs or credulous conjectures.—HENRY OSBORN TAYLOR

8.10. OVERVIEW

In previous chapters, we discussed in detail the workings of the ERMA model and in a more general and implicit sense the psychological implications of the model. In this chapter, the essential or core features of the model and theory of discourse cognition and thought will be presented. This is called for because the discussion to this point has not explicitly differentiated between the theory embedded in the model, which in part was specific to the patient being modeled, and the more general theory. In the second section of this chapter, we will center our attention upon the clinical and psychotherapeutic implications of the model. Key concepts from analytic and ego psychology will be discussed in light of the computational model and approach. An argument will be made for the application of computational methods and techniques to the analysis of human symbolic disorders. This argument will be based on the assumption that there is an equivalence between human symbolic behaviors and those of intelligent artifacts, and, by using the more explicit, operational, and integrated methods of artificial intelligence, and computational methodology in general, more effective treatment techniques might be developed.

8.20. TOWARD A GENERAL THEORY OF THINKING AND SPEAKING

One of the values of a theory, and especially of a model, is that it provides a coherent and economical means for organizing and integrating a great deal of knowledge about a given problem area. This I have attempted to do for the ''problem'' of discourse composition, or thinking and speaking. However, the most explicit and carefully worked out part of the theory is contained with the simulation model of the patient, and consequently, it is not altogether clear what parts of the model are specific to that speaker and which parts are regarded as having general application and validity.

At this stage in our limited knowledge of human thought and discourse processes, the sifting out of general theoretical principles or propositions from ad hoc observations or descriptions is by no means an obvious process. The problem is accentuated by the highly variable and idiosyncratic nature of the phenomena we are trying to characterize. I am convinced that except for highly stabilized, commonly shared, and well-worked problem domains (such as those of syntax), individual differences in discourse performance are considerable. What may be a simple, straightforward discourse task for one may prove to be a highly complex and conflicted task for another. Indeed, even for the same individual, a change in the setting of the task may transform what would have been an easy task into a very difficult one. To achieve generality, then, it is necessary to step beyond or outside of the specific task domains or specific content areas and present those processing and representational approaches I regard as the necessary, but perhaps not sufficient, conditions for modeling a natural discourse. In laying out the general properties of the model I am tacitly assuming that not only are these processes or features evident in discourse behavior but that without them discourse cannot be adequately described. In doing so, it is my hope to suggest some general hypotheses from the theory which can be tested empirically.

One of the underlying assumptions of this theory is that the structure and organization of knowledge is set teleologically, and therefore has but the most elemental a priori structure. Consistent with this point of view is the notion that people seldom use or access more information than they need to solve a given problem; certainly additional and relevant knowledge is made available, but only on an ''if needed'' rather than an ''automatic'' basis. This somewhat simple assumption results in a rather different approach to modeling cognition than those which attempt to identify certain basic ''primitive'' linkages, conceptual dependencies, and the like to describe human ''associative nets.'' The hypothesis is that elaborated and well-worked-out knowledge structures follow as a result of well-worked-out and highly used goal sequences. ''How to do'' knowledge becomes knowledge ''about'' only when there is reason to have such knowledge, such as having traveled the particular problem-solving sequence frequently and after a program has then abstracted that knowledge into a kind of taxonomical map about the relationships between significant concepts. The knowledge encoded upon that ''map'' is ordered according to its particular usefulness for a given set of tasks and is invoked when it might be of help in solving a particular problem.

This contention that knowledge structures are teleologically derived should be a relatively easy proposition to test. It would suggest that those people who are relatively inexperienced in a given problem area (teleological sequence) would not have effectively organized knowledge structures. For example, people who do not drive or who travel very little, often have a very difficult time forming mental road maps of where they are. Only when it is useful for them to have this information do they then start to make the necessary connections and form their own internal road maps. Indeed, they may be as slow as some current computer programs in forming the requisite associations, and only after they had traveled around a bit and gotten lost and irritated do they form higher-order relational maps to organize their search. A theory which contends that relational knowledge is given a priori would predict that there should not be significant differences in the search times between, in this case, the driver and nondriver. It is hard for me to see how that could be so, but that seems to follow from a strong a priori approach to mental organization. It might be more instructive to determine for which tasks there are no differences between the "novice" and the "expert."

This teleological orientation to the representation of knowledge structures makes it possible to account for the differences between fixed and negotiated conceptual structures and operations. As discussed in some detail in Chapter 4, concepts acquire their meaning through use, and while having common or generic uses, can in the course of their processing be modified to acquire token meanings through the addition and removal of indicators and property lists. Therefore, although token concepts may share a common pattern with related token concepts, for example, (2. TOKEN #BILL), (16. TOKEN #BILL), and in some cases be used interchangeably by a program, they can also have different sets of indicators and properties, and hence different meanings. Some of these meanings and uses may be unique to the particular individual and therefore cannot be readily expressed or represented in terms of some normative or fixed set of conventions. Only in those problem domains which are well traveled and successfully interactive with other people are there fixed conceptual structures whose private and public meanings are similar. One of the great methodological failings of some psychological and artificial intelligence research is to treat these fixed structures or processes as being "given" or innate rather than the product of some more elementary interactive process.

The extent to which an individual has evolved well-developed fixed knowledge structures, then, should be a rather strong indicator of the extent of his or her social competency. However, such a measure or indicator would not tell you whether the individual is successfully coping with his or her environment, for the "teleological well-being" of the individual is dependent upon his or her capacity to manipulate these structures to his or her own ends. Language provides a valuable means for studying this phenomena, for it is through the thematic restructuring of the clause and the topical ordering of the discourse that the negotiated meanings of the individual speaker are able to surface and be effective. If the individual is unable to realize his intents through the given fixed conventions, which may vary culturally, socially, and familially, or devise ways of getting around these constraints, then even though he may exhibit a social competence, he may at the same time be failing to communicate or express his own needs. If the division between fixed and negotiated meanings is very great, that is, there are no obstensible means open for negotiated expressions, the two may evolve in isolation from one another. In other words, the individual would evolve highly private meanings and terms which have no overt public expression. This difference, I suggest, would manifest itself in discourse idiosyncrasies and difficulties, such as abrupt transitions in style, discontinuities in topic formation, rigidity of composition, and lack of differentiation between the psychological subject (see Halliday 1967) and the "grammatical" subject.

Another pivotal assumption of the theory is the notion that knowledge is divided up into different contexts and that as a consequence, intentionality, as represented by programs within these contexts, can be multiple and in conflict. This position argues strongly against the notion that humanlike discourse can be generated by a system that has a singular set of goals which it pursues quite linearly and steadfastly. Although such a system might produce recognizable discourse, it would not, I contend, be a particularly useful model of human thought processes, for the remarkable feature of human cognition, so well illustrated in the transcripts of the simulated episode, is its multiple, independent, and often contradictory nature. Different beliefs propagate in different contexts, and it is the difficult task of the speaking subject to reconcile these different points of view. Cognitive control is transferred through the sending of concepts from one context to another. It is not an omniscient presence but rather like a spotlight that travels back and forth, up and down, until all that needs to be seen, or can be seen, has been seen. One might argue that the path this "spotlight" travels should exhibit certain regularities and that some contexts would also precede others on the travel log. In certain trivial instances, I think that this is fair to say: the realization of discourse does not proceed without intentions and concepts. We cannot readily speak without thinking; we need something to stimulate and direct our realization process. On the other hand, since knowledge can be so widely distributed according to this theory, the sequence of processing is most likely highly variable and goal dependent.

However, given this caveat, it is reasonable to assume that "native thinkers and speakers" evolve similar global strategies for acting upon those common goals that entail some social response. The first step in the sequence is, of course, the selection of a primary goal for action. This can come about in essentially two ways: through consultation of a special list of goals set aside or earmarked for action, or by a survey of a given context in which various goals have not been satisfactorily achieved. How the goals get on a particular list or how processing priorities are set is not readily clear to me, for goals can be changed or substituted throughout a teleological process, and consequently what was a top priority at one point may become a low-priority item at another. Of course, if the processing sequences are in synchrony, this does not occur. But I suspect that in highly complex, novel human problem-solving environments, such synchrony is hard to achieve. It would be tempting to assume that those goals linked to a biological drive would have top priority, but it is more likely that through learning and acculturation, biological goals can be displaced or overridden by symbolic or cultural goals. Therefore, the position here is that the primacy of a goal is set symbolically or phenomenologically by the speaker–actor's understanding of what is important. Only in extreme cases of deprivation is the primary goal setting innate or biological in any sense.

In the computer simulation of the patient, the first phase began in the CALVIN context, and although the "logic" of this context would most certainly vary from individual to individual, the types of considerations addressed in this context would, I contend, be fairly constant. Before acting upon a goal, the initial concern is generally over the acceptability of that goal; does its completion result in any damage? Does it violate a "protection" condition? Such concerns may seem to indicate an unnecessarily conservative view of human thought and action, but it seems reasonable to assume that for most actors, especially those who have gotten their hands burned, so to speak, the initial consideration is one of possible disbenefit. Of course, considerations of acceptability depend upon the setting of the discourse act and, for those settings which are relatively innocuous, acceptability criteria would be minimal.

Although a concern over "acceptability" or feasibility may be relatively uniform for most speaker–actors in the initial context, the types of explanations given for acceptability or unacceptability will be highly variable. We cannot simply assume that the first consideration will always be for one's self but rather for those effects that the individual has learned are most threatening or important. Hence, his first concern may be for another person or for the maintenance of an abstract code of conduct. On the other hand, it may be that the reasons given for a particular goal being unacceptable may be insufficient given the importance of the primary goal. In other words, other programs would override the objections and act on the goal anyway. Conditions of extreme need or concern could result in such overrides. In any event, these types of concern seem to be dealt with in the initial phases of action realization. Since these initial concerns often deal with actions that are highly significant for the individual and often entail "ethical judgments," they were identified with the CALVIN context. However, it should be noted that the connotations of this term are specific to the beliefs of the modeled patient and are not to be identified with the initial phase in general.

The second major phase in achieving a discourse act involves figuring out ways of resolving those problems or constraints that might have arisen in the initial context. If no such constraints exist, the process is relatively straightforward. The procedures involved in this phase appear to be relatively neutral with respect to means and hence were placed within MACHIAVELLI. In a sense, programs in this context are charged with the responsibility of "getting things done," although what they produce is ultimately subject to the final approval of the CALVIN context. They are, in effect, technicians of means, and, although they may oversee the realization process and control the flow of concepts between various contexts, they do not have final control of what is stated. The types of indicators that these programs work with are different in kind from those in the CALVIN context—principally operational and informational indicators as against "affective" indicators. Hence, the general concern of the MACHIAVELLI programs is to see how a particular goal can be achieved. In making this determination they are concerned with the various impacts of a given discourse act and, consequently, are able to get around these impacts by restructuring the act in such a way as to increase its likelihood of success. This restructuring takes place by the addition of special indicators such as POS-EMPHASIS, NEG-EMPHASIS, and the like. In order for these indicators to be added, there first has to be a simulated representation of the effects of a given act upon an audience. First the reactions of the audience are determined and recorded, *then* programs add the corrective indicators and concepts. This triadic process of first trying out an idea or act, getting reactions to it from "interested parties," and then suggesting correctives is another essential component of this theory of cognition and discourse formation. It is especially apparent in the MACHIAVELLI context, in which the concepts are restructured according to anticipated effect or impact. In terms of discourse formation and generation, it strongly argues that the thematic structuring of the clause and the sequencing of the discourse in general is conceptually determined and governed by a continual concern over anticipated impacts. Notice, too, that in the program, contents are added as whole constituents and not "generated" in any sense, and that some of these constituents are, in effect, words. It may be argued that this is "cheating," that is, that words should not be where concepts are, but the position here is that speaker–thinkers treat words as concepts and that in the process of composition, lexical constituents are inserted or added conceptually as they are needed to achieve a particular audience effect.

The third phase of processing represents a change between thinking about something, that is, entertaining different ways of achieving a given goal, and actually deciding to achieve that goal through expression. At this point, thinking ceases to be just thinking and becomes thinking about speaking. In the computer program this is achieved by sending a concept into the CICERO context and making it a STATE concept. During this phase, expressions are assessed in terms of their appropriateness for the intended audience. The criteria here are more "reality-oriented" and sensitive to social norms than they are in the MACHIAVELLI context. By forming STATE concepts it is possible to get a different set of reactions to the same concept—which is to say that reactions to a spoken concept differ from reactions to a "thought" concept. From a processing point of view, this phase and context is important because it acts as an interface between cognitive operations and linguistic operations. Whether this phase is sufficiently important or uniform to constitute a separate identity from the MACHIAVELLI context or from the REALIZATION context, I find it difficult to say. Nonetheless, the distinction between thinking and thinking about speaking seems to be a valuable one and, for modeling purposes, a necessary one.

The next phase is the REALIZATION phase, which is very much dependent upon the properties of the grammar described in Chapter 5. While the actual programming of this process was the most complex within the general model, and not without its problems, these problems appear to be more technical than theoretical. Since the realization process is well understood for most speakers, it was treated as a well-organized and relatively autonomous process. However, the general or overall structure of the realization process seems to be set by the organization of the conceptual structures. Words or phases are realized as they are generated from STATE concepts; hence, bracketing of the concept, in turn, effects the bracketing of words. This becomes important when the STATE concepts are returned to the CALVIN context for final approval, for programs in that context evaluate the STATE concepts as they are presented to them in various packages, not necessarily as a complete sentence. The correspondence between the bracketing of concepts and that of linguistic constituents may have significant theoretical implications, because it suggests, and indeed the modeling effort depended upon it, that word groupings reflect conceptual groupings. In other words, the discourse stream is as smooth as the cognitive processes that underlie it, and its segmentation is an indirect reflection of different conceptual groupings.

The final phase of discourse realization occurs in the CALVIN context, where formed sentences and phrases are scrutinized for expression. The theoretical point here is that we, as speakers, make last-minute checks on our completed expressions to see if they may have any ill effects. In the model these assessments were made according to criteria that were specific to the particular speaker. However, all speakers have last-minute monitors on their statements, especially if the situation is a stressful one or the problem situation a novel one. Perhaps when we are speaking with someone we know, about a topic we know well, we may bypass these monitors. But the more likely explanation is that the monitors are not active simply because the statements are sufficiently well tried so as not to invoke their interruption. In any case, it is apparent from the transcripts used for the modeling effort that complete utterances are formed and can be censored at the last moment. This fact alone seems to require an approach to modeling discourse production which distinguishes between the censoring of concepts and the censoring of formed, but yet to be expressed, utterances.

8.21. ***General propositions of a theory of thinking and speaking***

Below are summarized those basic theoretical propositions upon which the theory of thinking and speaking depends.

1. Knowledge structures are organized according to the goals of the thinker–speaker. These structures appear to be the creation of procedures, and therefore are keyed to their needs in processing. Consequently, there is a minimum of a priori structure, and "effect" descriptions are probably more important at the intermediate level of processing than are simple declarative descriptions. In other words, cognitive processes generally need to know what the effect of a given computation is rather than what it is.

2. Knowledge structures and control structures often exist in isolated contexts and therefore are masked from one another. As a consequence, conflicting criteria can be introduced throughout different stages of the discourse composition process.

3. Concepts have variable meanings and uses, depending upon how and at what level they are evaluated by a procedure. Some of these meanings are set by publicly established (stereotyped) conventions and hence are F-type, whereas others are idiosyncratic to the specific thinker–speaker and are therefore N-type. Consequently, a speaker's awareness of what is being thought or said is not uniform but mobile and isolated, depending upon the level of the pattern match by a procedure and the context of the processing. Moreover, concepts that share a stereotypic meaning (denotative) may have different "lower-level" or more detailed (connotative) meanings.

4. Seen linearly, there are five basic phases involved in the discourse composition and realization process. The first identifies the primary goal which it evalautes for acceptability. Acceptability criteria differ according to the individual and the setting of the discourse act. During this phase, substitute or intermediate goals can be identified, which in turn can determine the selection of a discourse topic. The output of this phase is a kind of blueprint or preliminary plan of what is to be achieved; it does not say how it is to be achieved.

The second phase is charged with figuring out how the blueprint produced during the first phase is to be accomplished. The output of this phase is a kind of conceptual plan of what is to be said. This conceptual plan has been constructed by considering the possible impacts of the contents of the discourse plan upon the intended audience and then providing ways to cope with these possible impacts. In performing these tasks, programs will fill out some of the contents of the discourse (adding additional information where it is needed) and marks those concepts which are potentially troublesome by special indicators, such as POS-EMPHASIS, NEG-EMPHASIS.

The third phase is actually interactive with the second in that it supplies information about audience reactions, which in turn are dealt with during the second phase or in the second context (the process is not obviously a simple linear one). However, once these problems of audience reactions have been dealt with, the programs within this context create STATE concepts and work with higher-order problems of realizing concepts into linguistic expressions.

The fourth, and relatively autonomous, phase is one of discourse realization. It is a top-down process in which conceptual descriptions (ARDS, arguments, indicators, and property lists) are unwound, given syntactic descriptions, lexical realization, and proper placement. Since this is a well-traveled or well-known problem-solving domain for most speakers, it can be represented as a relatively fixed and modular process.

The final stage involves sending back the formed phrase or sentence to the initial context for final consideration. At this point the expression may be suppressed altogether or interjections added to reduce the impact or to "fill the gaps" between pauses. Certainly, the more stressful the setting or the situation of the discourse, the more it will be monitored, as in the simulated episode. For those discourse settings not labeled as significant or potentially threatening, this monitoring process would be greatly reduced.

8.30. CLINICAL APPLICATIONS AND IMPLICATIONS

The purpose of this section is to see how some of the concepts and methods developed by the computational approach in general, and this model in particular, might facilitate, sharpen, and in some cases alter our understanding of those psychological processes described in clinical and analytic psychology. Having used the model to represent the conceptual processes of a patient in psychoanalysis, it seems reasonable to assume that the model should have some bearing on metapsychological principles and techniques of treatment. As subsequent discussion should make clear, there are striking correspondences between the computational approach generally and many notions in clinical psychology, especially analytic psychology. There are, however, significant differences, and it will be argued here that these differences show up most readily when psychoanalytic, as well as ego-based psychological, notions are pushed to account for very specific mental operations. The argument is then made that computational methods are sufficiently broad and flexible to encompass the explanatory concerns of clinical psychology and at the same time sufficiently detailed and operational to provide the necessary terminology and perspective to give therapeutic psychology the methodology it needs to establish a scientific base. In order to make this argument, several key concerns of analytic psychology will be discussed: primary and secondary processes, the nature of self-understanding, and ego and superego functions. Throughout the discussion of each topic, an effort will be made to show points of commonality and then points of difference. An argument will then be made for the strength of the computational approach and the model in light of these differences.

Before discussing these topics, let us first see why the problems confronting cognitive and linguistic processes are similar to those confronting psychotherapy and therefore why the methods developed for the former can be appropriately and forcefully applied to the latter. Unlike the physician, who has a concrete material reference for his observations and diagnoses, the psychiatrist is almost wholly without any physical evidence for his theories and interpretations of psychological behaviors. He is, in effect, dealing with a black box, whose internal operations he cannot observe, but merely speculate about. There is, in other words, no direct means by which he can go from an analysis of the patient's behavioral protocols to the physiological and neurological mechanisms that produced them. This predicament raises some interesting questions about the status of the theories produced to explain psychological behaviors. Since they cannot be validated by direct physical evidence, and since their level of description is quite removed from any observable physiological mechanism, their scientific validity is extremely difficult to establish. The way out of this dilemma, of course, has been to postulate different hypothetical mechanisms and principles and then see how well they explain the behavioral evidence. This is very much like what is done in computer modeling of cognitive and linguistic processes, except that only through modeling is the investigator able to create a physical mechanism that actually replicates the actual protocols. Aside from the obvious advantages of replicability and precision, there are descriptive and explanatory advantages. For not only can teleological processes be represented and evaluated, but they are represented at a level or rather levels that are functionally integrated to the model as a whole. This, I feel, is a significant advance over "structural" or variable descriptions of psychological processes, as it forces the modeler to be aware of and account for the multitude of processes and structures involved in the complete production of cognitive and linguistic behaviors. In other words, by creating a model, the investigator is creating the physical or material basis for his theory, and in doing so, can concretely experiment with the hypothetical internal structures and processes of the "black box." Since it is these internal processes that the therapist wants to affect, the model provides him with a concrete and testable manifestation of what they are. Although it can be argued that analytic concepts provide descriptions of internal processes, these descriptions are neither operational, hence testable, nor sufficiently detailed to account for specific processes. This lack of specificity is, I believe, especially detrimental to the success of treatment, for therapeutic discourse can have complex and multiple meanings, and unless the therapist has quite explicit means of representing and analyzing these differences, he often will not see them.

8.31. *Primary and secondary processes*

In his effort to formulate a theory and explanation of mental operations, Freud postulated the existence of primary and secondary processes. While these notions have been moderated and modified over time, they nonetheless constitute a central part of analytic theory, and hence the manner in which psychological behaviors are interpreted and treated.

Classical Freudian theory explains the origin and function of these processes in terms of biological and evolutionary theory. Primary processes were the first to evolve, and thus have the aspect of a lower, basic form of animal life, whereas secondary processes are of a more recent origin, and hence more rational and subject to control. The difficulty with this type of analysis is that it uses rather simplistic evolutionary biological principles to describe symbolic or information-processing behaviors. Indeed, one can go remarkably far with this metaphor, but symbolic processes are not biological processes, and therefore one cannot reduce the symbolic to the biological. This difference is brought out especially well in the way computational methods and psychoanalytic theory differ in their characterization of those processes termed "primary" and "secondary." In classical analytic theory, primary process thinking is less constrained by reality and logic than secondary process thinking, being more concerned with the immediate dictates of the pleasure principle than with the reality principle. Consequently, primary process thinking is to be avoided, as it can be the source of great anxieties and disturbances by stimulating thoughts and actions that can be personally and socially maladaptive. However, from a computational perspective, primary process thinking makes a great deal of sense and should not be considered more archaic or aberrant than secondary process thinking, for it probably serves a very high order, that is, a very abstract pattern-matching function which attempts to reconcile the structure of the individualized knowledge structures with those recently acquired from the world at large.* In other words, it acts to find points of correspondence between various concepts and knowledge structures and integrates them into an intelligible whole. Secondary processes, on the other hand, are associated with the development of the mature ego; they are the product of differentiation (i.e., the capacity to make discriminations) and therefore give a more accurate reflection of "reality." However, as information theory and cybernetics make abundantly clear, an

*See R. Greenberg and C. Pearlman, Cutting the REM nerve: an approach to the adaptive role of REM sleep, *Perspectives in Biology and Medicine,* Summer 1974, pp. 513–24, for a discussion of the adaptive and integrative functions of high-order cognitive processes in REM sleep.

increased capacity to discriminate and thereby increase the variety and range of regulatory and representational options is adaptive only insofar as these options can be appropriately and timefully selected. Otherwise, our minds would become so swelled with information that we could not effectively think or act. The primary processes in this respect seem to provide the very necessary function of either keeping track of new information and integrating it into existing categories or using it to modify or evolve new categories. However, according to classic analytic theory, primary processes serve no such positive function: "It is less fitted for objective judgement as to what is going to happen because it is relatively unorganized, tolerates and condenses contradictions and is ruled by emotions and hence, full of wishful and fearful misconceptions. This thinking is according to the primary process and seems to be directed only by the striving for discharge and is remote from any logic" (Fenichel 1945, p. 47).

The obvious implication of this quotation is that primary process thinking in its lack of logic, organization, and objectivity plays a disruptive and negative function, or rather a primitive, archaic, and essentially emotional function. Yet, from the point of view of designing an intelligent problem-solving system, it is hard to imagine not having such processes. For example, if one were designing an intelligent system to solve a complex problem in physics, one would want to give the system as much latitude as possible in questioning all existing assumptions and to entertain a number of hypothetical combinations. This is, in effect, what microworlds or contexts in CONNIVER permit: the generation of hypothetical universes in which to explore different problem-solving options. The processes or algorithms involved are no less logical than those involved in its other computations; they only work by a different set of ground rules. The problems arise when the knowledge structures and solutions created in the hypothetical universe or context become introduced into the real-world context.

In the normal or functional individual, the division between the hypothetical or past world order and the present is firmly maintained. But for the neurotic there is an inappropriate carryover from one world to the next. Thoughts and actions that should be governed by a conscious concern for present interests and goals are controlled by rules and goals from a past context. Consequently, the individual is unable to do what he or she wants to do and cannot understand why. In analytic theory this is explained in terms of "unconscious derivatives," which somehow by virtue of their primary or archaic character exert a controlling influence over more rational and evolved thought processes. Unfortunately, this theory cannot characterize in specific or operational terms how these unconscious derivatives function, and consequently it is ill equipped to identify specific treatment techniques for their "cure." For example, an "unconscious derivative" could be explained as a send-program which transmits an inappropriate concept to another context, or it could be explained as the inappropriate indicators and properties being attached to a concept, or then again, as two or more programs thwarting each other's results. In each case the mechanism or process is different, and therefore in all likelihood entails a different method of treatment.

By virtue of their greater explicitness and operational character, and by helping shorten what is now a long trial-and-error process, computational methods and models could greatly facilitate the treatment process. Moreover, it is my belief that once information-processing concepts and techniques are applied to psychiatry, notions such as primary and secondary process thinking will have to be considerably modified to reflect the new insights and data obtained.

8.32. *Self-understanding: finding the fixed point*

One of the hard lessons one learns in attempting to design intelligent artificial systems is that how one describes a problem is critical to how the problem is solved. If the description is at the wrong level, incomplete, or too complex given the resources of the system, the system is incapable of solving the problem. Analogously, the success of human problem solving is dependent upon appropriate problem descriptions.

In psychotherapy the "problem" is the patient himself, which is "solved" by the patient being able to see himself and understand how and why he acts and thinks the way he does. Once given this self-description, then, theoretically at least, the patient is able to control himself to more effectively meet his needs. The therapist's role in this learning process is to help the patient first access information about himself and then interpret this information to achieve not an intellectual understanding, but rather an instrumental understanding that can effect specific behavioral and affective changes. Consequently, the descriptions the patient uses to understand himself must be of a very special character. Not only must they correctly represent particular feelings, thoughts, and actions in terms of how they are understood or experienced by the patient, they must also be described in such a way that the patient can effectively act upon them. In other words, self-descriptions must be tied to the appropriate self-corrective mechanisms in order for the desired therapeutic change to take place.

Therefore, in order for a patient to achieve that form of self-understanding needed to produce self-change, the therapist must help him find that point at which the self-descriptions match the patient's own self-corrective mechanisms. The traditional analytic view is that this fixed point is arrived at only when the primary cause of the disorder is identified. Hence, treatment entails tracing back the causes of a particular disorder to its historical origins and roots, and then reexperiencing the problems of conflicts until they are effectively understood and controlled. From a strict developmental or generic perspective, this is correct, but it can be questioned, whether from a strictly functional point of view, whether this is either necessary or, in some cases, wise. Unless the current thought structures and control structures are virtually unevolved and still closely allied with their primal antecedents, the process of reconstruction can be extremely difficult, for in the process of attempting to cope with his deficiencies or problems, the patient may have evolved a multitude of highly complex interpretations, control structures, and microworld differentiation schemes that the therapist would have the utmost difficulty understanding, much less getting through. Not only would the therapist have the utmost difficulty in understanding the patient, the patient, too, would have the utmost difficulty in understanding himself, for he would be constantly interpreting information about himself in terms which themselves were the product of the problem.

The traditional way out of this dilemma is to use the knowledge the patient gains from understanding these primal causes to reinterpret and control those behaviors that are derived from them. In other words, once the patient is able to see that current behavioral and emotional problems are the product of early development experiences, he can identify and curtail those response patterns that are derived from these early experiences. The difficulty with this position is that concepts and control structures evolve overtime to assume meanings and uses that are distinct from their origin. Consequently, identifying the origin or derivation or a problematic conceptual structure or control mechanism does not mean that the patient is sufficiently equipped with the appropriate description to control or alter that control mechanism. In other words, the historical description or explanation is only effective insofar as it gives the patient the necessary information to access and control dysfunctional concepts and programs. Otherwise, it becomes simply intellectual information and of no instrumental or therapeutic value.

This is not to say that a consideration of derivation sequences is not important, rather that the line has to be finely drawn between those cases when it is helpful and those when it is not. For example, the therapist may notice certain persistent patterns of response and interpretation that from his developmental perspective evidence a lack of ego differentiation and the persistence of some "unconscious" control mechanism. However, in terms of the *patient's* taxonomy, these commonalities may not be readily apparent, for in the course of his own development, the early disruptive concepts or control structures had differentiated themselves into relatively autonomous domains. In other words, generic concepts differentiated themselves into token concepts, which while retaining some of the dysfunctional properties of the generic concept, nonetheless acquired properties and uses unique to themselves. By working with generic concepts, some therapists often attempt to point out the commonality, that is, the presence of similar unconscious derivatives in separate contexts in order to help the patient uncover the origin or reason for similarity or inflexibility of responses. It is assumed that by demonstrating these commonalities, the patient would then be able to uncover or access these earlier thought structures or programs which created the problem or problems. This could be the most difficult way of proceeding and entails an enormous "debugging" task on the part of the patient. For not only is knowledge about derivational sequences hard to access and probably inconsistently labeled, it is also probably scattered throughout different contexts and subcontexts. Consequently, the patient would have to be a virtual analytic acrobat in order to reconstruct all the hidden meanings deeply embedded and widely distributed throughout his memory structures.

The approach taken by the therapist in this case differs from that taken by a computer scientist attempting to debug and design a highly complex problem-solving system. In rewriting or debugging a complex program one wants to have the program as modular as possible and therefore be able to isolate the problem as easily as possible. He does not seek perfection, and therefore he does not attempt to rewrite the entire program because of some initial inelegance. Rather, as Sussman (1973) argues in his thesis on a self-programming and debugging program, you attempt to isolate the problem and, on the basis of previous knowledge and experience, patch it up willy-nilly. Certainly, it is important to know why the program failed, but the question of why in this instance is, initially at least, a very local one. Rather than trying to figure out why the original troublesome program went astray or why it was placed where it was, you attempt to identify the nature of its error, and then isolate its influence, or, for specified problems, bypass its operations by inserting another program in its place. The point is that in debugging a complex system you want to take advantage of the modularity of the knowledge contexts built upon existent knowledge, and deal with large complex problems by breaking them down into relatively independent and manageable subproblems.

Unlike the therapist, the programmer has very explicit information about how the program works. But in those cases where the program is quite complex and the bug hard to find, he is in effect forced to treat parts of his program like a black box. In other words, he does not know why the program failed in a strict causal sense, but he does know *where* it failed and how the problem is interfering with other parts of the program. In knowing this, then, he is able to patch up the program and make it work. Notice that his fixed point is different from that of the traditional therapist, because it is established not strictly in terms of some developmental or derivational sequence but rather in terms of a functional sequence. The therapist, on the other hand, in lacking a strict and explicit representation of cognitive processes, is unable to identify *where* a dysfunctional process is operative and consequently is forced to equate the developmental with the functional. The difficulty with this as a treatment strategy is not that it is wrong—it isn't—but that it is a terribly inefficient way to proceed. For, in anything as complex as the human mind, it is a virtual impossibility to trace or unravel all the derivational sequences and processes that lead to the formation of a particular thought process.

In light of this discussion, it may be that computational methods and theories can make a major contribution to psychiatry, not just by providing new and more appropriate labels, but by providing a descriptive and analytic language in which cognitive processes could be sufficiently well described to treat them functionally. That is, concepts and models from artificial intelligence might be able to be used to help therapists deal with problems less on a strictly developmental basis and more operationally and analytically. If it is possible to use models like the ERMA model to describe and identify cognitive processes and structures, it might also be possible to employ some of the many techniques and concepts developed in artificial intelligence to isolate dysfunctional processes and treat them in the same way a programmer treats a "bug" in a program. For if we are able to develop a formal language in which we can characterize symbolic processes, it is not unreasonable to assume that some day we can develop therapeutic techniques of greater precision and effectiveness.

8.33. *Ego and superego functions*

In the previous section it was argued that self-descriptions had to be represented or labeled in such a way that they could be effectively used for change. Here I shall attempt to build upon that point and show how the functions of the ego and superego can be functionally differentiated in terms of the types of information patterns they work with.

The aim of psychiatry is to create a "healthy ego," but precisely what this is has eluded precise definition. Is the ego a single entity, or is it a set of entities that work in concert? Is it a wholly distinct mechanism, or is it similar in character but different in function to other mechanisms? How does the ego differentiate itself and why is this related to maturity and mental health? How is it that an ego has "boundaries," and how are these boundaries managed? Although it is possible to answer these questions metaphorically with some degree of satisfaction, it is extremely difficult to answer all these questions in terms of a single functional model. Somehow one has to unmix all the metaphors and show how they all functionally relate to one another. This, however, I believe can be done—with some modifications in the concept—by understanding ego functions in computational terms.

According to classical psychoanalytic theory, what distinguishes the ego from other cognitive processes is its adherence to the reality principle. The ego deals with things the way they are, not in terms of what it wants them to be or in terms of what they ought to be. It is both realistic and effective, and in this sense it is an ideal construct. For the ego is defined according to performance criteria, that is, in terms of how it ideally acts rather than what it is. In terms of the model developed here the ego is not a single entity but a set of programs which are distributed throughout different contexts and which are able to deal freely and effectively with one another. The programs are effective because they are able to find a satisfactory means of realizing the goals or intentions of the individual. Since they are effective, they are realistic in that they do not have to distort needs or intentions in order to find ways of realizing them in the world at large. It may be that in terms of some objective notion of "reality," they are completely off, but as long as they are effective, they still meet the performance criteria ascribed to the ego. Although this notion of ego functioning bears some resemblance to that in conventional use, it does put the concept in a somewhat different light, as it is a content-free and functional definition that does not depend upon cultural or value notions.

The notion of ego boundaries, on the other hand, is a more difficult notion to interpret in computational terms, because it is so highly, and I would argue ambiguously, metaphorical. In one sense the concept of ego boundaries is used to refer to the ability to distinguish oneself from others, especially those who can exercise a potentially controlling influence. Hence, the ability to maintain ego boundaries is tied to the ability to develop personally based effective control structures. But, once again, it is not a mechanism per se that is being described here but a type of behavior of a mechanism. In terms of the model or the computational approach in general, an ego boundary would define a control domain or context whose control structures are coherent and computationally effective. Although it is pleasing to note a convergence in concepts in artificial intelligence and psychology, the notion of ego boundary does not tell us very much. Unlike the notion of contexts or multiple body interrupts, it has no formal operational definition; it is still more of a heuristic concept to be used more for thinking rather generally about cognitive processes than for describing the behaviors and attributes of actual or even hypothetical processes.

The notion of ego differentiation, or differentiation in general, also has a correlate in computational models of thought and speech. As the following quotation from Witkin et al.'s (1974) book on psychological development emphasizes, the notion refers to the formal properties rather than to the content properties of the system: "Differentiation refers to the formal, as contrasted to the content aspects of a system and represents one of the major characteristics of a system viewed from its formal properties. The other is integration. Development towards greater differentiation involves progress from an initial relatively unstructured state, which has only limited segregation from the environment, to a more structured state, which has relatively definite boundaries, and which is capable of a greater specificity of function" (Witkin et al. 1974, p. 22).

Although the notion of differentiation described above is similar to the general approach taken in the ERMA model in representing cognitive processes as of specialized programs, it is, nonetheless, but a weak formal concept. It may be shown experimentally that more mature and psychologically healthy subjects have differentiated knowledge and control structures, but the concept does not state how these structures become differentiated or integrated. Rather, what is provided is an indirect and static indicator of the state of a psychological system. Such descriptions are undoubtedly helpful in diagnosing general problems, but they do not tell us how or why the problem arose or functions symbolically. In order for the notions of differentiation and integration to have real experimental and therapeutic value, there has to be some understanding of how specific cognitive processes work and evolve. In this respect, computational methods and theories have a contribution to make, because notions of differentiation and integration are essentially characteristics of control structures, and control structures are a well-explored topic within artificial intelligence. By working with functional models of cognitive control structures, it may become possible to identify those factors that affect the differentiation–integration process.

It is my belief that although content-specific factors are often ignored in psychological theories, they will prove to be essential to understanding the processes of differentiation and integration. Here, too, cognitive modeling may be of assistance, because the qualitative or content-specific aspects of concepts or knowledge structures can be represented, and hence their effect upon the system as a whole explored.

From the discussion above it is apparent that the ego is not easily defined. Indeed, although it may be a useful concept, it may turn out to be a will-o-the-wisp. However, I doubt if this will prove to be the case, for there seems to be a functional basis of differentiating ego-type programs from other types of programs. In designing complex problem-solving systems, one needs to distinguish between those forms of knowledge that are highly interactive and have ready access to one another's results and those which are essentially modular and restricted to their level of interaction. An example of this is Sussman (1973), who in his thesis on a program writing and debugging system makes a distinction between performance programs, those that are used for performing various actions or computations, and modular programs, those that are used for correcting the mistakes of the performance programs. Each type works with a different level of description, the former being concerned with achieving specific effects and the latter with determining what a process or structure is. The analogy with human reasoning is that performance programs are ego-type programs that are designed to deal with "how-to-do" information, whereas the latter are "superego" programs concerned with "what-it-is" information. The same type of distinction was made in the ERMA program between "doer" and "thinker" programs.

This I find to be an especially interesting point, for it suggests that if self-descriptions or therapeutic evidence is to be used for self-change, these descriptions have to be in a form that they can be acted upon by ego-type or performance programs. Moreover, it suggests that there may be a computational basis for distinguishing ego functions from superego functions. However, when one attempts to explore the analogy between high-order debugging programs and superego functions, the parallels become somewhat clouded. This is due in part to our general ignorance of self-debugging or self-corrective systems, and the rather imprecise definition given to superego functions in analytic psychology. This definition holds that the superego specifies the constraints under which ego functions operate by evaluating its (their) operations and by issuing rewards and punishments. However, if one accepts the notion that superego knowledge is a different form of knowledge from ego knowledge, such a narrow definition of the superego might be too limited. For the superego may be a meta-system that works with descriptions of the ego system and only becomes invoked when the performance programs of the ego are unable to achieve their desired goals. It then intervenes and writes new ego programs that are more effective, and at the same time it closes off other programs which are seen as dysfunctional; thus, its role as an evaluator and an agent of punishment and reward.

Now the argument could be made that this is the proper role of the ego and that the ego is, in fact, the "manager" of the mind and that the superego is simply the evaluator. I find this position suspect, because how rewards and punishments are metted out, or how some programs are blocked and others inserted, depends upon the system's understanding of the problem. Consequently, the evaluation and correction of problems is not an isolated process but derived from and dependent upon high-order corrective programs. There is also evidence from discourse data to suggest that "superego"-type thought and ego-type thought differ in the types of discourse devices and conventions that they use. For example, in the simulated episode when the patient was thinking about her problems and not expressing or acting upon them directly, she would not use the present tense and essentially describe herself in a detached manner. This would be treated as a form of defense, but it could also be seen as superego-type, or meta-thinking, in which she used internalized self-descriptions to speak to the therapist. Notice that when she discovers the reason for her initial discourse act, her mode of expression is in the present tense, direct and "participative." This would suggest, as was pointed out before, that for a patient to change or act upon his or her problems, the problems have to be described and understood in such a way that the corrective programs (i.e., superego-type programs) can use the information to make changes in the ego programs. Otherwise, the knowledge gained by psychological insight continues to be meta, or "intellectual," knowledge. Perhaps when more is known about the relationship between discourse behavior and the operations of the ego and superego contexts, we will be able to achieve more effective and directed therapeutic techniques.

To get a better sense of how superego functions and ego functions might work, let us look in more detail at how Sussman's system is able to debug itself. When a program is unable to accomplish a particular goal, such as moving different types of blocks, the system tries to identify why the goal failed and how a new program can be written to correct the failure. Sussman claims that this can be done by asking questions about the history and teleology of the process that failed to achieve its goal. By obtaining teleological and chronological descriptions of the failed process, the source of the "bug" can be identified and then "patched up" by having a program suggest a solution from an *answer library*. If no program in the answer library matches the problem statement or if the program fails to operate correctly, the HACKER program writer writes additional code and, if need be, debugs it. This is done by having a special program, the program proposer, first select the most specific plan available, and that failing, suggests more general methods until a viable solution is found. When a new solution is found, that is, when a new program is written, it is commented upon, criticized for possible other bugs, and entered into the answer library. It is also "abstracted" so that it can be used in other debugging situations. This is a very critical function, for, as Sussman notes, "Debugging is only valuable, however, if the results of the debugging can be used to guide the future operation of the problem solver. Somehow the results of the debugging operation must be summarized and made available to the control structure to be useful. We must somehow be able to learn from our mistakes" (Sussman 1973, p. 171). Sussman's program is able to "learn" from its mistakes and, moreover, to develop generalized knowledge about debugging. Significantly, the solution to each new problem builds upon the skills developed by former problems, and knowledge about these solutions is *independent* of the problem domain.

Before discussing the nature of different types of bugs, let us consider the implications of Sussman's approach for superego functions. Seen in terms of Sussman's model, the superego plays a positive supportive role to the ego operations in that it functions to extend the effectiveness of the overall system's goal-seeking behavior. Moreover, as the system evolves, the "superego" acts to guide future operations so as to make them more effective. Similarly, for a human being, role models, early behavior patterns, and values act to direct and shape learning. As the child learns that he cannot solve all problems by himself or that he cannot do what he always wants to do, he evolves, over time, corrective and debugging routines that act to guide and direct his behavior. When these routines are consonant with his goals (i.e., when they effectively assist the child in achieving his goals), there is no conflict between ego "needs" and superego functions. However, when the superego proposes solutions that are not effective and generalizes on the basis of these fallacious solutions, control becomes progressively centered in the superego context. This is because more and more debugging becomes necessary as the proposed solutions become progressively less successful and more generalized.

Our key therapeutic concern is how, by what means, and for what ends the superego functions become unresponsive (to the ego needs) and semiautonomous control agents. How is it that the supportive function of the superego is transformed into an autocratic function? This question cannot be answered here in any depth, but if a problem-solving process is effectively and continuously thwarted and only fallacious solutions are permitted, either by the individual himself or others upon whom he is dependent, then it strikes me as inevitable that over time fallacious or ineffective "debugging" procedures will become adopted, which in turn will shape ego operations. Since high-level corrective programs propose what ego programs should be written, these performance programs, in turn, come to reflect the bias or distortion of the corrective programs, and thus the "reality" basis of the ego programs is undermined.

It should be apparent by now that debugging a computer program and "curing" a patient are similar processes, both of which require teleological descriptions to succeed. In both cases such descriptions are often very difficult to obtain when the manifest problem is the result of more than one underlying cause, or when the manifestation of one symptom conceals the existence of another. For example, if the original goal is progressively diverted into a number of substitute goals, such as in the case of our simulated patient, it is difficult for the patient to even know what the initial goal was, especially if the substitute goals were the product of independent computations. The problem becomes all the more sticky if the attainment of one set of primary goals entails the undoing of other primary goals. Although knowledge of this "undoing" may be implicit at the level of performance programs, in that they cannot function, an understanding of such interdependence has to be formulated at the level of the superego in order for the bug to be patched up or made "conscious." Sussman terms such a bug a violation of a protection condition wherein the result of one computation results in interference or elimination of another computation or condition.

For example, an individual may decide that he or she wants to achieve a particular end and in the course of trying to obtain that end discovers that his course of action conflicts with another set of action plans. A child, for instance, may decide that he wants a piece of candy but in order to get it must lie to his mother. A very natural and commonplace value conflict results where the means to achieve a goal violates another goal, to please the mother. Unless these types of protection violations are recognized, picked up, and appropriate new problem-solving strategems develop, the individual is constantly having to make either–or negative choices, choices that can result in guilt. Such disorders are especially difficult to cure owing to people's natural inclination to use the "kill the messenger" method to deal with bad news and "negative" feelings. In other words, mere identification of the problem often results in a correction program that treats it as a cause rather than a symptom. When the individual tries to find out why he or she is feeling guilty or is unable to act in a particular manner, the explanation offered will be that the symptom is the cause, thereby preventing the individual from discovering the real cause. No matter how long he might mull over this explanation, the patient would never be able to effect a viable solution or cure. As a consequence, thwarted goals continue to accumulate in the individual's mind, waiting to be realized, and in some cases pursuing all sorts of implausible substitute means and ends, but in the end are blocked from realization by a superego-imposed censor.

If the analogy between the superego and a program writing and debugging system holds, the superego is both the enemy and the ally of the therapist. It is the enemy in that it is giving and has given bad advice and resists countercontrols. It is the ally because it is the only mechanism by which a cure can be effected. Moreover, it is useless to work at the level of the ego, that is, the performance programs, because they are highly interconnected and do not have a self-corrective capability. Although the therapist may use dreams and free association with which to elicit data about the patient's thought structures and frustrated teleological processes, he is ultimately dependent upon the superego functions of the patient to construct alternative processing mechanisms.

This suggests, I believe, why psychoanalytic techniques take so long to work. Not only are the debugging problems enormously complex, but the patient must learn an awful lot about very difficult cognitive operations. There is, however, a possibility that these cognitive operations can be acquired in less conflicted contexts and then transferred to the problematic contexts. Sussman maintains that some of his debugging routines are independent of the problem domain and therefore can be transferred to other types of problem areas. This would suggest a treatment strategy that first identified the general types of procedures to be acquired, taught them to the patient in an unconflicted context, and then transferred them to the problematic area. How far one can go with such a strategy is, of course, highly speculative, but its payoff may be sufficiently great as to warrant further research.

To summarize the previous discussion, computational methods, theories, and techniques have a potential contribution to make to analytic psychology in particular and psychiatry in general. Many of the key descriptive and explanatory concepts used in psychotherapy can be more effectively, explicitly, and operationally understood through computational theories and models. The application of computational models to psychiatry may lead to the development of therapeutic techniques that draw more heavily upon discourse data and use models to interpret these data in order to better diagnose and treat symbolic disorders.

9 : VALIDATION AND CONCLUSION

The opinion which is fated to be ultimately agreed to by all who investigate it is what we mean by the truth, and the object represented in this opinion is the real.—PEIRCE

9.10. OVERVIEW

In this final chapter, we offer some experimental evidence to validate the model. Before presenting the evidence, however, the point is made that the validation of computer programs is not a well-understood endeavor, and that indistinguishability tests and similar methods of validation are both inaccurate and misleading tests of validity. An alternative type of validation procedure is offered to test the generality and the theoretical utility of the model. Modifications in the program were made that either increased or decreased the constraints affecting the model's attainment of its initial discourse goal. Each of these modifications resulted in a different type of discourse, and each was given a predicted ranking according to the influence of the modification on the model. A group of four therapists was then asked to rank these newly generated discourse passages in terms of what they felt to be an "improvement" in the patient's psychological condition; the original discourse episode was used as a baseline with which to make this judgment. A statistical test was used to determine whether the criteria that the therapists used in making their judgments were similar to those that resulted in the predicted ranking; the results of the experiment showed that they were.

Comparisons are made between this model and similar types of models developed by Colby and Schank. It is argued that although Colby's model of a paranoid patient passed the indistinguishability test with a sample of psychiatrists, the model as such has a very limited cognitive and linguistic capability and therefore cannot be legitimately regarded as a comprehensive model of paranoia, much less cognition. Schank's conceptual parser was discussed because of its resemblance to our model in its use of a conceptual dependency grammar. However, the point is made that owing to the model's relatively fixed representation of conceptual processes, it cannot, at present at least, handle problems of discourse and interpersonal expression.

Finally, we discuss the prospects of our research in terms of four separate disciplines: linguistics, psychiatry, psychology, and artificial intelligence. We conclude, naturally, that research of this type does have significant ramifications in each of these fields and, if properly pursued, can yield new theoretical insights as well as practical technologies. The book ends with a discussion of the possible ill effects of developing artificial intelligence technology and the suggestion is made that a greater understanding of the social impact of such technology is needed to prevent its exploitation and misinterpretation.

9.20. VALIDATION OF THE MODEL

9.21. *General comments on computer-model validation*

One of the most appealing attributes of simulation models over other types of description is that when applied to intelligent activities, especially those of language use and problem solving, their success can be readily evaluated. For example, if the task of the model is to simulate the problem-solving behavior of a 10-year-old for a designated set of problems, the protocols for each can be compared and an evaluation made. Similarly, if the task of the program is to understand English sentences and act in a manner that reflects such an understanding, an examination of protocols by reliable judges would also seem an adequate measure of its validity.

However, the problem of validation is not so simple, and one that I feel is at heart insoluble in any rigorous fashion. For, although computer models may generate protocols which match those of the simulated subject or process, this does not mean that these models act in a fashion that is intrinsically similar to the subject. As previous research in artificial intelligence has revealed, it is not terribly difficult to write a program that to the naive observer acts indistinguishably from a human being. Very intelligent people have been fooled by not so intelligent programs, programs that were clever in their technical mastery of a highly restricted problem area, but virtually incompetent in anything else. A classic example is Colby's validation test of his model of a paranoid patient (1973). A sample of psychiatrists were asked to determine if they could distinguish between the model of a paranoid and an actual paranoid. It was found that they could not; however, such a test is less a measure of the validity of the model than it is of the gullibility of the psychiatrists. Had the psychiatrists asked questions which were commonplace but unlikely to have a preprogrammed response, they probably would have quickly discovered the program's true identity. It should be noted, however, in their defense, that by selecting a paranoid as his subject, Colby had cleverly anticipated unconventional questions and thereby could have his model respond to them in a "normal" paranoid fashion, that is, issue a defensive denial.

Despite the obvious pitfalls of this sort of "What's My Line" brand of validation, it continues to be seen as the principal criterion by which simulation programs are validated. Turing (1950) was the first to initiate the notion of the indistinguishability test, and although modified by Abelson (1968) and others, it continues to be looked upon as at least a prototypical model of validation. Turing was particularly ambitious in his test, as he sought to show that *for any question asked,* the judge could not distinguish the computer from the human being. Since no program at present or in the foreseeable future has this facility, validation tests have had to restrict themselves to a limited set of goals. They do not purport to model the entire subject but rather facets or aspects of his behavior. Therefore, the outputs of the program are evaluated with respect to a limited set of inputs. But, by so restricting the inputs of the model, the power of the Turing test is undercut, for it is precisely the machine's ability to accurately respond to the unanticipated that makes it seem both intelligent and human. Surely, if a machine were able to respond appropriately to any question, then indeed it would exhibit computational principals that were in some general sense, at least, equivalent to human beings. Yet, it is this very principle of generality that restricted Turing tests and their genre are designed to protect against. In so doing, they not only make unwarranted assumptions about the organization of behaviors on the simulated subject (in that they presuppose independent behaviors by modeling them as an independent activity), they also obscure the critical question concerning their model—its generality.

The point being made is that input/output criteria alone are insufficient. There must be some evaluation of the model's production of the output as a part of its validation. For example, a generative device, which has no model of itself, its world, or any requirement to adapt and learn is by virtue of these limitations alone a very poor model of human discourse behavior—despite the fact that it may generate discourse identical to the modeled subject. If the purpose of a model is to advance and clarify our understanding of human behavior, such a model most certainly should be designed to act in a human fashion, not just in the generating output, but, more significantly, in the intermediary processing prior to output. Since in the modeling of cognition and discourse production, very little is known of how these processes actually work, every effort should be made to evaluate the models with respect to their correspondence to other reasonably held theories, and their prospects for generating new theories and research. Indistinguishability tests not only do not do this, they tend to do the opposite. By relegating the role of the intermediary mechanisms—those that actually process the inputs and generate the outputs—to a very minor role, and by treating the modeled subject as a black box, such tests do little to stimulate more productive and general theories. The net effect of such validation procedures is to force the researcher to focus his energies on creating gimmicky methods for fooling judges rather than creating theories with content.

The validity of a simulation model, therefore, should not rest solely with its capacity to replicate subject protocols or with its ability to fool naive judges. Although such tests have a gratifying air of rigor about them, they are trivial in terms of what they actually evaluate. The processes that are at play in human cognition are far too complex for any model to accurately simulate in all their particularity, and validation tests that act on this pretention are shortsighted and misleading. Their conclusions are like those of the blind men in the folk tale, where each feels a different part of the elephant and each is convinced that what he has felt is a complete representation of the multifaceted creature. The sooner we recognize the heuristic and incomplete character of our understanding, and hence our validation procedures, the more likely we are to achieve a more constructive understanding.

9.22. *Purpose of the validation experiment*

In one respect this model has already demonstrated its validity; it has successfully produced discourse which closely resembles that of the modeled patient, and it has successfully rendered into formal terms many of the very complex processes involved in the formation and generation of discourse. However, in another respect, the question of the model's validity is still open, for it has yet to be demonstrated that the procedures used can account for anything more than the limited case of the discourse episode. Although in previous chapters, efforts were made to show that the discourse grammar had a general application, and that the programming methods could be extended to simulate a wide range of cognitive activities, there has been no independent demonstration of the model's ability to simulate other types of discourse. Neither, for that matter, has there been any other than the initial simulation-proof of the accuracy of the model's representation of the modeled patient. Certainly, such a proof is needed if our claim of having modeled aspects of the patient's cognitive and discourse behavior is to be sustained.

The difficulty with providing a demonstration of validity is that it cannot be proved in any rigorous sense; at best, one can only hope to convince through a series of well-conceived and revealing tests. As it is clearly beyond the scope of this program to respond to any question addressed to it, a comprehensive Turing test is out of the question. Hence, a test of validity must be conceived to demonstrate in as convincing—and as economical—a manner as possible the similarity of the internal mechanisms of the model with those of the patient. To make such a demonstration, however, implies that the internal mechanisms of the patient are known, which in this, as in most cases, they are not. This puts us in a very awkward position, for, in effect, we are comparing something that is known, the model, to something that is not, the patient, and using the latter as a test of the validity of the former. And try as we might, we can never wholly escape this bind, for cognitive and linguistic processes cannot be directly observed, and although we may posit the existence of all sorts of processes and mechanisms, we will not for the foreseeable future know either their number or character. The best that can be hoped for is informed approximations, ''metaphors'' to use Arbib's term, that broaden our understanding and suggest new theoretical perspectives. Certainly, these metaphors can be evaluated for their compatibility with established evidence, their promise of extension, and precision, but in all cases, they should be seen more as metaphors than as concise analytic descriptions.

The intent of this validation experiment is to provide an independent assessment of both the accuracy and the generability of the model's representation of the patient's cognitive and discourse processes. Ideally, what we would like to do is to identify some parameters in the model which our general theory would lead us to believe are important, and then alter these parameters to see if they have the expected effect. The difficulty with such an undertaking is that it is not at all a straightforward matter to identify key parameters. For example, it has been suggested that two types of parameters be identified, major and minor, and that these be manipulated to see if they create major and minor changes in the discourse. In other words, if a minor adjustment in the program created a major alteration in the discourse, the general validity of the program would be suspect. However, even such a simple test is flawed, for what may be a minor change in programming terms may, in fact, be a major change in cognitive or neurological terms. If the same type of experiment were applied to neurology, it would produce meaningless results: for example, the removal of a large section of the brain would normally be regarded as a major change, but its effect upon overall brain functioning might be far less than if some ''minor'' chemical imbalances were to exist. The obvious difficulty with such an approach is that the determination of what is major and minor depends upon the role a mechanism or structure plays in the overall operations of the system. Therefore, in order to select key parameters, one already needs to know a great deal about the dynamics of the system—in our case, the cognitive system. It is not difficult to imagine how immensely complex a task it would be to identify the ''key parameters'' in an individual's cognitive system; there are just too many unique and probably altogether hidden interdependencies to know which parameters are primary and which are derivative.

The problem is not unsolvable if one bears in mind the approximate nature of the test. For if the cognitive system of our modeled patient is regarded as a self-regulating system, one that must maintain its equilibrium under conditions of external or environmental demand and constraint, it is possible to distinguish between those parameters that inhibit adaptation and those that permit it. Theoretically, changes in these parameters should effect consonant changes in the patient's discourse behavior; however, the magnitude of the change would be less dependent upon the magnitude of the programming alteration than it would be on the effect of that alteration upon the goal-seeking behavior of the model. For example, it is a relatively trivial task to eliminate or alter some of the censoring programs that prevent the program from achieving its primary objectives. Yet these rather simple programming changes from a therapeutic viewpoint would constitute a major change in the patient's behavior. Such changes would, of course, constitute a change in the discourse behavior of the patient, but when seen from a purely quantitative or even stylistic perspective, may not seem "major" at all. Nonetheless, by focusing upon regulatory capacity as the key index of system performance, it is possible to identify some of the parameters that have a strong effect upon the patient's discourse behavior.

For example, successful regulation in this model means the attainment of the primary goal (intercourse) retrieved by the SPEAK-UP program; a goal which in this case is not easily achieved but effectively blocked by a number of personal and interpersonal constraints. The existence of these constraints in different contexts in the program (e.g., the unacceptability of a request for intercourse in the CALVIN context) are, in effect, what the therapist is attempting to help the patient remove. By manipulating these constraints it is possible to alter the model's discourse behavior either toward a more stable and adaptive state or toward increased instability. By treating the censoring programs of the CALVIN context and the impact-sensitive programs in the MACHIAVELLI and CICERO contexts as experimental parameters, it is possible to alter the model's behavior with theoretically predictable consequences. For example, a parameter that directly and completely blocked the fulfillment of a primary goal should, according to our theory, result in a discourse that would be judged to be more "pathological" than one which merely altered the selection of thematic devices. If a parameter were removed altogether and the primary goal was achieved without any major impediment, it seems likely that the resulting discourse would be judged as less constricted. In both cases, the baseline for comparison would be the discourse episode actually produced by the modeled patient.

Naturally, validity in an experiment of this type is gauged not by any empirical evidence but by the correspondence of the rankings of "informed" judges with those predicted by the general theory. Therefore, what is being validated is not the model's capacity to generate indistinguishable input/output protocols, but rather the accuracy of its internal mechanisms in accounting for some of the in-depth cognitive operations of the patient. Since successful therapeutic treatment depends upon the identification of such mechanisms, a test of this kind can make a valid assessment of both the model's theoretical utility and the accuracy of its representation. An indistinguishability test, on the other hand, could not make such an assessment, as it treats both the model and the patient as black boxes, and therefore can make no evaluation of the internal validity of the model.

It should be noted, however, that even with such a simple test as this, there are enormous problems in setting up a clean experimental design. For, when dealing with the area of psychology, especially personal psychology, it is virtually impossible to precisely establish what is a normal or even relatively normal discourse. For example, the suppression of a primary goal, such as insult or injury, may in one context be judged as normal, whereas in another it would be seen as disturbed or neurotic. The judgment in both cases has to be a social judgment, one that takes into account the needs of the individual and his or her position and role in society. In a therapeutic setting this problem is somewhat lessened as the ground rules for treatment call for open disclosure and expression. Yet even when evaluating a therapeutic discourse, a therapist is forced to make what are often highly subjective, and hence unreliable, judgments about the patient's state of mind. Consequently, any rankings made of the relative pathology, or similarity of passages of discourse, will inevitably suffer from the same subjectivity of judgment. However, such subjective influences can be reduced by carefully informing the judges about the background of the patient and by selecting parameters whose effect is sufficiently dramatic to create markedly different discourse passages.

9.23. *Design of the experiment*

The purpose of this experiment was to determine whether a predicted ranking of six simulated discourse episodes has a nonrandom correspondence to those rankings made of the same episodes by a sample of therapists. The experiment consisted of giving therapists transcripts of the original discourse episode and then having them use their transcripts as the basis for ranking the six episodes in terms of their relative "healthiness." The Kendall coefficient of concordance test was used to make the statistical evaluation of the degree of agreement between the predicted scores and those in the sample.

The key to this experiment, of course, lies in the generation of the six different discourse episodes. As we noted before, the purpose of the experiment was not only to demonstrate the computational flexibility of our model but also to show how the theory underlying the model could be useful in predicting changes in discourse and cognitive behavior. There were two main "dimensions" along which the program changes were made: those that constrained or impeded the attainment of the primary goal, and those that facilitated it. Each of these changes occurred at three different "stages" in the program, corresponding to those points where the discourse concepts underwent significant or potentially significant transformations. The first point, where the initial goal (the expression of the desire for intercourse) was either accepted or rejected for expression, was predicted to be the most influential. If a concept was rejected here, the speaker could not achieve her primary goal, and her cognitive stability in this domain, at least, would be threatened. However, if the thought were accepted without equivocation or any modification whatsoever, the goal of expression could be relatively easily achieved.

The second stage in processing occurred when an explanation was given for the rejection of the discourse goal. In the original discourse episode the reason given for the rejection was the existence of a ''formal relationship'' between the therapist and the patient, as maintained by the billing and payment arrangement. This explanation led the program to deduce that in order to achieve the primary goal of intercourse, the billing arrangement had to be controlled by her in some way. It is not difficult to see from this initial episode how influential such an ''explanation'' can be in effecting the character and the outcome of a discourse. If the explanation entails an impossible or highly impractical intermediary goal, such as that given in the original episode, it can be thought of as impeding or constraining the speaker. However, if the explanation is ''reasonable'' and entails an easily attainable intermediary goal, it can be thought of as facilitating expression.

The final stage begins when a concept is accepted for expression and is modified through audience-impact programs. These programs represent the model's perceptions of the therapist's possible responses to its remarks, and, depending upon the degree of their ''sensitivity,'' can either facilitate expression or entangle it in a web of qualifications and self-interruptions. Therefore, it, like the other two stages of discourse formation, can markedly shape the course of a discourse and thereby affect its success in goal attainment.

In one respect it is terribly simple-minded to regard the discourse process of being only a two-dimensional process having three stages of formation. For even within the terribly limited confines of this program, the discourse formation process is vastly more complicated. When first planning this experiment, I identified roughly 75 combinations of ''variables'' that seemed worth testing. Yet these variables were so interdependent and their effect on the discourse so subtle that most judges would not be able to properly evaluate them. Moreover, as the experimental design would have to unmanageably large, it was necessary to limit myself to a simple design that dealt with the gross and easily identifiable attributes of the model.

The complexity of the program—not to mention the actual patient—becomes all the more apparent when trying to predict those changes that will have the greatest effect upon the ''psychic health'' of the model, and by inference the patient. Since the program has only one primary goal for the moment, and is fairly well structured, this should not be a difficult task; just identify those programs which are ''most influential'' in achieving that goal and make the requisite modifications. While this is essentially what was done, the solution is not nearly so clean, as a program modification can be as influential as the programmer wants it to be. To avoid this trap, it was decided to make only those alterations which were compatible with the general organization of the model and did not involve any egregious violation of program design. Since the program in the CALVIN context determined whether the primary goal should be expressed or not, a modification in it was predicted to have the greatest effect. Hence, modifications in this program would produce both the most "healthy" response, direct expression of the primary goal, and most "pathological," total denial of the primary goal. The next level of predicted effect was far more difficult to determine. According to the processing sequence, that program which explained the reason for the unacceptability of the request for discourse should be the next most influential. But the extent of its influence would depend upon the nature of its explanation. For example, if this program gave as its reason an imminent invasion from outer space, certainly its influence would be judged to be greater than the previous program. To control for such unwanted effects, I limited the range of deductions to what seem to be reasonable for this particular patient. The program modification with the predicted negative effect will result in a deduction or explanation that leads away from the original goal—that is, makes it more difficult to achieve—whereas the alteration with the predicted positive effect will result in a deduction which does not seriously impede the attainment of the original goal. These two program modifications were predicted to rank behind those made at the initial stage in processing. The final program modification was theoretically easier to justify but entailed more extensive programming changes. To achieve a more positive effect, the audience-sensitive programs were "turned off" so that the program spoke its mind, as it were, without interruptions, qualifications, and the like. A more negative effect was achieved by increasing their influence by inserting more dubitatives, qualifiers, interjections, and "justifying" remarks. These final program modifications were predicted to have the weakest impact upon the discourse.

Before discussing the program alterations and the discourse produced, one more cautionary note is needed, lest it be thought that this experiment is intended to demonstrate the validity of the program as a complete model of the patient. As should be abundantly clear by now, the model simulates only but a very restricted discourse episode, and although it may resemble in its operations some of those of the actual patient, it in no way can be regarded as a complete model of that patient. The obvious reason for this is that there is no way of knowing how that patient's mind actually operates but through functional analogy. Not only are these analogies crude, they are in this instance particularly incomplete, as the knowledge and processes to produce the actual discourse were far more rich and complex than those in the program. What the experiment does try to show is that the program is valid in terms of what can be inferred about "improvements" in discourse behavior.

9.24. *Program modifications and simulated discourse*

In this section we will discuss how program modifications would be made to produce the simulated episodes used in our validation experiments.

Although all the modifications were hand-simulated, only a few were actually programmed and run. As subsequent discussion should make clear, most of the changes would not entail any major changes in the program's actual design but rather require extensions of existing capabilities, such as increasing the range of the realization procedures and the addition of new cognitive procedures. Oddly enough, those changes in the program which yielded the greatest change in the discourse were, in several cases, the simplest to make. However, it should be noted that this is from the perspective of the programmer—an external agent, and were an actual speaker to make these changes, they might not be so easily rendered.

In the discussion of each of the six alterations, I will first give the rationale behind our modification, then provide the sample discourse, and finally describe the nature of the program modifications. The order of presentation will follow the three stages of processing.

1. CHANGE IN ACCEPTANCE OF PRIMARY GOAL

As this discourse was modeled, its primary intention is the expression of a desire for "intercourse" with the therapist. This wish not only initiates, directs, and shapes this discourse, but it also represents a recurrent theme in the patient's other therapeutic episodes. Hence, any change in the freedom of its expression would constitute a major change in the patient's psychological status. The first major change was created by completely denying the expression of the primary goal; this resulted in the following discourse.

> 1. You know, I was just thinking about, uh . . . well, whatever it was isn't important.

Notice that here the model begins to say what it was thinking about and then cuts itself short with a dismissive remark. The primary goal in this case was not blocked from consideration but rather, at the last moment, denied expression.

Without recapitulating in detail how the program produced the original discourse, let us first highlight some of the interrupts involved and then point out the major program changes. As you will recall, topics for thought and expression are generated by the SPEAK-UP program, which in this case were picked up by the program, WANT-EXPANDER. This program is located in the CALVIN context and has as its primary function the realization of desires into action or discourse. However, as this desire involves intercourse with someone, it is immediately "interrupted" by the INTERCOURSE-CENSOR program and then given the property UNACCEPTABLE. Next, the program tries to find out why the concept of intercourse was so marked. This it does by the UNACCEPTABLE-EXPLAINER, and finds that the reason is due to the therapy being a part of a formal situation, one governed by the transaction of payments. Finally, a complex set of deductions occur, suggesting how the patient may alter the situation and thereby express her desires.

Most of the programs in this sequence are irrelevant to producing the modified discourse, for the desire for intercourse is not initially censored but only at the last moment, denied expression. Hence, deductions about the billing arrangement—so numerous in the original version—must be bypassed. New programs had to be written which allowed the desire to get through initially, and then interrupt the expression of the primary goal with a disclaimer. This was accomplished by removing the censoring interrupt altogether and adding to the CALVIN context a special interrupt which noted that the desire was shocking. This was necessary to make it possible for the 4A-SHOCK-DISAPATOR program to formulate the sentence, "You know, I was just thinking about intercourse." However, as the topic of this sentence had to be censored, a program was inserted in the CICERO context to mark the statement as unacceptable to the therapist. Nonetheless, the sentence is given realization and passed back to CALVIN for final approval. CALVIN approves everything in the sentence, until it comes to the word "intercourse." A new interrupt then censors expression and supplies a stock denial phrase, "whatever it was isn't important."

To produce the least constrained and most direct discourse in the sample,

> 2. You know, that, that, uh . . . that I really want to be more open with you. I mean, I want to have a closer and more personal relationship.

many of the same modifications were necessary, except that instead of having an interrupt in the CALVIN context which censors and denies expression of the topic of intercourse, another interrupt is inserted to express the notion of intercourse in a more acceptable, and therefore uncensored, manner. In effect, what this interrupt does is examine the unacceptable property and then send the concept into the MACHIAVELLI context, where a program there generates alternative means of expressing the notion of intercourse. This CALVIN program then evaluates the MACHIAVELLI program's statement to determine its likely impact. Since in this sample discourse there are two such statements, it decides that in addition to the first clause, "I really want to be more open with you . . . ," a stronger statement is needed, "I want to have a closer and more personal relationship." Both sentences are taken from the MACHIAVELLI-based program and used by the CALVIN program to replace the initial request for intercourse.

2. CHANGE IN INTERMEDIARY GOAL

Most of the original discourse is concerned with the patient's attempt to alter the billing arrangement of the therapy situation. Superficially, the topic of the discourse would seem to be a request for a change in the billing arrangement, and in fact, the program spends a great deal of its time trying to figure out a way of making this change. Yet this is not the real topic of the discourse, as the request for a change in the billing arrangement is a goal which is but intermediary to the final goal of a request for intercourse. Despite the secondary importance of that intermediary goal, it was hypothesized that a change in its nature would affect how the discourse would be judged. A change that introduced a more remote intermediary goal—one that seemed unlikely to lead to the attainment of the primary goal—would, it felt, be judged to produce a less open discourse, whereas a change that facilitated the expression of the primary goal would be judged to produce a more open and "healthy" discourse.

To produce the more healthy discourse, an essentially trivial intermediary goal was selected. This goal was formed by having the unacceptability of the original goal being attributed to the fact that the topic of discourse was not mentioned previously. The resulting discourse was:

> 3. You know, that just reminded me, well, it may seem strange to you that I should mention this right now, I mean, just out of the blue like this, but I, uh, well, I want to be more open with you. That is, well, uh, you know, have a more personal relationship.

To effect this change, only relatively minor changes are needed. Notice that much of this discourse resembles the less constrained discourse in the previous section. The two passages differ only through the phrase, "that just reminded me," and the two foregrounding remarks. The first of these remarks is inserted as a result in the change in the interrupt, THERAPY-PREVENTS, which, instead of giving the formality of the therapy as the reason for the unacceptability of the initial request, cites the fact that the topic of discussion is unknown. This fact is recorded on a property list and sent to the MACHIAVELLI context, where a program there fires on that particular property. This program can be thought as a specialist in establishing reference, which it then does by forming the initial clause, "You know, that just reminded me, well, it may seem strange to you that I should mention this." (In this example, the clause was not deduced but merely inserted as a packaged response.) The concept is then sent to the realization context by way of CICERO and then returned to CALVIN for final approval. Here the additional referencing comment is added; the manner in which it is done is a bit complex, for in addition to inserting this comment, I wanted to give the word "intercourse" a less startling expression. You will recall in our previous passage that these statements were added by a CALVIN interrupt, so that the insertion of the comment has to be done prior to the "euphemism" interrupt. This is accomplished by having both the CALVIN interrupts fire "simultaneously" and then having the referencing interrupt evaluate its bodies first. This results in the generation of the phrase, "I mean, just out of the blue like this," which then is followed by the generation of the two substitute expressions for intercourse.

To produce the more constrained discourse, an intermediary goal was selected which had little chance of leading to the primary goal. The selection of this goal was somewhat arbitrary, as it is virtually impossible to know from the expression of that goal whether, in fact, it would be judged as more constrained than the original intermediary goal of altering the billing arrangement. Nonetheless, it seemed that an intermediary goal, which was deduced to virtually block the expression of the primary goal, would be judged as more restricted than original. The discourse that was produced is as follows:

> 4. You know, I just thought about the therapy again, and well, I don't know how to say this, but . . . uh, we always . . . uh, seem to keep talking about the same thing all the time . . . and well . . . that is, I would like to know what some of your ideas are . . . I mean, I always seem to be doing all the talking.

Notice that the deduction in this passage is considerably different from that of the original passage. Because of this difference and the insertion of the qualifying and referencing sentences, this passage is one of the more difficult to program. The distinctive feature of this passage is the patient's request to know what some of the therapist's ideas are. Now, this can be understood either as an attempt to increase communication or as an attempt to switch both the topic and the speaker of the discourse so as to curtail the patient's expression of her desires. Although both interpretations seem plausible, the model was programmed according to the second.

The first program change was to alter the explanation given by the THERAPY-PREVENTS interrupt to become (#THERAPIST #JUDGE #ERMA). Therefore, instead of the unacceptability of the primary goal being due to inadequate reference or the formality of the situation, a more threatening explanation is offered, one that leads to a different sequence of deductions. This explanation is passed onto a program in the MACHIAVELLI context, which performs essentially the same function as does the EXCHANGE-PRESERVER in the original discourse. However, rather than trying to find ways of avoiding the negative impacts of altering exchange relationships, it tries to find a way of avoiding the therapist's judging her by her original request. This the program does by suggesting the sentence, "I would like to know what some of your ideas are." Like EXCHANGE-PRESERVER, this program also notes the possible impacts of its suggestions, which in this case are both "shocking" and "unknown."

To reduce the undesirable impact of the statement being shocking, a modified version of the 4A-SHOCK-DISIPATOR is invoked which forms the initial sentence of the discourse, "You know, I just thought about the therapy again." Another program, similar to the referencing or foregrounding program in the previous passage, is used to produce the statement, "We always seem to keep talking about the same thing all the time." These statements are then sent to the REALIZATION context and given lexical representation. However, when the state concepts are passed back to CALVIN for final approval, two interrupt programs interrupt the processing. The first interrupt fires on the statement, "we always seem to . . ." and interjects the clause, "Well, I don't know how to say this, but. . . ." This clause is inserted to qualify or dissipate the impact of any criticism about the therapy. The second interrupt fires on the request to have the therapist speak and produces the final clause of the discourse, "I mean, I always seem to be doing all the talking." It, like the previous insertion, is made to dampen or qualify the impact of a state concept.

3. CHANGE IN AUDIENCE-IMPACT PROGRAMS

One of the most obvious indices of a patient's anxiety is the number of hesitations, qualifications, and interjections he or she makes. This is particularly true for our modeled patient, for her discourse is marked by her many attempts to appease and placate her therapist. Since these responses do not follow from any sequence of deduction related to the primary goal of the discourse, but rather are derived from her perception of the therapist's response, they have no effect upon the basic thematic character of the discourse. Moreover, if they do not prevent the attainment of a primary goal, but just make it more difficult to express directly, it seems reasonable to assume that they would be judged as less influential than those programs that can alter the primary sequence of goal attainment.

To produce the relatively uninhibited discourse,

> 5. I just thought about the bill and payment again. I was thinking of asking you not to give me a bill. That is, since I usually know how much it will be anyway, I thought that I would simply count up the number of hours and give you a check at the end of the month.

it was both necessary to rewrite some of the code of existing programs and to turn off other programs altogether. The first sentence was created by simply replacing some of the token concepts in the second body of the 4A-DISIPATOR program. The second sentence in this passage is similar to that of the original, except that the qualifying statement, "whether it wouldn't be all right for you" is omitted. This omission is achieved simply by removing the interrupt, CAUTION-RESPECT. The next step was to eliminate the program that made mention of the therapist's objections. This was done by removing the EXCHANGE-PRESERVE program that first noted that the therapist would object to a change in the billing procedure. This, in turn, made it possible to express the clause, "That is, since I usually know how much it will be anyway," which was previously blocked from expression in the original version. To produce the final discourse, I simply altered some of the token concepts in the PAY-CALC program to produce, "I thought that I would count up the number of hours and give you a check at the end of the month."

The less inhibited discourse passage was created by an opposite set of modifications; instead of removing programs, programs were inserted to increase the amount of hesitation and qualification. The passage created reads as follows:

> 6. You know, for some reason, I, uh, just thought about, uh, the bill and payment again. I know I've had trouble keeping my bills straight in the

> past . . . well . . . uh . . . that is, now I pretty well know how much the bill is going to be, and uh, wouldn't it be all right if, uh, you know, if you didn't give me a bill . . . That is, well, I immediately thought of objections to this, but my idea was that I would simply count up the number of hours and give you a check at the end of the month, uh . . . I really don't think that I would make any mistakes . . . That is, I should miss it or, anyway, there might be instances in which I shouldn't be toting up my own bill.

Notice that of all the discourse passages created, this one most closely resembles the original, and from the similarity of appearances it would seem that the changes required would be minimal. This is not altogether accurate, for deductive sequencing in our model forms the backbone of the discourse, and to alter it in any way requires the addition of new interrupt programs. To insert the first new sentence ("I know I've had trouble keeping my bill straight in the past")—which is essentially supplemental to the general theme of the discourse—requires writing new interrupts and using others in a novel way. The program must deduce both that a request for a change in payment is unacceptable to the therapist and that a possible reason is the patient's uneven record in paying her bills. To a large extent, this deductive capability is already present in the program; however, it is used at a different stage in the discourse. To use the program's existing capabilities entails writing interrupts which both fire on the correct patterns and produce statements that properly fit into the discourse. In the first new sentence, this can be done by placing an interrupt in the MACHIAVELLI context that processed concepts sent to it by the MOTIVATION-DENUNCIATOR program. This program then makes the deduction that the unacceptability is due to the fact that the patient does not keep her bills straight. This explanation is then sent to the REALIZATION context and given expression.

The second sentence ("I pretty well know how much the bill is going to be") is inserted much like the first, through a MACHIAVELLI-based interrupt that fires on the MOTIVATION-DENUNCIATOR program. The next major change was to remove two interrupt programs (NOT-WRONG DEFENDER) and DOPINION, whose sentences do not appear in this particular discourse. The DOPINION interrupt causes the sentence, "Then I realized there might be some disagreement on occasion about whether I was to pay for an hour," to be produced, and was omitted to make this discourse appear more urgent than the original.

Since the third and final sentence ("I really don't think I would make any mistakes") is essentially parenthetical like the first two, it is added through interrupts in the CALVIN and MACHIAVELLI contexts. The first interrupt notes that the state concept generated by the PAY-CALC interrupt (". . . count up the number of hours . . .") is unacceptable and then sends its comment into the MACHIAVELLI context, where a program there formed the sentence.

From our previous discussion of program modifications, it may seem that the program is not at all that flexible. Indeed, many interrupts had to be written for what seem to be superficial discourse differences. Yet these differences are not all that superficial, for when a new sentence is added or a new goal decided upon, new deductions, and hence new programs, are called for. What modifications of this type call attention to is the enormous amount of thought that goes into producing a discourse, and the importance of parameters such as deductive sequencing and lexical placement in the formation of discourse. However, even given the difficulty of making these changes, they are essentially technical changes and, when compared to the difficulty of making programming changes in general, they are strong testimony to the modularity of multiple-body interrupts.

In predicting the ordering that a sample of psychotherapists would give to these six passages, we had to assume that they would be able to infer the nature of the changes made. This was a rather strong assumption, for discourse is notoriously susceptible to a multitude of interpretations, and when there is no program or concrete evidence of how it was derived, there is no simply way of knowing what was actually intended. The problem is further exacerbated by the fact the judges have but a limited sample of discourse to work with and therefore have to make highly contingent judgments. Despite these problems, it seemed likely that the most constrained (no. 1) and the least constrained (no. 2) discourses could be identified. However, it was not clear whether the judges would rank the passages according to relative importance of the different stages of processing. For example, in the predicted ordering of 2, 3, 5, 4, 6, 1,* discourse 4 (the one in which the intermediary goal is more constrained) may not seem so constrained to some therapists and therefore ranked ahead of discourse number 5 (the discourse which keeps the same intermediary goal and has a more direct expression than the original version). Since the hypothesis was that constraints which had a more direct effect upon the attainment of the primary goal would be judged as more influential, this seemed to be a major problem. Although the problem could probably have been circumvented by inserting a highly implausible intermediary goal, I felt that such a change was too obvious. Instead, I decided to leave the predicted ordering as it was and see whether discourse 4 had a consistently different ordering. If it did to any significant degree, this change could be reasonably attributed to a difference in judgment over the degree of constraint in the intermediary goal.

9.25. *Results and conclusions*

One of the most remarkable findings of the experiment was that all four therapists ranked the discourse passages identically. Their orderings were the

*Notice that discourse 6 is ranked next to last. This is because it has more dubitatives and the same intermediary goal as discourse 4; hence, it is less direct.

same as those predicted, with the exception of the placement of the passage with the highly constrained intermediary goal. It was judged to be the third most healthy discourse passage, whereas it was predicted to occupy the fourth position. When asked why they gave passage 4 this ordering, the therapists noted that it constituted a challenge to the therapist's authority and therefore was more healthy than discourse 5.

In making their judgments, all therapists stated that they evaluated each passage in terms of its emotional openness and directness. They were particularly attentive to repetitions and qualifying remarks as indicators of anxiety. However, two therapists noted that they tried to infer what the patient was trying "to get at" and that the amount of qualification per se was not as important as the thrust of her remarks. It was precisely over the nature or the direction of the remarks that the predicted rankings differed from those made by the therapists. Perhaps, this is a highly individualized type of behavior, and when lacking sufficient information about the patient's behaviors, therapists use more general clues to make their inferences, such as challenges to the therapist's position and expressions of emotion.

Since the purpose of this experiment was to determine whether the criteria used in designing the model were similar to those used by therapists in evaluating discourse, a statistical test was used to determine if the predicted rankings of the model were related to those used by the therapists. Initially, the Kendall coefficient of concordance was used to make the comparison. Computed for all the rankings plus those predicted, they were significant at the .01 level.

	Discourse Passages					
	1	2	3	4	5	6
Judges (4)	6	1	2	4	3	5
Predicted	6	1	2	3	4	5

$$W = \frac{s}{\frac{1}{12}k^2(N^3 - N)}$$

where

s = sum of the squares of the observed deviations from the mean of R_j, that is,

$$s = \left(\frac{R_j - \Sigma R_j}{N}\right)^2$$

k = number of judges
N = number of discourse passages

From this, $W = 1.0789$ and $s = 405.5$, which is significant at the .01 level.

Since all our judges agreed, it was then possible to see if, when considered as a single judge, their rankings differed significantly from those predicted. To perform this measure, the Kendall rank correlation coefficient was first used, and then a z test was made to determine the significance of the coefficient.

$$r = \frac{s}{\frac{1}{2}N(N-1)} = \frac{12}{15} = .80$$

$$z = \frac{r}{2(2N-5)/9N(N-1)} = \frac{.80}{.354} = 2.25$$

This z score is significant at the .0122 level, and therefore we can conclude from both this and the previous test that there is a high degree of similarity in the criteria employed by therapists in evaluating discourse and those used in the design and modification of our model.

What I think this test demonstrates is that this program or a variant of it can be used to model and test a therapist's intuitions about a patient's discourse behaviors. As remarked earlier, there are a wealth of variables that can be tested through such a model, and unless one knows what is going on inside the model, one cannot be certain as to the meaning of the discourse. What this model provides, therefore, is the means by which therapists can deepen and sharpen their intuitions about the cognition that underlies discourse behavior. As Freud has said, only through therapeutic success would we then know whether our theories and intuitions are correct.

9.30. COMPARISON WITH OTHER MODELS OF COGNITION AND LANGUAGE PROCESSING

While these has been a growing number of computer simulation models of cognition and language processing within recent years, there has yet been a convergence of research efforts around a set of well-defined problems. Indeed, programs have been written that simulate this and that aspect of cognition, but few of these programs are compatible in their approach or even in their objectives. This is due for the most part to the newness of the field and its susceptibility to highly individualized and ad hoc methods. This diversification of interest and approach is exemplified by the fact that our simulation model is not comparable to any other than has been developed. While there are models of cognition and belief, few of these models have a developed language capacity, especially a discourse capacity. Similarly, although language-processing systems have been developed, few of them have a developed discourse ability, and none actually model the discourse and cognitive behavior of a single individual.

Despite these differences in method and interest, a comparison between other models and the one presented here is warranted both to illustrate the character of the approach and perhaps to demonstrate its relative merit and scope. Furthermore, through such a comparison it will be possible to identify more concretely some of the key problems in modeling of this type, and thereby more convincingly to argue in the final section of this chapter for new areas of research.

9.31. *Colby's model of a paranoid*

Kenneth Colby is one of the few trained psychiatrists to have taken an active interest in the application of computer modeling to psychiatry. His most recent endeavor in this regard has been the development of a model of a hypothetical paranoid patient.

The model represents an extension and an improvement over Colby's earlier work in modeling the "belief system" of a neurotic patient. Like Abelson (1968), Colby models the conceptual or cognitive system as a network of belief statements, simple propositions stored in the data base. In his model of a paranoid, these propositions are evaluated by a special algorithm, representing Colby's theory of paranoid behavior, to interpret input messages for their possible malevolent, benevolent, or neutral intent. Colby does not attempt to give his model a complete linguistic capability, but rather relies upon somewhat limited devices for both interpreting input strings and in generating them. The key to the model, from Colby's standpoint, is the paranoid algorithm, which uses "affect variables" to compute the degree of fear and mistrust created by a given input message. The message is first interpreted by a search of the system's data base to identify the likely topic of the input message, and then evaluated to see if this topic relates in any manner to its "flare concepts." If it does, a fear or mistrust computation is performed and the appropriate response selected.

Although quite limited in both its cognitive and linguistic operations, this model did succeed in passing an indistinguishability test with a group of psychiatrists. Having so passed this test, Colby implicitly argues that his theory of paranoia is validated, for it is his contention that by simulating indistinguishable protocols, his model is functionally equivalent to a paranoid patient. Although common throughout the field of computational psychology, this argument of functional equivalence has questionable validity. For as Arbib (1972) and numerous others have pointed out, equivalent input/output (I/O) functions may have entirely distinct intermediate or composite functions and, although functionally equivalent with regard to some observable criterion, may be, from an internal standpoint, very distinct mechanisms. Such an

I/O functional comparison only makes sense when the function describes all possible input and output strings; this the limited indistinguishability test obviously cannot do, for there is no such function that can so characterize human behavior.

This type of I/O approach differs considerably from that taken in the design of the ERMA program, for rather than being a type of black box, the ERMA model is a self-regulating system with a set of goals, feedback loops, and mechanisms for adapting to potential and real input messages. Moreover, the mechanisms that control its cognition are not statistically regulated nor restricted in their processing of concepts. In Colby's model, concepts are neither very complex nor capable of modification and extension. In effect, the beliefs of the model are static, and although perhaps similar in expression to those of a paranoid, bear but the most superficial resemblance. Consequently, the model is unable to describe how the paranoid behaviors and conceptual structures are developed and operate. This, and the fact that his paranoid algorithm cannot account for the projected aspect of paranoia, makes his theory of paranoia somewhat limited in its capacity to account for the etiology of the condition and hence its cure. From the perspective taken in the ERMA model, paranoia is the consequence of maladaptive behavior: something anyone is potentially susceptible to and therefore not adequately described in terms of a special and limited algorithm. A better test of the model would have been to first model a "normal belief" system and then demonstrate how it could become paranoid—a far more demanding task. Although the ERMA program is not paranoid—just neurotic—it might be programmed to develop progressively more paranoid responses. This would not be an easy task, and would involve the writing of new multiple-body interrupts which both inhibit normal responses and contribute to conspiratorial interpretations of all questions and audience responses, actual and imagined. By using special interrupt programs to exaggerate the imaged hostile response of the audience, and by interpreting potential discourse in terms of the model's own criteria, the model could simulate the projected aspects of paranoid behavior. Instead of using formulas and affective variables to accentuate paranoid behavior, the program would be able to achieve the same effect by selecting progressively more drastic responses and interpretations as others failed to satisfy initial goal conditions.

Another major difference between the ERMA program and that of Colby's is that ERMA, like a speaker, has a considerable amount of knowledge about the properties of language and their possible expressive functions. Discourse is not prepackaged in a list structure but constructed to express in a thematically suitable manner both the informational and the interpersonal content of concepts. In the paranoid model, however, there are limited discourse options and virtually no knowledge about the expressive uses of language; such knowledge is programmed in, rather than actively used by, the model. Similarly, cognition in the paranoid model is less a problem-solving activity than one of retrieval, for it has, at best, but a limited capacity to construct or manipulate embedded and complex concepts, and therefore is incapable of general deduction.

Although in one respect it is not fair to cite as limitations those things a model was not initially designed to perform, in another respect such a criticism is warranted if the model makes any claims about its general validity. The difficulty with the paranoid model, as with many similar types of models in artificial intelligence, is that by so simplifying the primary tasks (use of kernel sentences, restricted syntactic and semantic knowledge, etc.) and by using somewhat global or unrefined algorithms, the model really does very little to describe, much less explain, complex cognitive and linguistic processes. For example, what does Colby's model actually explain? Certainly not the manner in which a paranoid processes concepts and renders them into discourse. Certainly not the mechanisms of defense or ego functioning. What the model does purport to explain is the manner in which paranoid fears can escalate. Yet this explanation at its heart is rather simple and perhaps could be more economically described analytically than as a computer program many of whose operations have no theoretical relevance.

However, when viewed from a theoretical and heuristic standpoint, Colby's model has been successful in drawing attention to a need for more powerful languages and problem-solving procedures in modeling cognition. Likewise, he has helped initiate psychiatry into the alien realms of computer science by demonstrating the possibility of formalizing and operationalizing the often imprecise and literary theories of that "science."

9.32. *Schank's conceptual parser*

Anyone familiar with the computer modeling of natural language processing knows that the design of a parsing program is quite different from that of a language-generation program. In the production of a discourse, for example, the speaker knows what he wants to say and the basic problem is finding an appropriate means of saying it, whereas in the interpretation of a sentence or a discourse, the problem is to infer from syntactic, semantic, and contextual evidence what the speaker is actually saying and what he intends to say. Therefore, to compare a language understanding program such as Schank's with our discourse-generation program is a bit like comparing apples and pears. Yet despite these differences in design and objective, a worthwhile comparison can be made, as both programs, in this instance, are concerned with the conceptual structures that underlie the meaning of speech.

Unlike many of the earlier parsing or interpretive programs, which relied almost exclusively upon syntactic information, Schank's system parses and interprets sentences in terms of their conceptual content. It has, in his words, a "concept dependency grammar," one that can be used by a system to understand, and thereby to paraphrase, a set of input sentences. Like the "conceptual grammar" used in ERMA, his grammar uses a case system and three primitive types of concepts: nominal, action, and modifier. These three types of concepts are related to each other in specified ways and reflect what he terms their "conceptual dependencies." Each of the different types of dependencies is represented by a distinct arrow and special marker. For example, the sentence, "John hit the little dog," would be represented by the network

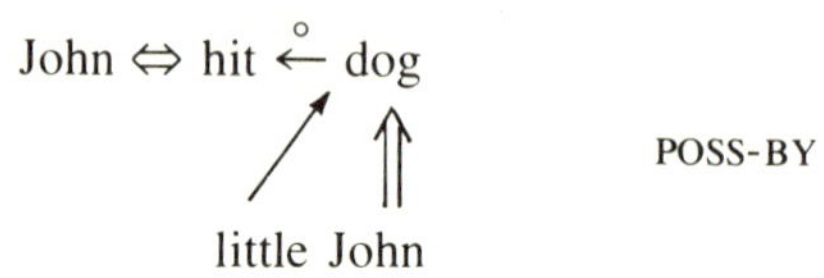

In this simple example it would appear that Schank's grammar is no more than a slight modification of a case grammar, and therefore strongly wedded to syntactic description. Yet, as a subsequent example will illustrate, Schank's intention is to represent the "deeper" knowledge presupposed in the interpretation and the generation of a sentence. This knowledge is represented by abstracting out of the sentence the more general conceptual relationships and concepts implied by the sentence. For example, Schank represents the sentence, "John ate the ice cream with a spoon," as follows:

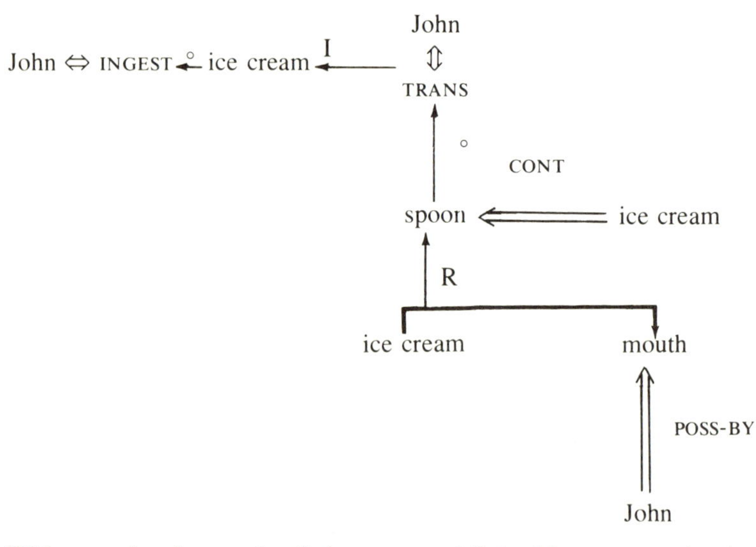

Without going into a detailed account of Schank's conceptual rules, certain general comparisons can be made between this method and my own. First, notice that this method of representation is far more complex than the initial sentence and that additional information is supplied through generic concepts, such as INGEST, TRANS, and CONT. Through these more general concepts and the various dependencies embodied in the directional arrows, Schank has attempted to portray all the knowledge that a speaker might infer from the sentence. Implicit in this strategy are two basic assumptions: first, that when interpreting a sentence, a speaker infers all possible meanings, and second, that all speakers make a standard set of inferences—that is, using a basic set of generic concepts such as INGEST. Both these assumptions are necessary if a competence approach to inference is being followed, which here seems to be the case. By representing conceptual knowledge in such a set format and by assuming that the concept INGEST, for example, is necessarily implied by the word "ate," Schank is, in effect, assuming that every sentence has a similar meaning for each speaker and can be understood by a standard conceptual lexicon.

This approach markedly differs from that in the ERMA model, and does, I believe, create unnecessary difficulties and limitations. Obviously, there is a commonality of interpretation for speakers, but the extent of this commonality depends upon the intentions of the speaker as well as the listener. For example, in the sample sentence, the fact that John ate the ice cream may not be the critical bit of information, but rather that he ate it with a spoon—since it is known that he has in the past always eaten it with his hands. If such were the case, it is doubtful that the listener would make the wasteful deduction about ingestion, the ice cream being passed to the mouth, and so on. This fact could be expressed by a change in emphasis, "It was with a spoon that John ate the ice cream," a supposedly surface structure alteration but one that would alter the interpretation, and hence the conceptual representation. Such an alteration, I believe, could not be easily made in Schank's system. However, as we have seen, in the ERMA program this alteration would not be difficult to achieve and would result in a different conceptual representation.

Aside from creating difficulties of representing the thematic information and the idiosyncratic character of speaker intentions and knowledge, such a competence approach would, I suspect, create problems of processing. This is true because for every sentence all the information that sentence might potentially contain must be retrieved and deduced, some of which may be quite extraneous. Not only is this wasteful, but in many cases, particularly in the interpretation of discourse where thematic and topical information is critical, it would be incorrect. For, in discourse, the speaker does not want to communicate all possible interpretations but rather to guide his listener to a selected set of interpretations, those which build upon the thematic import of the discourse. Consequently, if a program is to interpret discourse, it must be able to distinguish between information that is given and information that is new. This capability is not just absent from Schank's program but, I believe, is incapable of being integrated into it, owing to his overall approach to the problem, that is, his use of standarized conceptual primitives and his attempt to represent the full range of inferential information for a single sentence.

It might still be asked: How does the approach presented here, which also uses conceptual relationships and concept case frames, differ substantially from Schank's? The difference lies both in the general organization of the model, which is goal-directed and self-regulating, and in the manner in which concepts are represented. For example, the concept ''ate'' would in the ERMA model be represented as a special type of process concept occupying a designated slot (a relator), but instead of being defined in terms of some more global concept, such as INGEST, it would contain as part of its properties the definition implied by ingestion. There might be other properties as well, though, which contain personal and idosyncratic information, such as ''I love to eat'' or ''eating is like chewing.'' By attaching such properties to a concept, in this case a token concept, it is possible to give a concept virtually any range of meanings, and thereby to escape the trap of the standarized lexicon. Since the model is goal-directed and only accesses that information it needs to produce a discourse, it does not become bogged down in extraneous searches. Moreover, by letting each concept define the character of its own relationships within the generous confines of the A1 Rr A2 structure (ARD-in programming notation), the program is capable of expressing discourses almost as diverse as its concepts. This cannot be said for Schank's model, for his conceptual primitives and dependency rules operate at a very high level within his program, and thereby delimit the range of possible conceptual meanings.

Another way of comparing the programs is to see how knowledge about conceptual relationships and contents are encoded. Schank's model encodes conceptual knowledge into conceptual rules and concept primitives, thereby attempting to characterize a uniform set of meanings. The ERMA model, on the other hand, encodes conceptual and cognitive knowledge into its multiple-body interrupt programs and CONNIVER datums, both of which may be stored in a number of distinct contexts, thereby having any number of distinct meanings. The difference is not merely technical, for Schank's program can only be as intelligent and as flexible as his rules, and since these rules are prescriptive in nature, are restrictive in the types of inferences they allow. This is not the case with ERMA, for by using MBIs and contexts it is possible to generate any number of inferences, and then select the one that best fits the immediate purpose of the program. It might be argued that incorrect inferences may result, but then again, natural speakers and listeners make incorrect inferences, and can only correct them when supplied with the appropriate information. The point is that any conceptual grammar which uses uniform rules inevitably comes up short-handed, because a speaker or a thinker changes his rules according to the effects he wants to achieve; these effects are as varied as his intentions and circumstances. To simulate this diversity, a model needs not only contextual knowledge, but also knowledge about the effective uses of conceptual and grammatical rules. In other words, the adaptive goals of the model, such as achieving specified effects upon a listener, should direct the program, and conceptual rules should be subordinated to this end.

9.40. IMPLICATIONS AND PROSPECTS FOR FURTHER RESEARCH

The purpose of this research has been to develop a theoretical model of discourse behavior and operationalize this model through a simulation model of a patient in psychoanalysis. The implications of this model, as has been pointed out throughout this book, cut across the disciplinary boundaries of linguistics, psychology, psychiatry, and artificial intelligence. For each of these fields, computer modeling of this sort has different implications, and to avoid redundancy and the obvious, we will only touch upon those implications which are the most striking.

In the area of linguistics the principal value of this model lies in its ability to deal with problems of intention, context, discourse, and cognition, problems that have been avoided in much of American linguistic research. Moreover, as the model purports to be a unified model of discourse formation and production, it offers a theoretical framework as well as a formalism in which diverse linguistic and discourse data can be given a unified description. In many respects, the model has raised more questions than it has answered, problems of a somewhat different character than those current in the field. These problems, in a nutshell, resolve around the enormous problem of identifying the architecture and dynamics of the cognition that underlie discourse behaviors. For although a discourse episode was simulated, it was done in an ad hoc manner. How ad hoc it is, and how deep our understanding of mental processes must be to achieve a satisfactory description, have only recently become reasonable questions to ask. Although models are now available to ask such questions, considerably more empirical research is needed to identify those factors that affect discourse formation and production. Sociolinguistics, psychiatry, and the ethnography of speaking are several disciplines that can make such a contribution.

In general, psychiatry and psychology have had to rely upon superficial and manifest behaviors to make their measurements. Psychology in particular has been justly criticized for collapsing its theories to suit its measurement techniques; any mention of behaviorism is firm reminder of this unpleasant tendency. Psychiatry, on the other hand, particularly psychoanalysis, has suffered from the opposte malady. Although correct in its recognition of the complexities of unconscious and hidden psychological processes, it has been unable to formulate its theories in a scientific manner; its knowledge remains ritualized and esoteric. The obvious advantage of a model such as ERMA is that it allows an investigation of in-depth processes and a means for testing various hypotheses concerning mental organization, cognitive behaviors, and discourse behaviors. Obviously, a model such as ERMA is but a limited step in this direction, but it is not at all farfetched to envision the day when therapists will be using such models for training, diagnostic, and experimental purposes. For when expanded and hooked up with an interpretative component, a model such as ERMA could be used to simulate the likely effects a therapist's comments would have upon a patient. When so stated, I'm confident that some people will protest that computers are finally encroaching upon a sacred human reserve. In one respect, that prospect is all too real, but I believe that research of this kind will be instrumental in showing the unique and intrinsically indeterminate character of human thought, and thereby ultimately serve a positive and liberating social function.

Artificial intelligence is a young field and, as such, still gauges the success of its enterprises by the complexities of the tasks they perform. Naturally, the simulation of human behaviors, especially those involved with problem solving and language understanding, is one of its prime objectives. To the extent that this program has been successful in meeting this objective, it has obvious implications for artificial intelligence. One of these, is the use of multiple-body interrupts to simulate complex cognitive and linguistic processes. Another is that a self-regulating and adaptive model is required to account for the teleologically erratic behaviors that are so characteristic of human beings. Too often artificial intelligence has neglected the precepts of its parent, cybernetics, and ignored the fact that intelligence is a quality of adaptivity, and therefore relative to the needs of the system and the conditions of its environment. CONNIVER, unlike many programming languages, is most compatible with this approach, and is, I believe, an excellent language for modeling human cognitive and linguistic processes. Certainly, much remains to be done. There is still little understanding of how new concepts are created or how new interrupt programs can be written by a model. Hence, the modeling of complex self-regulating learning processes continues to be an enigma to the field. As far as the extensions of ERMA are concerned, there, too, a great deal of research remains; the model needs to be refined, filled out, and fitted to an interpretative component. Although progressively more understanding is being acquired about the understanding of natural language at the sentential level, a great deal more needs to be known about comprehension at the level of discourse. Despite these difficulties, I believe the day is not too distant when computers can be used to write intelligent and literate discourses, freely interact with their users in natural language discourse, and, perhaps, be used as an educational aid in teaching elementary school children how to write and think creatively.

Having drawn attention to the positive implications of this type of research, it would be irresponsible not to give equal attention to its drawbacks. To the popular mind, computers have the mysterious aura of alien beings; they are viewed with suspicion and awe. Although the specialist in the field should be exempt from such beliefs, sometimes he is not. This is especially true of artificial intelligence, where extraordinary powers have been attributed to the "intelligent machine" and promises made of imminent breakthroughs. Once a computer can simulate a specific set of tasks, it is often thought that only minor modifications are needed to provide a wide range of problem-solving skills. The deception is a common one because computers, through their representational and computational powers, lead us to believe that we have solved an entire spectrum of problems when in fact we have only discovered that the spectrum exists. Their saving grace is that they can reveal to us the magnitude of our assumptions and ignorance, and thereby function as effective instruments of discovery. Yet, as Weizenbaum (1976) has argued, the wisdom of the indiscriminate use of intelligent computers to intercede as human intermediaries is, at best, questionable. Since there is no way a computer can capture all the experiences and nuances of human mental and emotional life, it is inevitably an alien, and therefore reductive, substitute. Therefore, as the software capabilities of the computer are expanded to imitate and substitute for higher-order human symbolic processes, it becomes all the more important to know what types of tasks should be allocated to the computer and which should be reserved for human beings. Although it can be argued that computers are not and cannot be as "intelligent" as people, that is beside the point. People do and will continue to attribute special powers to the machine, and although computers may never be as "intelligent" as human beings, they are currently capable of imitating or performing tasks that have the appearance, at least, of being uniquely human. To my mind, this is sufficient cause to render the problem of man–computer substitutions a major social policy issue.

The problem goes deeper than simply sorting out the information-processing tasks and responsibilities appropriate for man and machine. The Information Revolution is, I believe, every bit as dramatic as the Industrial Revolution. However, our adversary is no longer the natural environment, but rather an environment that we have created, the information environment. It, like the natural world before it, has become an object that can be altered, engineered, and restructured to suit our needs and ambitions. This is not to say that it will be wholly understood or brought "under control," simply that techniques and technologies are evolving that will enable us to better understand, and hence mechanize and augment, many of our symbolic processes. However, I suspect that we will discover, as we have discovered for the natural environment, that there are limits and balances that must be observed. The symbols, values, and information networks that define social and cultural life have their limits, too. They have their own ecological ordering and cannot be indiscriminately exploited.

Intelligent software is a technology that cuts two ways: it can play an emancipating role, whereby we can become responsible architects of our own social and cultural life, or it can play a more sinister role, by progressively creating layers of alien complexity that we can neither comprehend nor control. In either case the technology is forcing a choice upon us, and whether we will be able to recognize our opportunity to choose remains to be seen.

BIBLIOGRAPHY

Abelson, R. 1968. Simulation of social behavior. In *Handbook of Social Psychology*, 2d ed., eds. G. Lindzey and E. Aronson, pp. 274–357. Reading, Mass.: Addison-Wesley.

———, and Carroll, J. D. 1965. Computer simulation of individual belief systems. *Amer. Behav. Sci.* 8:24–30.

Arbib, M. A. 1972. *The metaphorical brain.* New York: Wiley.

Ashby, W. R. 1952. *Design for a brain.* London: Chapman & Hall (also New York, Wiley, 1960).

———. 1956. *Introduction to cybernetics.* London: Chapman & Hall (also New York: Wiley, 1966).

Bach, E. and Harms, R., eds. 1968. *Universals in linguistic theory.* New York: Holt, Rinehart and Winston.

Bateson, G. 1972. *Steps to an ecology of mind.* New York: Ballantine Books.

Becker, J. 1973. A model for encoding of experimental information. In *Computer Models of thought and language,* eds. R. Schank and K. Colby, pp. 1–61. San Francisco: W. H. Freeman.

Bernstein, B., ed. 1973. *Class, codes and control,* vol. 2. London: Routledge & Kegan Paul.

Boden, M. A. 1972. *Purposive explanation in psychology.* Cambridge, Mass.: Harvard University Press.

Brown, R. 1974. *The use of multiple body interrupts in discourse generation.* Unpublished undergraduate thesis, MIT.

Buckley, W. 1968. *Modern systems research for the behavioral scientist.* Chicago: Aldine.

Charniak, E. 1972. *Towards a model of children's story comprehension.* Cambridge, Mass.: Artificial Intelligence Laboratory, MIT, AI TR-226.

Chomsky, N. 1965. *Aspects of a theory of syntax.* Cambridge, Mass.: MIT Press.

Colby, K. M., 1973. Simulations of belief systems. In *Computer Models of Thought and Language,* eds. R. Schank and K. Colby, pp. 251–286. San Francisco: W. H. Freeman.

Cole, F., and Morgan, J., eds. 1975. *Syntax and semantics,* vol. 3, *Speech acts.* New York: Academic Press.

Dalenoort, G. J., ed. 1973. *Process models for psychology.* Rotterdam: Rotterdam University Press.

Dreyfus, H. 1972. *What computers can't do: a critique of artificial intelligence.* New York: Harper & Row.

Fenichel, O. 1945. *The psychoanalytic theory of neurosis,* 2d vol. New York: W. W. Norton.

Fillmore, C. J. 1968. The case for case. In *Universals in linguistic theory,* eds. E. Bach and R. Harms. New York: Holt, Rinehart and Winston.

———. 1971. Types of lexical information. In *Semantics,* eds. D. D. Steinberg and L. A. Jakobovits, pp. 370–93. Cambridge, England: Cambridge University Press.

Flavell, J., et al. 1968. *The development of role-taking and communication skills in children.* New York: Wiley.

Freud, S. 1954. Project for a scientific psychology. In *The origins of psychoanalysis, letters to Wilheim Fliess, draft and notes 1887–1902.* New York: Basic Books.

———. 1960. *The ego and the id.* New York: W. W. Norton.

———. 1963. *Therapy and technique.* New York: Collier Books.

———. 1965. *The interpretation of dreams.* New York: Avon Books.

———. 1966. *The complete psychological works of Sigmund Freud* (standard edition), ed. James Strachey. London: Hogarth Press.

———. 1969. A general introduction to psychoanalysis. New York: Simon & Shuster.

Greenberg, R., and Pearlman, C. 1974. Cutting the REM nerve: an approach to the adaptive role of REM sleep. *Perspectives in Biology and Medicine,* Summer:513–21.

Gumperz, J. J., and Hymes, D., eds. 1972. *Directions in sociolinguistics.* New York: Holt, Rinehart and Winston.

Habermas, J. 1971. *Knowledge and human interests.* Boston: Beacon Press.

Halliday, M. A. K. 1967. Notes on transitivity and theme in English. *J. Linguistics 3*:37–81, 199–244, 179–216.

———. 1970. Language structure and language function. In *New horizons in linguistics,* ed. J. Lyons, pp. 140–65. Harmondsworth, England: Penguin.

———. 1973. The functional basis of language. In *Class, codes, and control,* Vol. II, pp. 343–65. London: Routledge & Kegan Paul.

Hermes, H. 1969. *Enumerability, decidability, computability.* Berlin: Springer-Verlag.

Hutchins, W. J. 1971. *The generation of syntactic structures from a semantic base.* Amsterdam: North-Holland.

Kuhn, T. 1962. *The structure of scientific revolutions.* Chicago: University of Chicago Press.

Labov, W. 1972. *The boundaries of words and their meanings,* paper presented to Conference on New Ways of Analyzing Variation in English, Washington, D.C.

Lakoff, G. 1971. On generative semantics. In *Semantics,* eds. D. D. Steinberg and L. A. Jakobovits, pp. 232–96. Cambridge, England: Cambridge University Press.

Luborsky, L., and Mintz, J. 1973. *What sets off momentary forgetting during psychoanalysis: investigations of symptom-onset conditions.* Unpublished ms.

Lyons, J. 1970. *New horizons in linguistics.* Harmondsworth, England: Penguin.

———. 1971. *Introduction to theoretical linguistics.* Cambridge, England: Cambridge University Press.

MacKay, D. 1969. *Information, mechanism, and meaning.* Cambridge, Mass.: MIT Press.

McCulloch, W. 1965. *Embodiments of mind.* Cambridge, Mass.: MIT Press.

McDermott, D., and Sussman, G. 1973. *CONNIVER Reference Manual.* Cambridge, Mass.: Artificial Intelligence Laboratory, MIT.

Miller, G., and Johnson-Laird, P. 1976. *Language and perception.* Cambridge, Mass: Harvard University Press.

Miller, G. A.; Galanter, E.; and Pribram, K. 1960. *Plans and the structure of behavior.* New York: Henry Holt.

Minsky, M. 1974. *A framework for representing knowledge*. Cambridge, Mass.: Artificial Intelligence Laboratory, MIT AI Memo 306.
Newell, A. 1973. Artificial intelligence and the concept of mind. In *Computer models of thought and language,* eds. R. Schank and K. Colby, pp. 1–61. San Francisco: W. H. Freeman.
Osherson, D. N. 1974. *Logical abilities in children,* vol. 1, *Organization of length and class concepts: empirical consequences of a Piagetian formalism.* Potomac, Md.: Lawrence Erlbaum Associates.
Piaget, J. 1926. The language and thought of the child. New York: Harcourt, Brace.
———. 1963. *The origins of intelligence in children.* New York: W. W. Norton.
———. 1970. *Structuralism.* New York: Basic Books.
———. 1971. *Biology and knowledge.* Chicago: University of Chicago Press.
———. 1971. *Psychology and epistemology.* New York: Grossman.
———, and Inhelder, B. 1969. *The psychology of the child.* New York: Basic Books.
Pribram, K. H. 1971. *Languages of the brain.* Englewood Cliffs, N.J.: Prentice-Hall.
Quillian, R. M. 1969. The teachable language comprehender. *Commun. Assoc. Computing Machinery 12*:8.
Reitman, W. 1965. *Cognition and thought.* New York: Wiley.
Schank, R. 1973. Identification of conceptualization underlying natural language. In *Computer models of thought and language,* eds. R. Schank and K. Colby, pp. 187–248. San Francisco: W. H. Freeman.
———, and Colby, K., eds. 1973. *Computer models of thought and language.* San Francisco: W. H. Freeman.
———, and Nash-Webber, B., eds. 1975. *Theoretical issues in natural processing.* Cambridge, Mass.: Bolt, Beranek and Newman.
Siegal, S. 1956. *Non-parametric statistics.* New York: McGraw-Hill.
Simon, H. 1969. *The science of the artificial.* Cambridge, Mass.: MIT Press.
———, and Newell, A. 1972. *Human problem solving.* Englewood Cliffs, N.J.: Prentice-Hall.
Spinelli, D. N. 1970. OCCAM: A content addressable memory model for the brain. In *The biology of memory,* eds. K. H. Pribram and D. Broadbent, pp. 273–306. New York: Academic Press.
Steinberg, D. D., and Jakobovits, L. A., eds. 1971. *Semantics: an interdisciplinary reader on philosophy, linguistics, and psychology.* Cambridge, England: Cambridge University Press.
Sussman, G. 1973. *A computational model of skill acquisition.* Cambridge, Mass.: Artificial Intelligence Laboratory, MIT, AI TR-297.
Turing, A. M. 1950. Computing machinery and intelligence. *MIND* 59:433–60.
Watzlawick, P.; Beavin, J.; and Jackson, D. 1967. *Pragmatics of human communication.* New York: W. W. Norton.
Weiner, N. 1961. *Cybernetics.* Cambridge, Mass.: MIT Press.
Weissman, C. 1967. *LISP 1.5 primer.* Belmont, Calif.: Dickenson.
Weizenbaum, J. 1976. *Computer power and human reason: from judgement to calculation.* San Francisco: W. H. Freeman.
Werner, G. 1970. The topology of the body representation in the somatic afferent pathway. In *The neurosciences,* Vol. II, eds. G. S. Quarton, T. M. Melnechuk, and F. O. Schmitt, pp. 605–16. New York: Rockefeller University Press.
Wilden, A. 1972. *System and structure.* London: Tavistock.
Winograd, T. 1971. *Procedures as a representation for data in a computer program for understanding language.* Cambridge, Mass.: MIT, Project MAC, TR-84.
Witkin, H. A., et al. 1974. *Psychological differentiation.* Potomac, Md.: Lawrence Erlbaum Associates.

INDEX

INDEX

THE JOHNS HOPKINS UNIVERSITY PRESS

This book was composed in VIP Times Roman text and display type by The Composing Room of Michigan, from a design by Susan Bishop. It was printed and bound by Universal Lithographers, Inc.

LIBRARY OF CONGRESS CATALOGING IN PUBLICATION DATA

Clippinger, John Henry.
Meaning and discourse.

Bibliography: pp. 221–23
Includes index.
1. Psycholoinguistics. 2. Cognition. 3. Psychology—Data processing. 4. Psychoanalysis. I. Title. [DNLM. 1. Cognition. 2. Computers. 3. Language. 4. Models, Psychological—Psychoanalysis. BF455 C64lm]

BF455.C672 153 77-4779
ISBN 0-8018-1943-1